Saw Swee-Hock

D1081281

Population Policies and Programmes in Singapore

LSEAS Institute of Southeast Asian Studies
Singapore

First published in Singapore in 2005 by ISEAS Publications
Institute of Southeast Asian Studies
30 Heng Mui Keng Terrace
Pasir Panjang
Singapore 119614

E-mail: publish@iseas.edu.sg
Website: <http://bookshop.iseas.edu.sg>

Chapters 2 to 8 originally published in Saw Swee-Hock, *Population Control for Zero Growth in Singapore* (Singapore: Oxford University Press, 1980).

ISEAS Library Cataloguing-in-Publication Data

Saw, Swee-Hock, 1931–
   Population policies and programmes in Singapore.
   1. Singapore—Population policy.
   2. Birth control—Singapore.
   3. Fertility, Human—Singapore.
   4. Singapore—Population.
   I. Title
HB3645 A3S272   2005

ISBN 981-230-318-9 (soft cover)
ISBN 981-230-319-7 (hard cover)

Typeset by Superskill Graphics Pte Ltd
Printed in Singapore by Utopia Press Pte Ltd

Population Policies and Programmes in Singapore

The **Institute of Southeast Asian Studies (ISEAS)** was established as an autonomous organization in 1968. It is a regional centre dedicated to the study of socio-political, security and economic trends and developments in Southeast Asia and its wider geostrategic and economic environment.

The Institute's research programmes are the Regional Economic Studies (RES, including ASEAN and APEC), Regional Strategic and Political Studies (RSPS), and Regional Social and Cultural Studies (RSCS).

ISEAS Publications, an established academic press, has issued more than 1,000 books and journals. It is the largest scholarly publisher of research about Southeast Asia from within the region. ISEAS Publications works with many other academic and trade publishers and distributors to disseminate important research and analyses from and about Southeast Asia to the rest of the world.

Contents

List of Tables

List of Figures

Preface

Population Policies and Programmes in Singapore is a vastly expanded version of my earlier book published some twenty-five years ago by Oxford University Press under the old title of *Population Control for Zero Growth in Singapore*. This revised edition of the book has been divided into two distinct sections — Part One: Antinatalist Period and Part Two: Pronatalist Period. The former deals with the period when the main concern was the need to lower the high and above-replacement fertility in the early years, and the latter covers the more recent period when the focus of attention was centred on preventing fertility from continuing to move forward at a level too low below-replacement fertility. The chapters included in Part One have been reproduced, with some revisions, from my earlier book, while Part Two contains the new chapters and appendices.

The enlarged book has therefore been structured in such a manner as to present a comprehensive account of the initiatives undertaken by the government to influence the course of fertility, and hence the rate of population growth, in the island state of Singapore during the last four decades or so. The book may be viewed as a case study of the public policy of a country in the area of population with regard to fertility and population growth. Hopefully, the book will enable the people of Singapore to comprehend the fundamental population issue of the day and to recognize the rather low below-replacement fertility, coupled with its adverse consequences, that will persist during their whole lifetime. More specifically, the book will be useful to married couples with children or planning to have babies since it constitutes a convenient source of detailed information on all the existing pronatalist incentives, financial or otherwise, that they are entitled to claim.

In the preparation of the two editions of the book, I was fortunate to receive the valuable assistance of many organizations and individuals.

My thanks go to the Government Statistics Department, the then Family Planning and Population Board, and the Family Planning Association for supplying me with the statistical data and other relevant materials. My research has been enormously facilitated by the conducive facilities offered at the London School of Economics Library, the National University of Singapore Library, and the Institute of Southeast Asian Studies. I wish to thank Mr K. Kesavapany, Director of ISEAS, for his generous hospitality and for providing me with a research assistant, Mr Benjamin Loh, while I was deeply immersed in writing the latest edition of the book. My thanks are also due to Mrs Triena Ong, Managing Editor of ISEAS Publications Unit, for her tireless effort in bringing out this book so expeditiously. Finally, I am indebted to my wife, Cheng Siok Hwa, for reading and commenting on the manuscripts of both editions. Needless to say, any opinions and shortcomings in the book are entirely my own.

Saw Swee-Hock

Part One

Antinatalist Period

1

Background

The Republic of Singapore comprises the main island of Singapore and some 54 small islets within its territorial waters and jurisdiction. The country has a total land area of only 697.1 square kilometres, 550 of which are taken up by the diamond-shaped main island which is 41.8 kilometres in length and 22.5 kilometres in breadth. Singapore is situated at the southern extremity of Peninsular Malaysia to which it is linked by the 1,056-metre rail-and-road causeway spanning the Straits of Johore. In its wider context, the Republic occupies a strategic position of the principal sea, air and trade routes between Europe and the Far East and Oceania. Singapore, being only 136.8 kilometres north of the Equator, has an equatorial climate with uniform and high temperatures of about 28°C, high humidity of about 70 per cent, and fairly abundant rainfall of some 2,400 millimetres per year. There is an absence of marked seasonal changes though December is often the wettest and coolest month.

The topography of Singapore is one lacking in contrast as the whole country is of very low elevation with a few small hills no higher than 166 metres. There are many rivers, with the larger ones such as the Kranji and Seletar rivers used as catchment areas for reservoirs and of course the Singapore River which is the traditional busy waterway for small boats in the very heart of the city. The lowland forests that used to cover the island in the early days have retreated with the advance of roads, houses, factories and cultivated vegetation. What remain are some small pockets of protected reserves, such as the Bukit Timah Nature Reserve and the Kranji Nature Reserve, totalling some 2,797 hectares. The built-up area is dominated by public housing high-rise apartments and factories which are concentrated mainly in the industrial town of Jurong on the western side of the main island.

The early history of Singapore prior to the nineteenth century remains largely uncharted, being interwoven with that of the various Buddhist, Hindu and Islamic empires that existed in the Southeast Asian region. The British led by Stamford Raffles landed on the island on 29 January 1819 and soon signed a treaty with the Malay ruler, Sultan Hussein Mohamed Shah of Johor, and established a trading post. In 1826 Singapore joined the two other British settlements of Penang and Malacca in the Malay Peninsula to form the Colony of the Straits Settlements. This arrangement continued until after World War II in 1946 when Penang and Malacca became part of the Malayan Union and Singapore was governed as a separate colony. Singapore attained full internal self-government with a completely elected Legislative Assembly of 51 members in 1959 when the People's Action Party secured a majority in the May election.

Four years later, Singapore joined Malaya, Sabah and Sarawak to form the Federation of Malaysia, but this political union proved to be shortlived as Singapore separated from Malaysia on 9 August 1965 and became an independent and sovereign state within the Commonwealth. With full powers to manage the affairs of the state, the PAP government led by Prime Minister Lee Kuan Yew proceeded to embark on a series of measures designed to expedite the social and economic development. Since then, the PAP has remained in government, with Lee Kuan Yew continuing as Prime Minister until November 1990 when Goh Chok Tong took over. The latest leadership changeover occurred in August 2004 when Lee Hsien Loong became the third Prime Minister of Singapore.

After World War II, the population of Singapore was quickly enlarged from 938,144 in 1947 to 1,449,929 in 1957, an increase of 507,785 or an annual growth rate of 4.5 per cent. This rapid rate of population increase recorded in the early post-war years may be attributed to an accelerated decline in mortality and a persistently high level of fertility. Another factor was the net movement of people from the hinterland of Peninsular Malaysia to the island of Singapore. As mortality declined less slowly, fertility commenced to fall, and Malaysia-Singapore movement of people diminished, the rate of population increase began to slacken to 2.8 per cent during 1957–70 and to 1.5 per cent during 1970–80. With the importation of foreign guest workers to alleviate the shortage of labour, the population increased at a faster rate again, 2.3 per cent during 1980–90 and 2.9 per cent during 1990–2000. The economic difficulties in recent years led to a slow rate of population increase, 1.0 per cent in

2002, 0.3 per cent in 2003, and 1.3 per cent in 2004. The total population of Singapore numbered 4,240,300 in 2004, with 3,486,900 or 83.0 per cent resident population defined to include Singapore citizens and permanent residents. The racial composition of this resident population consists of Chinese with 2,650,100 or 76.0 per cent, Malays with 479,300 or 13.7 per cent, and Indians with 293,100 or 8.4 per cent.

The economy of Singapore has undergone dramatic changes from an entrepôt centre in the early sixties to a very advanced economy nowadays viewed in terms of the economic structure and per capita income. Transport, communications, power and other basic facilities are well developed; standards of public administration are high and efficient; and social institutions and services are modern and adequate. The proportion of the work-force engaged in the main occupational groups amounted to 28.9 per cent in professional and technical, 13.3 per cent in administrative and managerial, 17.9 per cent in manufacturing, 11.9 per cent in business services, and 5.2 per cent in financial services. The per capita income was estimated to reach the high of $38,023 in 2003, which propels Singapore into the small club of rich countries in the world.

An integral part of the overall development strategy in the early post-war years to raise the standard of living of the people in the small island state devoid of most natural resources has been the government population control programme. The principal component of this programme was first introduced in 1966 when the Singapore Family Planning and Population Board was established by the government. Prior to this there was the Private Family Planning Programme operated by the Family Planning Association since 1949. The national programme was strengthened in the late sixties with the introduction of measures that go beyond family planning to achieve its demographic goals. In 1970 the restrictive laws concerning induced abortion and sterilization were legalized and liberalized. They were further amended in December 1974 to make abortion and sterilization freely available on request. Stringent social and financial incentives and disincentives introduced in the late sixties and early seventies constitute the final component of the national programme.

The comprehensive population control programme has been responsible for sustaining and accelerating the decline in fertility first commenced in 1958, and the eventual attainment of the replacement fertility level in 1975. The attainment of replacement fertility is a pre-condition for achieving its stated demographic goal of zero population growth in the future. But the second condition of maintaining fertility at the replacement level was never fulfilled as fertility was allowed to remain well below replacement level since 1975. The key reason is that the strong antinatalist policies and programmes were not relaxed or reversed until the mid-eighties. Some relaxation of the old antinatalist policies and the introduction of limited pronatalist policies were made in 1984. In the meantime, fertility as measured by the total fertility rate (TFR) continued to fall well below the replacement level to touch the record low 1.33 in 2003, with only 37,485 births. This led the government to introduce by far the most comprehensive pronatalist measures in 2004 aimed at raising fertility to a less dangerously low level, but recognizing the futility of trying to push it back to replacement level.

The term "population policies" is usually used to refer to those policies adopted by a government to influence the course of population trends and patterns in the country. Some examples of such explicit population policies are immigration policy regulating the inflow of foreigners into the country, population distribution or redistribution policy governing the movement of people within the country, mortality policy affecting the general health of the people, and fertility policy affecting the reproductive behaviour of the people. There are two types of fertility policy — those designed to encourage childbearing and those designed to discourage childbearing. Those policies adopted by government to persuade their people to produce fewer children in order to lower the rate of population growth are known as *antinatalist* policies, while those meant to do the exact opposite are known as *pronatalist* policies. The adoption of a population policy will normally lead to a population programme being implemented to achieve the objective of the policy. For example, the adoption of an antinatalist policy in the early days resulted in the implementation of a national family planning programme in Singapore to provide island-wide family planning services to the people.

This book is devoted to a detailed account of the national population policies and programmes in Singapore during the period of some forty years. The first part deals with the population control programme aimed at lowering fertility and hence the rate of population growth. The second part discusses the various attempts at raising fertility by relaxing the early antinatalist measures and introducing some pronatalist measures in the new millennium.

2

A Private Programme

FORMATION OF THE FPA

Birth control as a means of spacing children and limiting family size has long been practised by couples in Singapore on an individual basis, with sometimes the advice of doctors and friends and the use of family planning literature. However, this practice was confined only to a small group of persons belonging mainly to the more educated and wealthier classes. The idea of providing family planning services to the general public was first discussed by a major correspondence in the *Straits Times* in January 1935, and this attracted some public comments from various interested groups about the pros and cons of family planning.[1] Public interest in this subject was revived during the visit of Mrs M. Sanger to Singapore in February 1936 when she advocated that, among other things, family planning should be an essential part of the official public health programme.[2] In December 1936 the Chinese Christian Association debated the matter and voted, with only three against, that birth control clinics should be established in Singapore.[3] Some time before World War II the establishment of a private family planning society was in fact recommended by a leading article in an English newspaper published on 21 September 1938.[4] This suggestion did not result in any positive action and it was not until a decade later that such a society was formed.

The idea of providing family planning services for the general public on a large and organized scale was debated again during the post-war years when the country was faced with serious social and economic dislocations. Apart from housing and educational problems, the government was confronted with the problem of feeding a large number of undernourished persons, especially children roaming the streets, because of rampant food shortages. The Social Welfare Department set up numerous centres to feed the hungry children, but it soon became apparent to the group of voluntary workers assisting in this scheme that, instead of feeding the children, the parents should be given family planning advice to plan their family size according to their means.[5]

At the invitation of the YWCA International Club, a series of lectures on birth control was delivered in April 1949 by the Head of the Social Welfare Department, the Municipal Lady Health Officer, and the wife of a senior missionary to some sixty women.[6] At the end of the series, they voiced their support for the formation of a voluntary family planning society and the three speakers prepared a report which urged the provision of family planning services to mothers attending infant welfare clinics.[7] This was followed by a long and heated debate in the Municipal Council Chamber on 28 May 1949, and it was urged by a majority vote of twelve to ten to allow the infant welfare clinics to give family planning advice on request after the other work of the clinic had ended for the day.[8] The new service was limited to only once a week in three of the five clinics. Since this fell short of the work envisaged, a group of doctors, social workers and other interested individuals held a public meeting on 22 July 1949 to form the Family Planning Association (FPA) with the immediate aim of setting up clinics in areas not served by the municipal clinics. The account of the development of the private family planning programme by the Association presented in the rest of this chapter is essentially based on information and data extracted from its annual reports.

OBJECTS

The immediate task of the Association at the time of its formation was to expand the family planning services in as many areas as possible. The primary objective of the Association as envisaged by its founders was to improve the welfare of the family by providing contraceptive education and services so that planned births could be spaced and unplanned births avoided. The Association also wished to assist women with sterility and minor gynaecological problems. These were made clear by the aims of the Association as stated in its constitution. In due course, however, it was realized that the family planning programme could not be divorced from the wider national issue of population problems resulting from unchecked rapid population growth.

The following are the objects of the Association as spelled out in its constitution:[9]

(1) To educate the people in healthy family planning and to provide facilities for scientific contraception so that married people may space or limit their families and thus promote their happiness in married life and mitigate the evils of ill-health and overcrowding.

(2) To advocate and promote the establishment of Family Planning Centres at which, in addition to advice on scientific contraception, women can get advice on, and, when necessary, treatment for any or all of the following:
   (a) involuntary sterility;
   (b) minor gynaecological ailments;
   (c) difficulties connected with the marriage relationship.

(3) To encourage the production of healthy children who are an asset to the nation, provided that their parents have the health and means to give them a reasonable chance in life.

(4) To examine such other problems as are relevant to the above, and to take such action as may be considered advisable.

ORGANIZATION

The organizational structure of the Association was determined by the fact that, being a non-profit private body, it depended largely on voluntary contributions and manpower for its daily management and development. The Association therefore operated through a system of committees, the number and nature of which varied over the years. The general affairs of the Association were mainly entrusted to an Executive Committee, while the other specialized areas of work were handled from time to time by other committees such as the Medical Sub-Committee, Management and Planning Sub-Committee, Membership Sub-Committee, Publicity Sub-Committee, Finance Sub-Committee, Research Sub-Committee, Building Sub-Committee, and Appeals and Entertainment Sub-Committee. The individuals serving in these committees were drawn from the list of members of the Association itself, supplemented by a few other volunteers who provided their expertise as and when the need arose.

In the early days the Association depended entirely on voluntary personnel to perform the daily administrative work and to staff the clinics. These volunteers came from every spectrum of occupation but the majority were social workers, doctors, nurses, teachers and interpreters. As the number of clinics and patients became too large to handle, employees paid on a part-time basis were first engaged, and this was soon followed by the recruitment of full-time employees. The first two paid workers were engaged on a part-time basis in 1950, and the following year witnessed the recruitment of a part-time paid doctor to take charge of the sessions, especially in the rural clinics. Over the years the number of paid workers, both full-time and part-time, had to be enlarged to handle the increased work load due to the expansion of clinics and patients. By 1966 the number of paid employees totalled about forty-two. However, the Association continued to rely heavily on voluntary workers to provide assistance in the committees, in the headquarters, and in the clinics. In a way this helped to reduce the financial burden of the Association since staff salaries constituted a very high proportion of the total annual expenditure. In later years the bulk of the income was spent on employees' salaries which in 1965 accounted for about 88 per cent of the total expenditure of $168,000.

The funds of the Association, which ultimately determined the size and scope of the services it could offer, came from various sources. There was the annual grant from the government, $5,000 in the first year, provided as a gesture of official blessing on what the Association was attempting to do for the good of the people. As can be observed from the figures in Table 2.1, the grant was progressively increased to $60,000 in 1955 and finally to the highest figure of $120,000 in 1958, but from 1959 to 1965 it was stabilized at $100,000. After the takeover of most of its clinics in 1966 by the Singapore Family Planning and Population Board, the Association received a reduced annual grant of $10,000 during the period 1966–68 to manage its headquarters and the remaining three clinics. The government grant constituted by far the major portion of the income of the Association, though other smaller and sometimes less regular sources had to be relied upon to maintain the expanding programme of services offered.[10] These were the annual membership subscriptions, private donations, and funds raised through special fund-raising campaigns. Funds for specific purposes were received from the Asia Foundation, the Ford Foundation and the International Planned Parenthood Federation.

In the mid-fifties the work of the Association, geared towards the welfare of the family unit, was soon affected by the extremely high

TABLE 2.1

Annual Government Grants to the Family Planning Association

Year	Amount ($)	Year	Amount ($)
1949–50	5,000	1960	100,000
1951	10,000	1961	100,000
1952	20,000	1962	100,000
1953	30,000	1963	100,000
1954	45,000	1964	100,000
1955	60,000	1965	100,000
1956	85,000	1966	10,000
1957	100,000	1967	10,000
1958	120,000	1968	10,000
1959	100,000		

annual rate of population increase of about 5 per cent which created considerable pressure in the fields of education, housing and employment. The increasing number of children born after World War II reaching school-age and entering school imposed a tremendous strain on the government in its efforts to provide enough facilities, especially schools and teachers. The strain on housing, badly neglected during the War, was made worse by the swelling population. More serious still was the large army of unemployed resulting from the rapid population growth on the one hand, and the inability of the then predominantly entrepôt economy to absorb them on the other. These problems attracted the widespread attention of the public, especially the press and the political parties, in the late fifties when negotiators for the political independence movement made known their concern for the welfare of the masses in terms of housing, education and employment. By 1957 the Association, because of its inadequate financial resources, had found it impossible to cope with the increasing demand for its clinical services.

In its annual report for the year 1957, the Association made an official appeal to the government to take a more direct role in the provision of family planning services. The President, Sir Percy McNeice, declared, "The time may well come when the Singapore Government may think fit to take over the responsibility for providing family planning services for the population. If so, the Association will feel that its efforts have been well rewarded and will be happy to hand over this work and to give it as devoted and loyal support as it has done in the past."[11] In

September 1958, the Vice-President, Mrs H. B. Amstutz, took the opportunity to request the government to take over the clinical work in response to the statement of the Minister for Education, Mr Chew Swee Kee, that it was increasingly difficult to find jobs for youths leaving school.[12] With no positive reaction forthcoming from the government, Sir Percy echoed his earlier plea for the government take-over of the clinics in the 1958 annual report, but still to no avail. In the meanwhile Singapore was embroiled in profound political changes that soon led to self-government and a new emphasis on family planning.

The most positive enunciation of an official policy came from the People's Action Party which stated openly its support for family planning in its party manifesto in the May 1959 election. On page 232 the manifesto states: "The present family planning arrangements are totally inadequate for the task of spreading knowledge among the masses. The PAP intend to expand the family Planning organization considerably so that it will effectively reach the people all over the island."[13] On 22 June 1959 the Association lost no time in calling upon the newly elected PAP Government to take over the clinics of the Association while it carried on the educational component of its programme. This press statement was issued by Mrs Joanna Moore in her capacity as publicity officer of the Association, and was supported by Mrs Goh Kok Kee who was Chairman of the Far East and Australasia Region of the IPPF with its headquarters situated in Singapore.[14] There was no positive response though the PAP Government began to play a more active role in the promotion of family planning.

The government continued to provide the annual grant of $100,000 to the Association and to permit it to offer family planning services in twenty-seven Government Maternal and Child Health Centres and in the outpatient clinics of Kandang Kerbau Hospital. In November 1960 the government, in conjunction with the Association, organized a concentrated three-month family planning campaign as part of its Mass Health Education Programme. The first government-sponsored Exhibition was held in the Victoria Memorial Hall from 26 November to 6 December 1960, with emphasis on the need for family planning in terms of the welfare of the family and the state. Subsequently, the Exhibition went on tour to all Community Centres in the outlying areas, with the co-operation of the People's Association and local leaders. This direct government participation in educational and motivational work was followed by a government grant of a valuable piece of land at the junction of Dunearn Road and Gilstead Road in September 1963 to the Association at a nominal fee of $1 per annum for 99 years for the construction of its permanent building. Another significant event took place in 1963 when Singapore acted as host for the Seventh Conference of the International Planned Parenthood Federation in February in Singapore, which undoubtedly enhanced the prestige of the Association in the eyes of the delegates.

In the early sixties the Association, with rather limited personnel and financial resources, found it increasingly difficult to cater for the growing demand for family planning services generated by the government's policy of direct involvement in "motivational" work. Inevitably, the Association renewed its request in November 1964 and again in January 1965 to the government to take over all family planning activities conducted in government institutions on the conviction that only the state could ever hope to satisfy the endless demand for such services. This led to the formation of a Review Committee on 13 March 1965 and eventually to the establishment of the Singapore Family Planning and Population Board in January 1966, charged with the responsibility for administering the national programme. However, the government continued its policy of supporting the Association but decreased the grant to $10,000 in 1966 in view of its reduced functions.

CLINICS, ACCEPTORS, AND ATTENDANCES

Although the Association was established in July 1949, it was not until the first week of November that the first three clinics came into operation, and they functioned after office hours between 4.30 and 6.00 p.m. in private dispensaries kindly put at the disposal of the Association by three of its own members. They were the Queen's Dispensary in Geylang Road, Union Dispensary in North Bridge Road, and the Victory Dispensary in South Bridge Road.[15] The second batch of three clinics was soon opened but this time at Municipal clinics through the influence of its members working in the Municipality. By December the Association had successfully negotiated with the government for family planning work in the North Canal government outpatient dispensary. During the first six months the Association, being a small voluntary body, had to overcome some major obstacles connected with accommodation, personnel and finance. What was reassuring to its members was that the services provided in the clinics opened so far were fairly well received by the patients, notwithstanding certain age-old problems arising out of ignorance, superstition, prejudice and tradition.

In early 1950 it was felt that the demand for family planning services was great enough to justify the setting up of more clinics, and accordingly such services were provided at two more Municipal clinics. In June another two were established at Government Infant Welfare Centres at Nee Soon and Bukit Panjang to cater to the people in these rural districts. By the end of 1950 the Association was providing family planning services in a total of eleven clinics, nine situated in the Municipal area and two in the rural areas.

The number of clinics functioning at the end of each year is shown in Table 2.2. The fluctuating feature of the figures is due to the fact that they were taken at year-end, and in any year some clinics would cease operating, some former clinics might be reopened, and new ones might be formed. However, it is evident that over the first seventeen years the number of clinics has generally increased. Most of the clinics were in the rural areas, operating in Government Maternal and Child Health Centres. On the eve of the government take-over in January 1966, the Association was managing all in all thirty-four clinics widely dispersed over the country. The newly established Singapore Family Planning and Population Board took over all the clinics operating in the Government Maternal and Child Health Centres, except the three situated in the Association's headquarters in Cuppage Road, in the rented premises in Tiong Bahru Road, and in the Singapore Anti-Tuberculosis Association building. On 2 November 1968 these remaining clinics were also transferred to the SFPPB.

The growth of the family planning programme can best be examined in terms of the number of women seeking birth control services annually. It is necessary to classify the women into new acceptors and old acceptors; the latter refers to women who attended the clinics on second and subsequent occasions. In the first two months of November–December 1949 the clinics were visited by about 600 women, while in the first full year of the Association's existence in 1950 a total of 1,871 new acceptors were registered. The annual figure rose steadily over the years, reaching about 5,900 new acceptors ten years later in 1959 and finally 9,800 in 1965. The sharp drop to 2,100 new acceptors in 1966 was due to the government take-over in January 1966. As can be seen in Table 2.2, for the period from November 1949 to December 1968 a total of 88,000 acceptors were recruited by the Association.

TABLE 2.2
Annual Number of Clinics, Acceptors and Visits, 1949–68

Year	No. of Clinics	Acceptors			Total Visits	Average Visits per	
		New	Old	Total		Clinic	Acceptor
1949	7	600	*	*	*	*	*
1950	11	1,871	*	*	*	*	*
1951	12	1,880	*	*	*	*	*
1952	8	1,787	*	*	3,841	*	*
1953	9	2,302	*	*	5,548	*	*
1954	12	2,966	*	*	9,223	*	*
1955	14	2,850	*	*	10,072	*	*
1956	25	3,772	*	*	14,393	*	*
1957	29	3,820	*	*	18,443	*	*
1958	25	5,280	*	*	27,522	*	*
1959	27	5,938	9,235	15,173	34,445	1,276	2.3
1960	28	7,472	10,135	17,607	37,757	1,348	2.1
1961	30	8,070	11,473	19,543	43,724	1,457	2.2
1962	28	7,189	13,083	20,272	48,916	1,747	2.4
1963	31	8,429	15,006	23,435	60,194	1,942	2.6
1964	30	9,339	16,243	25,582	78,368	2,612	3.1
1965	34	9,845	17,109	27,054	103,986	3,058	3.8
1966	3	2,145	4,214	6,359	26,403	8,801	4.2
1967	3	1,349	*	*	22,643	7,548	*
1968[+]	3	1,017	*	*	17,301	5,767	*

Notes:
* Not available.
[+] Up to 31 October 1968.

A substantial proportion of the new acceptors continued to attend the clinics after their first visit, which was most reassuring as attendance by old acceptors is a good indication of the acceptance and use of family planning services. Figures for these old acceptors are available for 1959 onwards (see Table 2.2), and they show that in every year the number of old acceptors exceeded the number of new acceptors. In 1959 there were about 5,900 new acceptors as compared with 9,200 old acceptors; during the 1960s the proportion oscillated around a fairly constant ratio of one new acceptor to about 1.6 old acceptors.

The total number of visits made by both the new and old acceptors
in any particular year gives a good idea of the work-load that the
Association had to cope with. Table 2.2 shows that the number of visits
in any year increased very much faster than the total number of clinics
or new acceptors. In 1952 about 3,800 visits were recorded, in 1959
about 34,400, and in 1965 the figure reached the peak of 104,000.
Dividing the number of visits by the total number of clinics gives us the
average number of visits that each clinic had to handle. In 1959 the
average was 1,276 visits, increasing gradually until 1965 when the figure
stood at 3,058. After the government take-over, the average was 8,801 in
1966, which was due to acceptors shifting from the other clinics to the
remaining three operated by the Association. It is evident that the work
of the Association as a whole expanded rapidly over the years, and all the
time the clinics had to cater to an increasing level of activity. To some
extent this was caused by the acceptors making more frequent visits, as
reflected by the figures showing the average number of visits made by
each woman. In 1959 the average was 2.3 visits per woman, increasing
gradually until 1966 when the figure was 4.2. The rise in recent years
was partly due to the re-visits of patients to obtain their regular supply
of cheap oral pills, first introduced in 1961.

It is possible to ascertain in which year the old acceptors first visited
the clinics by examining the statistics of old acceptors tabulated by the
year in which they had paid their first visit. The 1963 figures presented
in Table 2.3 show that the old acceptors dated from past years as far back
as 1949. Out of the total of 15,006 old acceptors registered in 1963, 4,063
paid their first call in the previous year when 7,189 new acceptors were
registered. Therefore about 56 per cent of the new acceptors served in
the previous year appeared again in 1963. Similarly, the table shows that
40 per cent of the new acceptors contacted in 1961 appeared again in
1963. As was to be expected, this percentage decreased consistently over
the years as one moves back into the past as shown in the last column
of the table. Some women would have passed the reproductive age by
1963, some would have been sterilized, some would be able to practise
birth control on their own without any further visits, and others would
have become pregnant and hence did not appear again for some time.

CHARACTERISTICS OF NEW ACCEPTORS

A study of the characteristics of new acceptors must necessarily be
constrained by the kind of statistics obtainable from the annual reports

TABLE 2.3

Distribution of Old Acceptors Attending in 1963
by Year of First Registration

Year of Registration	New Acceptors	1963 Old Acceptors	Percentage
1949	600	1	0.16
1950	1,871	41	2.19
1951	1,880	88	4.68
1952	1,787	138	7.72
1953	2,302	190	8.25
1954	2,966	306	10.32
1955	2,850	412	14.45
1956	3,772	654	17.34
1957	3,820	752	19.68
1958	5,820	1,215	23.01
1959	5,938	1,612	17.15
1960	7,472	2,270	30.38
1961	8,070	3,264	40.44
1962	7,189	4,063	56.52
Total	55,797	15,006	26.89

and the unpublished records maintained by the Association. It is only natural that the Association did not regard the compilation of comprehensive statistics as an important job because its paramount concern was to manage and expand the clinic services to meet the increasing number of women attending. The statistical information was compiled by staff, both full-time and voluntary, who did not have the prerequisite training and experience in statistical work and who were subject to rapid turnover. Some of the figures were inaccurate, inconsistent or incomplete. Notwithstanding the inherent shortcomings of the statistical system operated by the Association, the data that we managed to obtain do provide some indication of the characteristics of new acceptors.

Among the 3,820 new acceptors recruited in 1957, 84.8 per cent were Chinese, 5.5 per cent Malays, 5.6 per cent Indians and 4.1 per cent other races. Since then the racial composition has moved towards a more normal one in line with the racial composition of the general population. In 1965 the Chinese acceptors accounted for 75.0 per cent of the total number, the Malay acceptors 12.2 per cent, the Indian acceptors 4.6 per cent and the other races 8.2 per cent. Statistics on the age at marriage are available for a few years only, from 1954 to 1959. In these years the average age at marriage of the new acceptors was about 18.5 years, somewhat lower than that of the women in the general population.

Data on the income of the new acceptors are again published for the years of 1954 to 1959 only; during this period the figures indicated a definite swing towards the lower income group (see Table 2.4). In 1954 acceptors with family incomes of less than $100 per month amounted to 27 per cent, and those between $100 and $200 accounted for 44 per cent. The two corresponding figures rose to 32 per cent and 53 per cent by 1959. In terms of the average family income of the new acceptors, the average fell from $195 in 1954 to $146 in 1959. Assuming the statistics can be trusted, this trend suggests that the free or highly subsidized contraceptives offered by the Association tended to attract more and more women from the lower income group. The family income of the new acceptors was very low compared with that of the general population, which is to be expected since persons in the high income group would have the means and the knowledge to practise birth control on their own. However, there is a possibility that the new acceptors had intentionally understated their family income in order to benefit from the sliding scale of charges or the free services offered by the clinics.

Figures on the source of information through which the new acceptors became aware of the services provided in the Association's clinics show that about 67 per cent were influenced by the Association's workers, publicity work, and old acceptors. The remaining 33 per cent were referred by government doctors and private doctors. As attitudes towards

TABLE 2.4
Per Cent Distribution of New Acceptors by Monthly Family Income, 1954–59

Income ($)	1954	1955	1956	1957	1958	1959
Under 100	26.8	25.7	29.6	24.1	29.3	32.4
101–200	44.1	52.2	49.3	53.6	52.7	52.6
201–300	13.1	12.9	11.3	12.1	10.0	8.8
301–400	5.1	3.2	3.7	3.3	2.7	2.2
401–500	1.6	1.5	1.7	1.9	1.5	1.3
Above 500	8.5	4.6	4.4	5.1	3.8	2.7
Total	100.0	100.0	100.0	100.0	100.0	100.0

TABLE 2.5
Per Cent Distribution of New Acceptors by
Source of Referral, 1959–65

Year	Medical Staff		Family Planning Association			Others	Total
	Govt.	Private	Workers	Publicity	Acceptors		
1959	27.7	3.4	41.4	5.0	20.5	2.0	100.0
1960	37.4	4.3	35.0	3.4	18.4	1.4	100.0
1961	39.2	4.4	33.2	3.5	18.9	0.8	100.0
1962	31.6	5.0	39.6	2.5	20.6	1.6	100.0
1963	31.8	4.2	34.1	5.6	22.9	1.3	100.0
1964	51.5	2.5	18.0	4.9	22.1	1.0	100.0
1965	54.6	3.2	11.9	4.9	24.4	1.0	100.0

family planning changed, birth control knowledge spread and new contraceptive methods came into wider use, the pattern of the sources of referral underwent a radical change (see Table 2.5). By 1965 the source of information attributable to the Association's own efforts had been lowered to 41 per cent, the reduction due largely to the reduced proportion of acceptors brought in by the Association's workers. By now the doctors were the principal source of referral, accounting for about 54 per cent of the new acceptors in 1965. Since the government did not operate any family planning clinics, the government doctors, on receiving inquiries about birth control from their patients, usually referred them to the Association's clinics.

In examining the information on the methods selected by the new acceptors on their first visit shown in Table 2.6, we should bear in mind that some of them may have switched to other methods at a later stage. In 1959 nearly 60 per cent of the new acceptors preferred diaphragms and 21 per cent preferred condoms; the rest chose foam tablets. Diaphragms declined in popularity very markedly as new and better methods like the oral pill and intra-uterine device (IUD) were introduced. Thus only 3 per cent of the new acceptors preferred diaphragms in 1965. When the oral pill was made available in 1961, hardly 1 per cent of the women took to it, and it did not become popular until 1964 when 20 per cent of the women decided to take it. In the following year the proportion shot up to 33 per cent. The intra-uterine device was first offered to women in 1965 and at once attracted about 11 per cent of the new acceptors.

TABLE 2.6
Per Cent Distribution of New Acceptors by
Method Chosen, 1959–65

Method	1959	1960	1961	1962	1963	1964	1965
Diaphragm	59.4	35.8	24.7	21.6	15.2	7.2	3.2
Condom	21.3	32.7	41.4	45.4	47.5	46.1	36.1
Foam Tablet	16.1	25.9	24.6	21.4	13.6	9.1	5.9
Applicator/Paste	3.2	5.1	4.6	5.1	3.7	2.7	1.5
General	0.2	0.4	4.0	3.5	12.8	14.6	9.4
Oral Pill	—	—	0.7	3.0	6.7	20.2	33.0
IUD	—	—	—	—	—	—	10.9
Others	0.1	0.0	0.0	0.0	0.5	0.0	0.1
Total	100.0	100.0	100.0	100.0	100.0	100.0	100.0

TARGETS AND ACHIEVEMENTS

As in the case of most private programmes, the Association did not lay down any target number of new acceptors to be recruited during specified periods. Every year it proceeded to recruit as many new acceptors as possible through the offer of maximum clinic services in accordance with the resources, financial or otherwise, at its disposal. As noted earlier, the annual number of new acceptors that the Association managed to recruit is by no means negligible or insignificant, and the number increased steadily over the years. By October 1968 a total of 87,921 new acceptors had been recruited by the Association. It is abundantly clear that the work of the Association has been largely responsible for precipitating the decline in fertility in 1958 as well as for the continuous decline without any interruption up to the time when its clinics were handed over to the government in 1966.[16]

In many respects the Association was a pioneer organization in the field of family planning. It was one of the earliest to be established in Asia and it was one of the founder members of the International Planned Parenthood Federation in its inaugural meeting held in Bombay on 29 November 1952. In the early years many member-countries of the IPPF sought the advice of the Association,[17] and mainly in recognition of the pioneering work of the Association, the Southeast Asia Regional Headquarters of the IPPF was located in Singapore. For seventeen years the Association was the only organized agency responsible for providing the vital and much needed family planning services to the people of Singapore during its most crucial demographic history when high rates of population increase were the order of the day. Through its increasing activities over the years, the Association was certainly responsible for laying down the much needed basis for the widespread acceptance of family planning ideas and practice by the general public, and hence played a significant role in bringing about a favourable climate for the eventual introduction of the national family planning programme. By voicing the needs of the community and repeatedly requesting the government to take over its clinics, the Association was directly instrumental in helping to persuade the PAP Government to adopt an official population policy in 1966.

THE RE-ESTABLISHMENT OF THE FPA

Following the misappropriation of funds by an official in the Association, the government directed the Singapore Family Planning and Population Board to take over the functions and assets of the Association on 1 November 1968.[18] After a lapse of about three years, the Family Planning Association was re-established in November 1971 and was registered in due course with the SFPPB in accordance with Section 11 of the Singapore Family Planning and Population Board Act, 1965. The objectives of this revived Association are as follows:

1. To disseminate knowledge of healthy family planning and to provide facilities for scientific contraception so that married couples may space or limit their families and thus promote their happiness in married life and mitigate the evils of ill health and overcrowding.
2. To advocate and promote the establishment of family planning centres at which, in addition to advice on scientific contraception, advice may be obtained and, if necessary, treatment given for any or all of the following:
   a. involuntary sterility;
   b. minor gynaecological ailments;
   c. difficulties connected with the marital relationship.
3. To encourage the production and rearing of healthy children who will be an asset to the nation.
4. To examine such other problems as are relevant to the above and to take such actions as may be considered advisable.

5. To cooperate with other organizations in the course of family planning.
6. To acquire property both movable and immovable for the use of the organization.

The government lent its moral and financial support to the revival of the Association by providing an initial grant of $10,000, half of which was given in 1972 and the other half in 1973. But the major source of income had always been generous grants by the International Planned Parenthood Federation, amounting to, for instance, $89,000 in 1975, $82,000 in 1976 and $97,764 in 1977. The other regular donor is the Singapore Turf Club which has been giving $10,000 per year since 1974.

The Association is governed by a Council of 21 elected members, with three government representatives acting as ex-officio members from the three Ministries of Health, Education and Social Affairs. The office bearers are the President, two Vice-Presidents, an Honorary Secretary and an Honorary Treasurer, while the full-time paid staff consists of an Executive Director, an Information and Education Officer, an Executive Assistant, an Accounts Clerk, a Project Coordinator, two Clerical Officers, and a Technician. As was the case in the early years prior to November 1968, the Association depends a great deal on volunteers to assist in giving talks and in providing professional services through the various Committees. There are eight committees dealing with Management, Finance, Medical, Information and Education, Research and Evaluation, Media, Resource Development, and Youth.

Since family planning services were adequately provided by the SFPPB, the Association has decided not to offer clinic services in order to avoid duplication. Instead it complements and supplements the activities of the SFPPB in primarily motivational and educational work in planned parenthood and family life education through talks, workshops, seminars, reference materials and films. In 1977 a new programme was launched by the Association in collaboration with the IPPF and the East and Southeast Asia and Oceania Region. This was the three-week IPPF-ESEAO Regional Training Course for Trainers in Sterilization which constitutes part of the IPPF's effort to facilitate the smooth expansion of sterilization programmes in the Federation.[19] The first two courses were conducted in 1977 and another two in 1978, when some thirty-eight doctors and paramedical personnel from Malaysia, Indonesia, the Philippines, Thailand, Hong Kong and Korea attended.

Notes

1. George G. Thomson and T. E. Smith, "Singapore: Family Planning in an Urban Environment", in *The Politics of Family Planning in the Third World*, edited by T. E. Smith (London: George Allen & Unwin, 1973), p. 219.
2. *Straits Times*, 15 February 1936.
3. Thomson and Smith, "Singapore: Family Planning", p. 219.
4. *Straits Times*, 21 September 1938.
5. Hena Sinha, "Singapore: Family Planning Association", in *Proceedings of the Seventh Conference of the International Planned Parenthood Federation, Singapore 1963* (Amsterdam: Excerpta Medica, International Congress Series, No. 72, 1964), p. 714.
6. These three persons were Dr Mary Tan, the Municipal Lady Health Officer, Mr T. P. F. McNeice, the First Secretary for Social Welfare, and Mrs C. Amstutz, wife of a leading Methodist pastor.
7. Thomson and Smith, "Singapore: Family Planning", p. 222.
8. Hena Sinha, "Singapore: Family Planning Association", p. 714.
9. See, for instance, *Fifth Annual Report of the Family Planning Association of Singapore, 1954* (Singapore: Malaya Publishing House Ltd, n.d.).
10. Maggie Lim, "Malaysia and Singapore", in *Family Planning and Population Programs*, edited by Bernard Berelson et. al. (Chicago: University of Chicago Press, 1966), p. 91.
11. *Eighth Annual Report of the Family Planning Association of Singapore, 1957* (Singapore: Malaya Publishing House Ltd, n.d.).
12. *Straits Times*, 6 September 1958.
13. *The Task Ahead: PAP's Five-Year Plan 1959–65*. This manifesto consisted of a collection of speeches published in May 1959.
14. *The Free Press*, 22 June 1959.
15. *First Annual Report of the Family Planning Association of Singapore, 1949–50* (Singapore: Malaysia Publishing House Ltd, n.d.). The dispensaries were owned by Drs Loh Poon Lip, C. J. Poh, and Goh Kok Kee.
16. See, for example, the speech delivered by Dr Goh Keng Swee, then Minister for Finance, to the Annual Meeting of the International Monetary Fund in Washington on 1 October 1969, and *Annual Report of the Family Planning Association of Singapore 1975* (Singapore: Stamford College Press, n.d.), p. 8.
17. Hena Sinha, "Singapore: Family Planning Association".
18. *Sixth Annual Report of the Singapore Family Planning and Population Board, 1971* (Singapore: Yeat Sing Art Printing, 1972).
19. *Annual Report of the Family Planning Association of Singapore, 1977* (Singapore: Stamford College Press, n.d.), p. 21.

3

The Government Programme

FORMATION OF THE SFPPB

It was noted in the preceding chapter that since 1957 the Family Planning Association had on numerous occasions requested the Ministry of Health to take over all the family planning activities it conducted in government institutions, but the government had consistently turned down the request. It was in response to the request submitted by the Association in January 1965 that the government finally announced on 13 March 1965 the appointment of a three-man Review Committee to look into this matter.[1] The terms of reference were to determine which of the family planning activities were to be transferred from the Association to the Health Ministry, to fix the quantum of annual grant for 1965 and subsequent years for the Association, and to resolve the disposition of the staff employed by the Association. The Review Committee held a total of seven meetings between 8 April 1965 and 9 June 1965 and submitted its unanimous report to the Minister for Health on 29 June 1965. Briefly, the report recommended that all except three of the clinics should be transferred to the government and a grant of $100,000 for 1965 and $10,000 for 1966 and subsequent years be given to the Association.

Some three months later, on 27 September 1965, a *White Paper on Family Planning* was tabled in Parliament, generally endorsing the recommendations of the Review Committee.[2] In addition to including the report of the Review Committee as an appendix, the 25-page White Paper spelled out in considerable detail the various aspects of a national population policy which the PAP Government proposed to implement. It announced, among other things, a five-year plan to recruit 180,000 new acceptors during the period 1966 to 1970 and the establishment of a statutory authority to take charge of the proposed government family planning programme. The aim of the plan was "to liberate our women from the burden of bearing and raising an unnecessarily large number of children and as a consequence to increase human happiness for all".[3]

Thus in December 1965 the *Singapore Family Planning and Population Board Act, 1965* was passed by Parliament without any debate and came into force on 7 January 1966.[4] The Singapore Family Planning and Population Board was formally established with its inauguration by the Minister for Health, Mr Yong Nyuk Lin, on 12 January 1966. In the inaugural ceremony the Minister stated,

> Singapore, as we all know, is a very overcrowded little island of nearly 2 million people living in an area of just over 2 hundred square miles or a density of population around 8,000 people per square mile. Family planning is therefore a matter of national importance and indeed, one of urgency for us. Our best chances for survival in an independent Singapore is stress on quality and not quantity.[5]

The establishment and activities of the Board expressed full government endorsement of family planning with all the prestige and authority that necessarily follow.

The change in government policy from one of indirect participation to one of direct provider of family planning services as enunciated in the White Paper was proclaimed a few weeks after the momentous political event of the separation of Singapore from the Federation of Malaysia on 9 August 1965 and with the full knowledge that the newly independent state had to survive alone without the traditional economic hinterland. The separation certainly highlighted the limited small land area of Singapore and the economic difficulties and lack of viability of the island state devoid of natural resources. This focused serious attention on the dire need to check the rapid population growth in planning for social and economic development. At that time the crude birth rate was in the neighbourhood of 30 per thousand population and the annual rate of population increase was no less than 2.5 per cent.

OBJECTIVES

The responsibilities of the SFPPB as stated in the Singapore Family Planning and Population Board Act are as follows:

(i) to act as the sole agency for promotion and dissemination of information pertaining to Family Planning in Singapore;

(ii) to initiate and undertake the population control programme;
(iii) to stimulate interest in demography in Singapore;
(iv) to advise the Government on all matters relating to family planning and population control.

The family planning programme has been essentially an integral part of the social and economic development strategy of the government aimed at improving the general standard of living of the people. More specifically, the programme has been designed to reduce the rate of population increase so as to facilitate and reinforce government efforts in advancing rapid economic development geared towards raising the per capita income of the masses. The programme constitutes the principal component of the overall population control programme directed at the maintenance of fertility at replacement level so that zero population growth can be attained as quickly as possible to stabilize the population. This policy was first promulgated by the Singapore Government in the World Population Conference held in Bucharest in August 1974 when the Minister for Finance stated, "It is within the context of total development that the Singapore Government adopts a population policy to achieve zero population growth as soon as possible."[6]

ORGANIZATION

The Singapore Family Planning and Population Board, which was directly responsible to the Minister for Health, was composed of fifteen members, of whom seven were ex-officio members drawn from government departments and two were representatives from the University of Singapore. Of the remaining six appointed by the Health Minister among members of the public, two or three were normally from government departments. The Chairman was the Republic's Deputy Director of Medical Services (Health) and he reported directly to the Health Minister. Various committees such as Executive Committee, Medical Committee, Information and Education Committee, Research and Evaluation Committee, and Training Committee existed to help in the implementation of the general policies formulated by the Board.

The work of the SFPPB was organized under six units. The Clinical Services Unit was responsible for organizing the family planning services, including male sterilization, while the Cytology Unit provided a cancer screening service. The Information, Education and Communications Unit developed and administered family planning education and publicity activities. Training programmes were formulated and operated by the Training Unit. The Research and Evaluation Unit took care of the routine statistical work and conducted special surveys or research to evaluate the various activities of the Board. Administrative support was supplied by the Administrative Services Unit. A diagrammatic presentation of the organization is given in Figure 3.1.

The senior professional staff of the SFPPB included medical officers, nursing officers, statisticians, health education officers, communications officers, an administrative secretary and an accountant. The junior staff members were the family planning assistants, general clerical assistants, statistical assistants, stenographers, typists and other supporting staff. At the end of 1977 there was a total of 183 established posts, out of which 164 were filled. Despite the rapid expansion of staff, the SFPPB relied heavily on support from government staff, particularly officers from the Maternal and Child Health Service and the Training, Health Education and Special Services Branch of the Health Ministry. Furthermore, valuable assistance and co-operation were provided by the staff of the government Maternity Hospitals and the Ministry of Culture, especially staff attached to its Radio and Television Service. These are further indications of the strong integrated character of the national programme.

The SFPPB has received appropriations from the Ministry of Finance since 1966. The annual expenditure and the proportion of the expenditure devoted to salaries are as shown in Table 3.1.

In addition to the annual government grant, the SFPPB received donations in cash and kind from various outside bodies. From the Population Council Inc., New York, there was the gift of 30,000 pieces of Lippes type of IUD in 1966 and 5,000 cycles of contraceptives in 1967. The IPPF provided a grant of $25,000 for the purpose of developing the cytological services. Much larger sums were forthcoming from the Ford Foundation, $118,956 in 1968, $98,877 in 1969 and $61,300 in 1970. The Asia Foundation donated $41,185 in 1974 and $5,000 in 1975. The United Nations Fund for Population Activities (UNFPA) donated about $439,000 under the commodity aid programme and $144,000 for the setting up of the Training Unit within the Board.

The Information, Education and Communications Unit was responsible for information, education, and motivational activities which were conducted through various channels.[7] Some of these were approaches made to government ministries, statutory boards and other organizations to motivate their staff, assistance rendered to schools to educate the

FIGURE 3.1
Singapore Family Planning and Population Board Organization Chart#

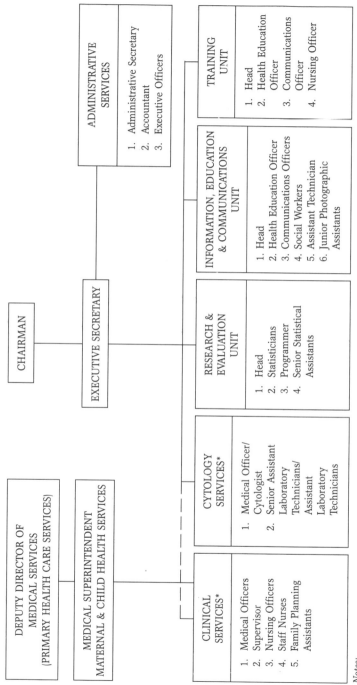

Notes:

Reflects SFPPB professional and technical staff only.

* Clinical Services and Cytology Services were under the administrative supervision of the Medical Superintendent, Maternal and Child Health Services, Ministry of Health.

TABLE 3.1

Singapore Family Planning and Population Board Annual Expenditure

Year	Expenditure ($)	% Spent on Salaries
1966	348,100	52.6
1967	338,600	72.9
1968	380,100	79.8
1969	433,600	80.2
1970	513,300	74.3
1971	538,200	82.6
1972	852,000	72.2
1973	*	*
1974	1,685,375	68.8
1975	2,002,854	67.7
1976	2,126,517	71.0
1977	2,203,240	71.4

Note: * Not available.

pupils, and contact made with community leaders through the Community Centres. Others were massive national family planning campaigns, mobile exhibitions and publicity through television, radio and newspapers. Still others included talks, film shows, forums and debates, pamphlets, posters, banners, car stickers and coasters. There was also the important face-to-face method in respect of post-partum women visiting the Maternal and Child Health clinics, women contacted through home visits, and couples contacted through the special services for newly-weds.

In the early phase of the national programme the emphasis in all these activities was on generating public awareness about the population problem and on stressing the need for family planning. By 1968 the message to "Plan Your Family" appeared to have been widely publicized, and the emphasis was accordingly shifted to "Singapore Wants Small Families" which became the overriding theme in the next few years.[8] Sometime in 1972 this gave way to "Two-Child Families for Singapore" and subsequently to "Boy or Girl — Two Is Enough" which was the theme employed to drive home the concept of the two-child family irrespective of the sex of the children. The activities of the Unit were also directed at the promotion of sterilization as the best method of family limitation among couples who have two or more children.[9]

The Research and Evaluation Unit was responsible for the routine compilation of statistics on acceptors, abortion, and sterilization and for undertaking special studies on certain important topics and surveys to gather basic data. Unlike the Family Planning Association, the SFPPB had a sound statistical system, managed by professional staff, to generate very comprehensive and accurate statistics on a routine basis. Special studies conducted in the past include oral pill follow-up studies to assess discontinuation rates, a cost-effect study in terms of cost per birth prevented, and participation in the comparative study on the administration of family planning programmes.[10] The last project constituted the Singapore component of the study sponsored by the Economic and Social Commission for Asia and the Pacific and was designed to ascertain the relationship between organizational variables and performance in the Maternal and Child Health/Family Planning clinics.[11]

The Unit, together with the National Statistical Commission, conducted the First National Survey on Family Planning in 1973 to gather data on knowledge, attitudes, and practice of family planning, abortion, and sterilization.[12] Also collected were data on knowledge and attitudes towards government incentive and disincentive policies and use of and attitudes towards clinical services provided by the SFPPB. The survey covers a sample of 2,078 currently married women aged fifteen to forty-four selected by means of stratified random sampling. The salient features of the survey results are discussed in Chapter 7. The Unit also processed the results of the Second National Survey on Family Planning conducted in 1977. The main departure of this survey is that a small sample of currently single women were also interviewed.

The Training Unit was established in the SFPPB in November 1972 with technical and financial assistance from the United Nations Fund for Population Activities (UNFPA). Prior to this, the staff were trained in the IPPF Southeast Asia and Oceania Region headquarters located in Singapore. After the transfer of the IPPF-SEAOR headquarters to Kuala Lumpur towards the end of 1970, the SFPPB undertook the provision of part-time in-service family planning training courses with the assistance of the Training, Health Education and Special Services Branch of the Ministry of Health.

After a year of preparation, the Unit launched its training programme in 1974 with the first family planning course conducted from 11 March to 6 April 1974. The first part of the course consists of classroom teaching in the form of lectures, group discussion and role play, and the second part was conducted in the field to observe sterilization and abortion techniques, IUD insertion and removal, to participate in home visits, and to observe the activities of the MCH/FP clinics. In 1974 the Unit conducted seven courses, attended by eighteen sisters, forty-four staff nurses, twenty midwives, six family planning assistants, and two social workers, followed in 1975 by nine courses attended by four nursing officers, sixty-seven staff nurses, forty-eight midwives, and seven family planning assistants. The objective of this training programme was "to strengthen the technical and motivational knowledge and skills of staff in family planning and related topics to improve job efficiency".[13]

CLINICAL SERVICES

The national programme operated by the SFPPB was strongly integrated into the work of the Ministry of Health. The clinical services for family planning were offered in the forty-six Maternal and Child Health clinics and the six purely Family Planning clinics. These fifty-two MCH/FP clinics, strategically located over the country, provided family planning advisory and clinical services free and contraceptives at nominal prices. In addition, a mobile clinic staffed by a doctor and nursing personnel visited certain places on request. Another special service was the male family planning clinic located in the National Family Planning Centre in Dunearn Road where a male doctor attended to the needs of male patients daily and a panel of qualified surgeons performed vasectomy as an outpatient procedure once a week. The methods available at all the clinics were provided on a menu system which included oral contraceptive pills, IUD, injectable contraceptive, spermicidal cream/tablets, diaphragms and condoms.

The post-partum programme, initiated in 1966, functioned in the Kandang Kerbau Hospital, Toa Payoh Hospital and Alexandra Hospital. The service was provided by family planning assistants who were midwives with family planning training. They specialize in motivation by individual interviews of post-natal and post-abortal women in the three government maternity institutions towards accepting contraception. The programme was the main source of recruitment of new family planning acceptors. For instance, in 1977 contacts under this programme were made with 33,467 women, 81 per cent of whom were post-partum and the other 19 per cent post-abortal cases. These women were interviewed in the hospitals for family planning, and 28,828 accepted family planning verbally after the interview and 19,488 actually accepted reversible contraceptive methods subsequently.[14] In addition, 2,817 women were sterilized after the interview.

As a complement to the family planning services, the Cytology Unit offered a free cervical cancer screening service to women registered at the MCH/FP clinics for family planning. This was considered a good public health practice for women. In 1977 the Unit screened a total of 31,035 smears for 29,902 women, out of whom thirty-nine were confirmed cases of cancer. The main type of cancer among these detected cases was carcinoma-in-situ.

Though all available methods were made known to potential acceptors, patients preferring a particular method would be given their choice. The condom has become the most popular method, followed closely by the contraceptive pill. Of the total of 16,158 new acceptors in 1977, no less than 52 per cent used the condom and 46 per cent the pill. Less than 1 per cent utilized the IUD and the remaining 1 per cent accepted injectable contraceptive, spermicidal cream/tablet or the diaphragms.[15] Sterilization was becoming a popular method of family planning. In 1977 the number of female sterilizations was 8,236, and vasectomies numbered 351.

Seven brands of oral pills were distributed to patients at a cost of $1.00 per cycle, while condoms were sold at $0.50 for six pieces. IUD were priced at $5.00 per person for insertion with free check-up, and diaphragms were available at $2.00 each. Depo-provera injectable contraceptive was provided at $2.50 per injection, and chemical contraceptive or spermicide was available at $1.00 per tube. Vasectomies were performed at the Vasectomy Clinic at $5.00 per patient.

CHARACTERISTICS OF NEW ACCEPTORS

An analysis of the major characteristics of new acceptors of the national programme is presented in Table 3.2. The racial composition of the new acceptors has remained somewhat stable, with about the same proportions as those prevailing among the general population in most years. This seems to suggest there is little difference in the extent of contraceptive acceptance among the various races. Apart from this, the profile of the new acceptors has undergone significant changes. For one thing, the age of the new acceptors has been lowered over the years as evidenced by

TABLE 3.2

Per Cent Distribution of New Acceptors
by Selected Characteristics, 1968–77

Characteristics	1968	1969	1970	1971	1972	1973	1974	1975	1976	1977
Race										
Chinese	77	73	71	75	75	77	78	76	79	79
Malays	15	16	16	13	16	15	15	17	15	15
Indians	6	5	5	5	5	5	5	5	5	5
Others	2	6	8	7	4	3	2	2	1	1
Age Group										
15–19	4	5	6	8	9	8	4	8	7	6
20–24	21	26	31	36	38	38	35	41	40	39
25–29	30	28	25	26	30	32	41	36	37	38
30–34	22	19	19	16	12	12	12	9	10	11
35–39	14	12	10	7	6	5	5	4	4	4
40 & above	7	8	7	4	4	3	2	2	2	2
Education										
No education	49	39	32	24	9	17	14	13	9	9
Primary	38	37	38	38	41	41	41	36	37	34
Secondary	12	22	28	36	37	39	42	48	50	54
Tertiary	1	2	2	2	3	3	3	3	4	3
No. of Living Children										
0	1	1	3	4	5	5	7	11	11	13
1	21	31	44	54	62	65	67	65	66	65
2	17	19	17	15	15	16	16	15	15	15
3	14	14	11	9	6	6	6	4	4	4
4	12	10	7	4	3	2	2	2	2	1
5 or more	35	25	18	14	9	6	3	3	2	2
Reason for Family Planning										
Limitation	46	37	29	17	13	12	9	8	9	9
Spacing	52	60	67	79	83	84	87	88	88	87
Unknown/ Undecided	2	3	4	4	4	4	4	4	3	4

the rise in the proportion below age 30 from 55 per cent in 1968 to 83 per cent in 1977. This trend towards younger acceptors may be attributed partly to the saturation effect at the older ages over time.

Another conspicuous change concerns the educational background of the new acceptors. In the early years the new acceptors were comparatively less educated since as high as 49 per cent had no education and only 12 per cent had a secondary education in 1968. By 1977 the proportion with no education had fallen to 9 per cent and slightly more than half now have been to secondary schools. This trend towards more educated acceptors is in a way a reflection of the rise in the educational level of women in Singapore.

With regard to the number of children, those with less than three children comprised 39 per cent of the total new acceptors in 1968, but this proportion was increased to 93 per cent in 1977. The mean number of children of new acceptors decreased from 3.8 children in 1968 to 1.2 in 1977. This was a natural consequence of the continuous decline of fertility to even below replacement level. The lower parity among new acceptors was related to the increasing tendency among women to practise family planning for child spacing rather than for family limitation. While in the early years of the national programme about half the women cited child spacing as the reason, this proportion has approached almost 90 per cent by 1977. The trend towards younger and lower parity women was a reflection of the usual feature of a national programme where the older, higher parity women were the first to adopt family planning for reasons of family limitation, followed by younger, lower parity women who were more interested in spacing births.

About 53 per cent of the new acceptors in 1977 were not working at the time of registration, and some 81 per cent had never practised any form of contraception. The others who had practised before serve to underline the important fact that the new acceptors are defined as new acceptors of the national programme and not necessarily new acceptors of family planning.

One method of measuring the extent of participation of women in the national programme is by means of the acceptance rate which can be defined as the number of new acceptors of the programme per thousand women aged 15 to 44.[16] The computed rates are shown in Table 3.3.

In the first year of the national programme the acceptance rate was 79.4 per thousand women aged fifteen to forty-four, and it fell a little to 78.1 the very next year and reached its peak of 84.9 in 1968.[17] In the

TABLE 3.3

Rate of Acceptance

Year	Rate	Year	Rate
1966	79.4	1972	35.8
1967	78.1	1973	37.4
1968	84.9	1974	34.6
1969	81.7	1975	30.5
1970	53.1	1976	31.5
1971	37.4	1977	27.8

fourth year the rate still remained high at 81.7 but it tumbled down to 53.1 in 1970 when abortion was legalized, and dipped down further to 37.4 in 1971. Thereafter, a new equilibrium at a lower level emerged with the rate staying between 35 and 37 up to 1974 and around 30 in the years 1975 and 1976. The year 1977 witnessed another noticeable drop in the rate to a new low of 27.8. It would appear that one cannot discount the relationship between the lower and generally declining acceptance rate from 1970 onwards and the legalization of both abortion and sterilization. Of course, sterilization has the permanent and cumulative effect of reducing the number from the total group of present and potential acceptors of family planning over the years.

TARGETS AND ACHIEVEMENTS

The First Five-Year Plan 1966–70 was aimed at motivating 180,000 eligible women to accept family planning during the first five years of the Board's existence. This target figure was calculated on the basis of certain assumptions concerning fertility, mortality and marriage patterns derived from data made available in the 1957 Population Census. It was assumed that out of the estimated total of 450,000 women in the reproductive age group 15 to 44, about 67 per cent or 300,000 were married. It was further assumed that among the latter about 20 per cent or 60,000 would not require family planning services. This leaves 180,000 eligible married women who would have to be catered for during the first five years.[18] The annual target of new family planning acceptors for each of these years is shown in Table 3.4. The ultimate aim of the five-year plan was to reduce the crude birth rate from 30 per thousand population to 20 by the end of the period.

TABLE 3.4

Targeted and Actual New Acceptors within the National Programme, 1966–77

Year	Targeted New Acceptors (1)	Actual New Acceptors (2)	Achievement (2) − (1) (3)
	First Five-Year Plan		
1966	25,000	30,410	+5,410
1967	30,000	30,935	+935
1968	35,000	35,338	+338
1969	45,000	35,643	−9,357
1970	45,000	24,230	−20,770
Total	180,000	156,556	−23,444
	Second Five-Year Plan		
1971	16,000	17,749	+1,749
1972	16,000	17,666	+1,666
1973	16,000	19,102	+3,102
1974	16,000	18,292	+2,292
1975	16,000	16,692	+692
Total	80,000	89,501	+9,501
	Third Five-Year Plan		
1976	*	17,674	*
1977	*	16,158	*

Note: * Unknown.

Though 1966 was essentially a year of planning and organizing for the Board, there was a steady increase in the number of acceptors from 411 in January to 2,234 in December. By the end of the year a total of 30,410 had become new acceptors of the programme, exceeding the 1966 target by 21 per cent. However, it should be pointed out that many of the new acceptors within the programme were in fact formerly patients of the Family Planning Association clinics, almost all of which were taken over by the Board, because the new acceptor figures shown in Table 3.4 refer to new programme acceptors rather than new family planning acceptors. This is reflected in the second year when the number of new acceptors rose only slightly to 30,935, exceeding the target by a mere 3 per cent in spite of massive publicity and educational programmes.

These included the First Anniversary Exhibition, a United Nations-sponsored international conference-cum-exhibition, extensive exhibitions at community level and widespread fieldwork by the Board's staff. During 1968, which can be considered as a year of consolidation, the number of new acceptors rose appreciably to 35,338 which just managed to reach the target with some 338 to spare. In the following year the number remained almost stationary at 35,643 and fell far short of the target figure of 45,000. The last year of the Plan witnessed a sharp drop in the number of new acceptors to 24,230, amounting to only 54 per cent of the 1970 target fixed at 45,000. In a way this drop was related to the legalization of abortion and sterilization in March 1970.

The setting of the overall target at 180,000 was subsequently proved to be on the high side according to the results of the 1970 Population Census. The projected female population of 450,000 aged fifteen to forty-four came close to the 1970 Census figure of 455,943. What went wrong was the use of the same percentage of married women within the age group 15–44 derived from the 1957 Census to estimate the number of married women for the years 1966 to 1970. This proportion, which stood at 67 per cent in 1957, has fallen consistently over the years so that by 1970 it stood at 53 per cent as evidenced by the 1970 Census. The nuptiality assumption has therefore led to an over-estimation of the overall target of eligible women. A more realistic figure would be about 150,000. Another criticism of the target-setting concerns the apportioning of the overall figure to each of the five years. Whilst the increase in the annual target by 5,000 in the first three years appears reasonable, the increase for the fourth year by 10,000 resulting in the annual target being fixed at 45,000 for 1969, and also for 1970, is not consonant with the saturation effect that is bound to take place a few years after the launching of a national programme. It is precisely this that accounts for the inevitable failure to achieve the annual target in the last two years by a wide margin.

When the First Five-Year Plan came to an end in 1970, the number of new acceptors had reached a total of 156,556. Though this figure did not quite approach the original target of 180,000, it exceeded the revised target of 150,000 based on the more up-to-date information obtained from the 1970 Census. It is also worth noting that during the five-year period the annual number averaged about 31,000 which was far above the annual figure registered by the Family Planning Association prior to 1966. For instance, the 1965 total amounted to only 9,845 and this was the highest ever recorded by the Association. Finally, the 1970 crude birth rate was brought down to 22.1 per thousand population as compared with the targeted rate of 20.0. Notwithstanding the failure to achieve the target, the drop in the crude birth rate by about 25 per cent from 29.5 in 1965 to 22.1 in 1970 was quite an achievement. Fertility as reflected by the total fertility rate was reduced at an accelerated speed amounting 33 per cent from 4.62 to 3.10 during the same period as compared to the 30 per cent decline during the nine-year period from 1957 to 1965.

While the details of the First Five-Year Plan were published in advance in the *White Paper on Family Planning* before its implementation date, the same cannot be said about the Second Five-Year Plan 1971–75. No mention of it was made in the 1971 Annual Report of the Board, and only in the 1972 Report was a reference made to this plan to the effect that the target was "to consolidate the efforts of the five years with an even annual recruitment of 16,000 new acceptors, to achieve a total of 80,000 registrants with the Board by the end of 1975".[19] The overall aim of the plan expressed in terms of a reduction in the crude birth rate was spelled out later in the 1974 Report to the effect that the rate was targeted to be brought down from 22.1 per thousand population to 18.0 during the plan period.[20]

The data provided at the bottom of Table 3.4 reveal that the annual target of 16,000 new acceptors was exceeded every year. At the end of the plan period the total number of new acceptors recruited amounted to 89,501 which exceeded the overall target by 9,501 or 12 per cent. However, at the beginning of the Second Plan there was an adverse trend in the number of births and the birth rate which had first become apparent in the last year of the First Five-Year Plan. For three consecutive years from 1970 to 1972, an upsurge in both the number of births and the crude birth rate was recorded, caused primarily by the increasing proportion of women in the reproductive ages. The total fertility rate even increased a little in 1972 which seems to suggest the appearance of births previously postponed by mothers who had earlier become programme acceptors for child-spacing reasons. But over the whole plan period the birth rate was reduced below the target level to 17.1 per thousand population in 1975 from 22.3 in 1971. During this same period the total fertility rate fell by 32.0 per cent from 3.06 in 1971 to slightly below replacement fertility level of 2.08 in 1975. Leaving aside the dynamics of this fertility decline which will be examined in a subsequent chapter, one can say that the Second Five-Year Plan has proved to be resoundingly successful in that replacement fertility was more than attained by the last year of the Plan. The SFPPB in fact had as its target the attainment of replacement fertility in 1980.

The fertility reduction of 32.0 per cent attained during the Second Plan in the context of an already low fertility base as compared with the lower 32.9 per cent recorded in the First Plan is indeed a remarkable achievement by any standard. This result was secured not only by the recruitment of new acceptors to the national programme but also by the introduction of a comprehensive range of effective population policies during the years coinciding with the Second Plan period. These policies include the complete liberalization of the restrictive laws concerning induced abortion, sterilization and the institutionalization of a series of tough social incentives and disincentives aimed at promoting the two-child family norm and sterilization.

The target of the Third Five-Year Plan in terms of the annual number of new acceptors to be recruited during the period 1976–80 was not announced. However, the 1976 Report of the SFPPB stated that the programme activities in the immediate years would be directed towards dissuading young people from early marriage and parenthood and encouraging wider spacing between births. "In this way, a steep rise in the number of births can be avoided. As the cohort fertility will be maintained at Replacement Level, the ultimate goal of Zero Population Growth is retained."[21] In another publication it was stated that the aim of the current plan is to maintain the net reproduction rate of 1.0 for the next five years from 1976 to 1980. "All activities are expected to continue at maintenance level without any change in policy, direction or intensity in 1976."[22] The 1977 Report still did not spell out the target number of new acceptors for the third plan, and it only stated that "With Replacement Level attained in 1975, the broad policy of the National Family Planning and Population Programme during the Third Five-Year Plan is to maintain fertility at this level."[23]

Notes

1. The Committee consisted of a Chairman in the person of Mr R. Quahe, Deputy Vice-Chancellor, University of Singapore, and, as members, Dr K. Kanagaratnam, Deputy Director of Medical Services (Health), Ministry of Health, and Mr A. D. Fraser, representative of the Family Planning Association.

2. *White Paper on Family Planning*, Command 22 of 1965, presented to the Legislative Assembly on 27 September 1965 (Singapore: Government Printer, 1965), 25 pp.

3. Ibid., p. 14.

4. *Singapore Family Planning and Population Board Act, 1965*, No. 32 of 1965 (Singapore: Government Printer, 1965).

5. Quoted on p. 17 of *First Annual Report of the Singapore Family Planning and Population Board, 1966* (Singapore: Government Printing Office, 1967).

6. "Speech by Mr Chua Sian Chin, Minister for Health and Home Affairs at the World Population Conference, Bucharest, Romania, 19–30 August 1974", *Singapore Public Health Bulletin*, No. 15, January 1975, pp. 4–5; and *Singapore — A County Statement for World Population Conference, Bucharest, 19–30 August 1974*, Singapore Family Planning and Population Board Paper 22, 13 pp.

7. For details, see Wan Fook Kee, *Communications Strategy in the Singapore National Family Planning Programme*, Singapore Family Planning and Population Board Paper 14. This is a paper prepared for the Seminar in Communication for Family Planning sponsored by the East-West Communication Institute, East-West Center, Honolulu, during 8–20 August 1971.

8. See, for example, K. Kanagaratnam, *The National Programme in Singapore — A Review of Two Years, 1966 and 1967*, Singapore Family Planning and Population Board Paper 1, p. 39.

9. *Ninth Annual Report of the Singapore Family Planning and Population Board, 1974* (Singapore: Eurasia Press, 1975), p. 29.

10. The results of some of these studies are provided in K. Kanagaratnam and Khoo Chian Kim, "Singapore: The Use of Oral Contraceptives in National Program", *Studies in Family Planning* 48 (December 1969): 1–9; Wan Fook Kee and Quah Siam Tee, "Singapore: A Study of Clinic Continuation Rates", *Studies in Family Planning* 2 (December 1971): 257–58; and "Singapore: A Cost-Effect Analysis of a Family Planning Program", *Studies in Family Planning* 3 (January 1972): 8–11; and Wan Fook Kee, Chen Ai Ju and Jessie Tan, "Oral Contraceptive Continuation Rates in the Singapore National Program, 1966–1972", *Studies in Family Planning* 6, no. 1 (January 1975): 17–21.

11. *Report of a Comparative Study on the Administration of Family Planning Programmes in the Escap Region: Organizational Determinants of Performance in Family Planning Services*, Asian Population Studies no. 29 (Bangkok: Economic and Social Commission for Asia and the Pacific, 1977).

12. *Annual Report of the National Statistical Commission, 1973* (Singapore: Photoplates Private Ltd., 1974), p. 8.

13. *Ninth Annual Report of the Singapore Family Planning and Population Board, 1974*, p. 34.

14. *Twelfth Annual Report of the Singapore Family Planning and Population Board, 1977* (Singapore: Secura Singapore, 1978), p. 28.
15. Ibid., p. 26.
16. *Assessment of Acceptance and Effectiveness of Family Planning Methods*, Asian Population Studies no. 4 (Bangkok: Economic and Social Commission for Asia and the Pacific, 1968).
17. See Chapter 4, footnote 37.
18. *White Paper on Family Planning*, p. 6.
19. *Seventh Annual Report of the Singapore Family Planning and Population Board, 1972* (Singapore: Singapore National Printers, 1973), pp. 3–4.
20. *Ninth Annual Report of the Singapore Family Planning and Population Board, 1974*, p. 1.
21. *Eleventh Annual Report of the Singapore Family Planning and Population Board, 1916* (Singapore: Secura Singapore, 1977), p. 2.
22. Wan Fook Kee and Margaret Loh, "Singapore", in *Family Planning in Developing World: A Review of Programs*, edited by Walter B. Watson, A Population Council Factbook (New York: The Population Council, 1977), p. 22.
23. *Twelfth Annual Report of the Singapore Family Planning and Population Board, 1977*, p. 2.

4

Induced Abortion

Until 1970 the performance of abortion in Singapore, like many other members of the British Commonwealth, was governed by laws based on legislation passed in the nineteenth century in Victorian England. It constituted a criminal act punishable under sections 312–316 of the Penal Code and could only be defended on the plea that the abortion was caused in good faith to safeguard the life of the woman concerned. Under such prohibitive laws, some pregnant women had no alternative but to resort to backlane illegal abortions as a means of terminating unwanted pregnancies. Though the incidence of such criminally induced abortions performed during any period of time will always remain a mystery, the existence of such abortions is common knowledge among the public and has been confirmed by cases clinically diagnosed as "abortions with sepsis" in Kandang Kerbau Hospital.[1] Moreover, there were numerous occasions when pregnant women approached the Family Planning Association for an abortion but were turned down.

During the early days of the national programme, some embarrassment was caused by women patients who approached the clinic staff of the SFPPB to terminate their pregnancies on account of contraceptive failure, especially from the IUD. This was particularly so in the case of women who had adopted family planning with IUD as a method of preventing further childbirth rather than spacing their children.[2] Nothing could be done to alleviate the suffering of the women and they were persuaded to continue with their pregnancies. It was felt that this category of contraceptive failure should merit sympathetic consideration for induced abortion had the law permitted such termination of pregnancies.[3]

MOVE TOWARDS LEGAL ABORTION

The review of the government policy concerning induced abortion was undertaken by the SFPPB soon after its establishment in January 1966. The role of induced abortion in the context of the family planning programme within the overall population control policy was discussed in some detail by the Board. It was generally agreed that induced abortion should be made available as a complement to this programme but not as an alternative to the other less drastic and preventive methods of family planning. By 1967 the Medical Committee of the SFPPB had resolved by a simple majority decision that failed sterilization and failed contraception could be accepted as criteria for legally induced abortion. Additional criteria agreed upon were (a) when the life of the mother is in danger, including both her mental and physical health, (b) eugenic cases such as German measles or congenital malformation, and (c) when the mother is a victim of sex crimes such as rape and incest.[4] It was felt very strongly at that time that induced abortion on demand would not be entirely acceptable in Singapore as there were likely to be professional, moral and religious objections.

The views of the SFPPB concerning the legalization of induced abortion were transmitted to the Health Ministry for consideration, and by the second half of 1967 the Singapore Government had arrived at a positive decision with regard to the abortion question. The first announcement in public about the government's intention to liberalize the restrictive abortion laws was made by the Minister for Health, Mr Yong Nyuk Lin, in an official statement released to the public on 10 August 1967. The statement observed that though the family planning programme had been proceeding satisfactorily under the auspices of the SFPPB for the past eighteen months, unwanted babies were still being brought into the world. It also viewed with concern the sizeable number of pregnant women still resorting to the dangerous method of illegal abortion to get rid of their unwanted babies. The statement added: "With the proposed legalizing of abortion, every child born in Singapore will henceforth be a wanted child and our women folk will thus be liberated from the clutches of nefarious people who are unscrupulous enough to exploit and profit in the anomalous situation which regards abortion as being illegal abortion."[5]

Less than a month later, Mr Yong Nyuk Lin took the opportunity to reiterate the government's desire to legalize induced abortion in his address delivered in the opening ceremony of the ECAFE-sponsored Working Group Meeting on Communication Aspects of Family Planning held in Singapore on 5 September 1967. Among other things, he stated:

> To date, there is no such thing as a 100 per cent effective contraceptive. That being so, there will be a number of "contraceptive failures" ending with pregnancy for the women — the classic unplanned pregnancy and the unwanted child! Such a situation must come as a grievous shock and a great let-down to the woman. Should we not lift a finger to help her out of her predicament? Must she be penalised to carry on with the unwanted pregnancy when she earnestly begs her termination of pregnancy? Can't she be given the choice of a legal abortion? Must she, in desperation, resort to the quack to perform an illegal abortion with all its attendant dangers?
>
> It is to be noted that there is one important difference where Singapore is concerned. For most of the countries which have legalised abortion the Family Planning movement would appear to come after abortion was legalised. For Singapore, we started off with family planning and family planning is a reasonable success and not a failure, and legalization of abortion is being brought in as our second line of defence, in waging the battle against hordes of unwanted children. It is not our first line of defence.[6]

Following the ministerial statement released on 10 August 1967 and the confirmation of the government's intention by the Health Minister on 5 September 1967, there was considerable public discussion of and interest in the various facets of the controversial issue of the legalization of abortion throughout the latter part of 1967 and well into 1968. Most of the comments came from interested individuals in the form of letters published in newspapers[7] and comments by the Singapore Medical Association,[8] the Conference of the Methodist Church and the Graduates' Christian Fellowship.[9] The reaction was somewhat divided between those in favour of legally induced abortion and those against it, some of those who came out in support of the government expressed concern and caution.

The final statement of the government's plan was made by Mr Chua Sian Chin, who was then the Health Minister, at the Fourth Asian Congress of Obstetrics and Gynaecology held in Singapore on 16 November 1968. The Minister said,

> A reform of the law on abortion will be undertaken. However, in Singapore, legalized abortion will not be a substitute for family planning but as a natural complement to provide that ultimate security for the

woman who does not wish to have the unwanted child. This piece of legislation will be introduced in Parliament before the end of the year.[10]

True enough, on 3 December 1968 the Health Minister introduced into Parliament for the first reading the Abortion Bill designed to reform and liberalize the laws relating to induced abortion.[11] According to an explanatory statement accompanying the Bill, the proposed legislation would, if passed, continue in force for four years but the Minister might extend it for a further year. The effect of this is that after five years, at most, a critical assessment could be made as to the effectiveness of the legislation and consideration could be given by Parliament as to the desirability of continuing the legislation.

THE ABORTION DEBATE

The release of the anxiously-awaited details of the Abortion Bill met strong criticism from various quarters, including certain members within the ruling People's Action Party. In order to allow the public to air their views and to suggest amendments, particularly when Parliament consisted of all PAP members with not a single opposition member, the controversial Bill together with the simultaneously presented Voluntary Sterilization Bill were referred to a Select Committee in order to provide interested groups with ample opportunities to make public representations, oral or written, in any of the four official languages of Parliament. The Committee held eight meetings between April and June 1969 to hear oral evidence from five different organizations and to consider thirty-three written submissions on the Bill.[12] Most of those presenting their oral or written views were from the medical profession and religious organizations. The Council of the Singapore Medical Association agreed on the need to reform the abortion laws, noted the success of the family planning programme, and pledged their continued support, but was against the idea of making induced abortion freely available to any woman who wanted it. They considered legalized abortion to be an unsuitable method of birth control in view of the higher health and mortality risks involved and the possible use of abortion instead of contraception to control family size. The Christian groups were more concerned with the moral issues of the matter, and argued that legalized abortion would condone laxity in sexual morality and would be tantamount to taking away a life. By and large, they accepted family planning but were against abortion as a method of population control.

After a lapse of about a year since its first reading, the Abortion Bill with a few amendments to take into account the Report of the Select Committee was put before Parliament on 24 December 1969 on the final lap of its passage. In presenting the Bill at its third reading, the Health Minister, Mr Chua Sian Chin, stressed that most of the representations were agreed on the need to reform and liberalize the laws relating to abortion though there was some disagreement on specific provisions of the Bill and its wording and on how far one should go in liberalizing it.[13] He further emphasized that the proposed amendments would in no way alter the aims and objectives of the Bill but would in fact improve and strengthen some of its provisions. The debate that ensued in the House, with all members coming from the ruling PAP, proved to be the most lively and critical in the history of Parliament since Independence in August 1965.[14]

The opponents of the Bill argued that there was no need to legalize abortion because family planning was already a great success, that there was no objection to induced abortion on medical grounds but not on socio-economic grounds, that some of the members were convinced that abortion was a bad thing, that widespread abortion would be disastrous for the nation and hence it should be confined and discouraged in every possible way.[15] The greatest opposition came from the only woman member in the House, Madam Chan Choy Siong, who described the Bill as a retrogressive step and the act of an irresponsible government.[16] Abortion, according to her, was tantamount to murder, more women would turn from practising family planning to abortion, and the government should promote sex education in schools rather than promoting promiscuity by relaxing the abortion laws. The Prime Minister, Mr Lee Kuan Yew, spoke at great length in support of the Bill, emphasizing the importance of raising the quality of the population by discouraging large families especially among the poorer classes who could least afford them. The Health Minister, Mr Chua Sian Chin, rounded up the debate by reminding the House that the Bill was not a means of controlling population but rather to "liberate women from the tyranny of unwanted pregnancies, and to ensure that every child born would be a wanted child". The Abortion Bill passed its second and third readings on 29 December 1969 by 33 votes to 10 with 1 abstention and 15 absentees.[17]

It should be emphasized that the decision to change the restrictive laws governing induced abortion was first announced by the government on 10 August 1967, and it was not until some eighteen months later that the Abortion Bill was presented to Parliament for its first reading on 3 December 1968.

Even so the Bill did not go any further and was committed to the Select Committee and finally appeared a year later with some amendments for its second and third readings in December 1969. From the time of its first announcement, the proposed Bill had generated a great deal of discussion and was eventually passed against a background of immense public and parliamentary controversy. The delay itself is an indication of the controversial nature of the Bill and the considerable care with which the Singapore Government formulated and developed its population control policy.

LEGAL ABORTION

Under the Abortion Act 1969, which came into force on 20 March 1970, an eleven-member Termination of Pregnancy Authorisation Board was set up to authorize the treatment to terminate pregnancy by registered medical practitioners.[18] Members of the Board comprised the Director of Medical Services, the Deputy Director of Medical Services in charge of Health, the Deputy Director of Medical Services in charge of Hospitals, the Director of Social Welfare, an obstetrician and gynaecologist and a psychiatrist employed in the Public Service and five other members to be appointed by the Minister for Health, three of whom were to be females, of whom two were to be professionally qualified social workers.[19]

Under the Abortion Act, which was in many respects based on the 1967 Abortion Act passed by the British Parliament on 27 October 1967, the Board could grant approval to a woman to have an abortion performed by a registered medical practitioner under defined circumstances.[20] These are spelled out in subsection (2) of section 5 of the Act as follows:

(a) that the continuance of the pregnancy would involve serious risk to the life of the pregnant woman or serious injury to the physical or mental health of the pregnant woman;

(b) that the environment of the pregnant woman, both at the time when the child would be born and thereafter so far as is foreseeable, justifies the termination of her pregnancy (the expression "environment" in this paragraph includes the family and financial circumstances of the pregnant woman);

(c) that there is substantial risk that if the child was born it would suffer from such physical or mental abnormalities as to be seriously handicapped; or

(d) that the pregnancy is the result of rape under section 375 of the Penal Code or of incest under section 376A of the Penal Code or of unlawful carnal connection under paragraph (j) of subsection (1) of section 128 of the Women's Charter or of intercourse with an insane or feebleminded person.

Furthermore, the Act also made provisions for abortion to be performed by registered medical practitioners without the authorization of the Board. Under section 5(3) a registered medical practitioner acting in consultation with another registered medical practitioner could perform an abortion, if they were of the opinion that the termination of pregnancy was necessary on the grounds indicated in section 5(2)(a) above, provided that the abortion was carried out in a government hospital or in an approved institution. Section 5(5) provided that if the medical practitioner considered that such treatment was immediately necessary to save the life of the patient, such treatment need not be carried out in a government hospital or an approved institution and did not require the second opinion of another medical practitioner. The Board had to be notified of abortions performed under these two circumstances within two weeks of such treatment, together with a statement setting forth the medical reasons for this type of abortion.

The most significant clause from the family planning point of view in this reform of the abortion laws was the social clause incorporated into section 5(2)(b) above, otherwise termed the environmental clause which included the family and financial circumstances of the pregnant woman. These socio-economic reasons for abortion received considerable opposition from those who voiced an opinion against the Act. It was expected that the majority of the applicants for abortion would be authorized under this clause which constituted the key component to the liberalized laws.

Certain conditions or safeguards were incorporated in the Act. Authorization would not be granted for grounds (a) and (c) of section 5(2) above if the pregnancy was of more than twenty-four weeks' duration unless such treatment was necessary to save the life or to prevent grave permanent injury to the physical or mental health of the pregnant woman.[21] Authorization would also not be given for grounds (a) and (d) of section 5(2) above if the pregnancy was of more than sixteen weeks.

In addition, authorization for the termination of pregnancy would only be given if the pregnant woman was a Singapore citizen, or the wife of a citizen, or had been resident in Singapore for a period of at least four months immediately preceding the date on which such treatment was to be carried out, except only if it was considered necessary to save the life of the patient. The aim of this clause was to prevent Singapore from becoming an abortion centre for, in particular, its neighbouring countries.

The Act also laid down that, except for the special case mentioned earlier, every treatment to terminate pregnancy would be carried out by a registered medical practitioner in a government hospital or in an approved institution. Another safeguard stipulated that no person could disclose any facts or information relating to treatment to terminate pregnancy unless the pregnant woman expressly gave her consent. Finally, the Act included a provision exempting any person participating in abortion treatment if he or she has any objection on moral grounds.

According to the Act there were certain procedures, both legal and administrative, that had to be followed before an abortion could be performed by a registered medical practitioner. The pregnant woman had first to arrange to be medically examined by a medical practitioner, complete the prescribed form of application, and hand it over to the practitioner who forwarded the completed form with a medical certificate stating the grounds for abortion, together with the relevant documents required, to the Board for its consideration. The applicant might be required to appear for an interview before the Board. In practice, an applicant would be informed of the Board's decision within one week of submission of the application, and, if approved, an appointment will be given for the abortion to be performed within seven days in a government hospital or an approved institution.

From 20 March 1970 to 31 December 1970, a total of 3,093 pregnant women applied for induced abortion in accordance with the provisions of the Abortion Act, and out of this total some 2,726 or 88 per cent were granted approval, though only 1,970 went through the treatment to terminate pregnancy.[22] Out of 367 unsuccessful applicants, 262 were rejected because the reasons given were not acceptable to the Board, 90 were too advanced in their pregnancy, and only 2 were refused for failing to satisfy the citizenship or residential qualification. Among the successful applicants, 88 were approved under section 5(2)(a), 2,596 under 5(2)(b), 12 under 5(2)(c), 4 under 5(2)(d), and 26 under 5(3). This shows that the Board has given approval to some 2,596 pregnant women,

or 95 per cent of the successful applicants, on the basis of socio-
economic reasons, the most common of which was "unable to afford
another child/too many children" cited by 1,946 pregnant women. Among
the successful applicants, 50 per cent had no formal education and 34
per cent had only primary education, 46 per cent had 5 or more living
children, and 80 per cent had total monthly income between $100 and
$400. The majority were married women and only 5 per cent were
unmarried or single. It would appear that the Act achieved one of its
main aims in permitting pregnant women, who could ill afford another
child or already had too many children, to have their pregnancy
terminated. By and large, the experience gained during the first ten
months or so showed that the implementation of the Act under the
watchful eye of the eleven-member Termination of Pregnancy
Authorization Board had worked satisfactorily without any major problems
being encountered. The comparatively low rate of abortion during this
period seems to suggest that the provisions of the Act and the supervision
of the Board were sufficiently stringent to compel attention to
contraception as a preferred method of family limitation, whilst allowing
abortion as a method of last resort.

ABORTION ON DEMAND

The 1969 Abortion Act which came into force on 20 January 1970 was
supposed to be temporary and subject to review in five years' time.[23]
Accordingly, the Act was reviewed in 1974. In view of the government's
determination at that time to have a comprehensive population control
programme to work towards replacement fertility and the satisfactory
working of the Act in the past, the government decided not only to
continue with the Act but to liberalize it further to make abortion on
demand possible and to make it a permanent feature of the laws of
Singapore. On 23 October 1974 the Abortion Bill which sought to
liberalize further the abortion laws contained in the old Act was presented
to Parliament by Mr Chua Sian Chin, the Minister for Health and Home
Affairs, for its first reading. As compared with the previous occasion
when the passage of the 1969 Act had generated considerable debate
both inside and outside the House, the proposed Bill attracted little
comment from the public and less heated debate in Parliament.

In presenting the new comprehensive Abortion Bill in its final
reading on 6 November 1974, Mr Chua Sian Chin reported to the House

that the exercise had been a huge success and that many of the fears expressed by opponents and critics earlier against the original Act had proved unfounded.[24] He quoted facts and figures, obtained since 20 March 1970 when the old Act came into force, to demonstrate that abortion was complementary to family planning and not a substitute, that legalized abortion had not led to an increase in promiscuity or a breakdown of moral standards, and that it had not led to an increase in maternal mortality and morbidity of pregnant women. With due respect to the religious and ethical beliefs of individual MPs in the House, he withdrew the government whip during the debate on the Bill so that they could speak freely. The opponents of the Bill were against liberalizing the laws further to make abortion easily available.[25] They argued that such easy abortions would encourage abortion instead of family planning and would lead to more permissiveness and promiscuity. The Abortion Act 1974 was passed by Parliament on 6 November 1974 and came into force on 27 December 1974, repealing the original Act.

The Abortion Act 1974 introduced the principle of abortion on demand subject to certain safeguards by incorporating very liberalized laws and extremely simplified procedures governing its operation.[26] Section 3(1), the key section to the Act, provides that "Subject to the provisions of this Act, a person shall not be guilty of an offence under the law relating to abortion when a pregnancy is terminated by a registered medical practitioner acting on the request of a pregnant woman and with her written consent." Abortion can now be provided on the request of the pregnant woman with her written consent, and the medical practitioner no longer has to be satisfied that the four grounds stipulated under section 5(2) of the old Act exist. In fact, these grounds have been deleted in the 1974 Act. Furthermore, the origin of the conception is now irrelevant for the purpose of the 1974 Act. There does not seem to be any requirement of a minimum age for giving consent; presumably any woman however young may lawfully ask for an abortion.

In many ways the 1974 Act has simplified the procedures by which pregnant women can obtain an abortion. Authorization for treatment for the termination of pregnancies no longer needs to be obtained from the eleven-member Termination of Pregnancy Authorization Board which was abolished forthwith. This certainly cuts out the cumbersome delaying procedures and the mandatory waiting period so characteristic of the original Act. Treatment to terminate pregnancy, if it consists solely of the use of drugs, need not be carried out in a government hospital or in an approved institution, neither is it necessary for the registered medical practitioner to hold the prescribed qualifications or to have acquired any special skills prescribed in the regulations as in the case of an abortion by means of surgical operation. The imposition of a fee of $5 no longer applies if the abortion is performed in an approved institution, though it continues to apply if performed in a government hospital.

The repealed Act required a registered medical practitioner to have certain obstetric and gynaecological qualifications to perform any abortion regardless of the gestation limitation. Now a distinction is made between those qualifications needed for a practitioner to perform earlier abortions and those needed to perform late abortions.[27] A practitioner doing abortions up to the sixteenth week of pregnancy requires at least six months' experience in an obstetrics and gynaecological unit of a Singapore government hospital or in a hospital recognized by the Minister. For doctors performing abortions between the sixteenth and twenty-fourth weeks, the law requires them to have certain higher degrees or specialist qualifications.

Most of the safeguards in the repealed Act have been retained in the 1974 Act. One important safeguard is that no treatment for the termination of pregnancy shall be carried out if the pregnancy is of more than twenty-four weeks' duration unless such treatment is immediately necessary to save the life or to prevent grave injury to the physical or mental health of the pregnant woman. Even so, in such a case a higher qualification is required for the medical practitioner before he is entitled to perform the operation. The original safeguard in respect of Singapore citizenship or four-month residential requirements, designed to prevent Singapore from becoming the abortion centre in South-East Asia, has been retained in the Act.[28] The 1974 Act also stipulates that every treatment to terminate pregnancy shall be carried out by a medical practitioner in a government hospital or in an approved institution. The safeguard against disclosure of information relating to treatment for abortion incorporated in the repealed Act has also been retained in the 1974 Act. So too is the provision exempting any person from participating in abortion treatment to which he or she has any objection on moral grounds.

The 1974 Abortion Act has been designed to make the services available at the earliest possible stage of pregnancy at the lowest cost to the clinic and the lowest price to the woman requesting an abortion. The recent legal and administrative changes were meant to eliminate the time-consuming procedures of approval and certification of the licensing board and to allow doctors to qualify through on-the-spot experience to perform abortion treatment. By and large, the problem of unwanted pregnancies has been brought out of the hands of the criminal abortionist and into the public arena, thus contributing to the improvement in birth control services. The existence of a highly liberalized Abortion Act has introduced an additional component to the population control programme in Singapore.

CHARACTERISTICS OF ABORTEES

An important consequence of the legalization of abortion in Singapore is the development of a statistical system of collecting, through the legally prescribed form, comprehensive and reliable statistical data relating to what is perhaps the most fundamental and least understood area of demographic behaviour and public health.[29] In the field of demography, information on the incidence of abortion and of the characteristics of women undergoing abortion permits the evaluation of the total number of conceptions, the evaluation of the impact of abortion on fertility, and the measurement of the role of abortion in birth prevention compared with contraception. From the point of view of public health, abortion statistics provide the basis required for the planning and administration of abortion services and for the measurement of mortality and morbidity associated with legally induced abortions.

Though the supervision of the operation of the Abortion Act is the direct responsibility of the Ministry of Health, the Research and Evaluation Unit of the SFPPB has been entrusted with the job of producing abortion statistics from the completed prescribed forms submitted to the Director of Medical Services by medical practitioners within thirty days of performing the abortion.[30] The abortion statistics have facilitated the government's monitoring of the performance of the Abortion Act during the first five years, and have enabled the Minister for Health to put up a good case in Parliament in November 1974 for not only the continuation but also the further liberalization of the abortion laws.[31] The statistics revealed that women have not abandoned contraceptive practice in favour of abortion because the number of women with more than one abortion formed only 7 per cent of the total number of abortions and the legal abortion ratio was only 110 per thousand live-births in 1973 as compared with the corresponding figure of 237 for Sweden, 799 for Bulgaria and 1,023 for Hungary. Legalization of abortion has not encouraged promiscuity since the number of single women who had abortions numbered only some 5 per cent of the total number performed in the first four years as against the 1973 figure of 43 per cent for Finland, 48 per cent for England and Wales, and 52 per cent for Sweden. With regard to mortality there had not been a single death from abortions performed under the Act during the four and a half years from March 1970. The vast majority of women who sought abortion were from the lower income group, with a median income of less than $300 per month. The Act, according to the Minister, has served to provide an avenue for married women, especially those in the lower income group, to be freed from the burden of an unwanted or unintended pregnancy without any great risk to the woman and without detriment to the nation.

In Table 4.1 are given the statistics for the past eight years, showing the per cent distribution of legal abortions by age of women and parity at the time of the treatment for the termination of pregnancy.[32] Among the women obtaining legal abortions, there was a persistent swing towards a younger age pattern during the eight-year period 1970 to 1977. The proportion of abortees between the ages of 30 and 39 decreased from 54 per cent in 1970 to 30 per cent in 1977, while the proportion between 20 and 29 rose from only 27 per cent to 55 per cent during the same period. A more concise indication is reflected by the mean age of abortees, which fell during this period from 32.8 to 28.0 years.

The per cent distribution of legal abortions by the number of living children parallels the pattern observed in the distribution by age of women. A conspicuous shift of great impact took place in the parity pattern of women seeking legal abortions in these years. Only 0.5 per cent of the abortees in 1970 were nulliparous, whereas 51 per cent had experienced at least five births. By 1974 the proportion of nulliparous women had increased to 7 per cent while women with five or more living children had dropped to 23 per cent. A more spectacular change was brought about by the 1974 Abortion Act in 1975 when the proportion of nulliparous women shot up to 20 per cent, and further increased to 26 per cent in 1977. Without any doubt this is the consequence of making legal abortion available on the request of the women. It is also important to note that the proportion of abortees with one living child has risen from 3 per cent in 1970 to 18 per cent in 1977; so has the proportion with two children which rose from 7 per cent to as high as 26 per cent.

TABLE 4.1

Per Cent Distribution of Legal Abortion by Age Group and Number of Living Children, 1970–77

Characteristics	1970	1971	1972	1973	1974	1975	1976	1977
				Age Group				
15–19	2	3	3	3	6	8	7	8
20–24	10	12	14	18	20	25	26	28
25–29	17	19	20	24	25	25	27	27
30–34	30	30	29	25	22	18	17	18
35–39	24	23	22	19	18	14	13	12
40–44	15	11	10	9	8	7	7	6
45 & above	2	2	2	2	1	2	2	1
Mean	32.8	32.1	31.6	30.7	29.8	28.6	28.5	28.0
				Number of Living Children				
0	0	1	1	4	7	20	24	26
1	3	3	4	10	13	15	15	18
2	7	10	15	21	22	23	24	26
3	16	18	19	19	17	15	15	14
4	18	17	18	14	12	10	8	7
5 or more	51	47	38	28	23	17	12	9
Unknown	5	4	5	4	6	0	1	0
Mean	5.2	5.0	4.6	3.7	3.4	2.9	2.4	2.0

During the 1970s the number of abortions performed among adolescent girls aged 15–19 has risen more than thirty-fold, from 35 in 1970 to 1,320 in 1977.[33] This increase has taken place in government hospitals as well as in private clinics. In the former the number increased from 7 in 1971 to 340 in 1977 while in the latter it rose from 91 to 793 during the same period. A more noteworthy feature refers to the consistently larger number of teenage abortions performed annually by private practitioners. For instance, in 1977 teenage abortions constituted 20.7 per cent of the total abortions performed by private practitioners as compared with the small proportion of 2.9 per cent performed by doctors in government hospitals. The reason is not difficult to find. In many respects, the private clinics can provide the teenagers, very often unmarried, the secrecy and convenience which a government hospital cannot possibly offer. It was reported that some 77 per cent of the teenage abortees in 1976 were unmarried.[34]

The incidence of abortions among teenage girls may be measured in terms of the abortion rate which is defined as the number of teenage abortions per thousand female population aged 15 to 19. The abortion rate among teenage girls had remained somewhat constant at 0.8 for the first three years, and rose to 1.4 in 1973 and 3.2 in 1974. It shot up to 7.5 in 1975 and the upward trend continued in 1976 when it reached 8.1 and 9.4 in 1977. The complete liberalization of the laws concerning abortion on 27 December 1974 was responsible for the sharp rise in 1975. Since this date abortion can be provided at the request of a pregnant woman with her written consent, and there is no stipulated minimum age requirement. Of late, there is some concern about the tendency towards teenage abortion and the ways and means of arresting this trend in view of the traumatic experience, psychologically and physically, entailed in an abortion.[35] However, the teenage abortion rate in Singapore is still not as high as that prevailing in other countries where abortion has also been liberalized. Taking the figures for 1975, we may observe that the rate was 29.7 in Sweden, 26.6 in Hungary, 25.1 in Denmark, 21.2 in Finland, 16.2 in England and Wales, and 11.0 in Czechoslovakia.[36] In contrast, the rate stood at only 7.5 in Singapore in the same year.

INCIDENCE OF ABORTION

In Table 4.2 the figures for abortions have been divided into two types: spontaneous abortions and legal abortions. The latter refers to induced abortions performed under the Abortion Act since 20 March 1970, while the former refers to those treated in government hospitals but outside the ambit of the Act. They are generally reported as spontaneous on admission to the hospitals though some were most probably induced by the women themselves or by criminal abortionists. It should be emphasized that the combined total for spontaneous and legal abortions does not represent the actual number of abortions performed in Singapore since there will always be illegally induced abortions, the number of which can never be ascertained.

In contrast to sterilizations, abortions have been treated in government hospitals in significant numbers even before it was legalized in 1970. Such spontaneous abortions numbered slightly more than 3,300 per year

TABLE 4.2

Number of Abortions, Abortion Ratio, and Abortion Rate, 1965–77

Year	Legal Abortion		Spontaneous Abortions	Total	Abortion Ratio	Abortion Rate
	Government Hospitals	Private Practitioners				
1965	—	—	3,386	3,386	60.8	9.2
1966	—	—	3,432	3,432	62.8	9.0
1967	—	—	3,327	3,327	65.8	8.4
1968	—	—	2,922	2,922	61.9	7.0
1969	—	—	2,929	2,929	65.7	6.7
1970	1,886	27	3,414	5,327	116.0	11.7
1971	3,343	64	2,673	6,080	129.1	12.8
1972	3,694	112	2,041	5,847	117.7	11.8
1973	5,089	163	1,413	6,665	138.1	13.0
1974	6,681	494	2,396	9,571	221.2	18.1
1975	8,891	2,214	2,929*	14,034	351.3	25.7
1976	9,099	3,831	4,377*	17,307	404.5	30.7
1977	10,063	3,699	4,548*	18,310	477.3	31.5

Note: * Includes menstrual regulation cases.

during 1965–67 but dropped to just below 3,000 in the next two years as contraceptives for preventing unwanted babies were readily available from the national programme. In 1970 when the 1969 Abortion Act came into operation some 1,886 legal abortions were performed in government hospitals which also treated no less than 3,414 spontaneous abortions, apart from the 27 performed by private practitioners. The combined total of 5,327 is a clear indication of the effect of legalizing abortion in Singapore. Thenceforth there emerged a definite pattern which shows a continuous increase in legal abortions and a fall in spontaneous abortions. To a limited extent this is a reflection of the swing away from criminal abortions towards the cheaper and safer legal abortions available in government hospitals and approved institutions.

The next major development took place in 1975 when the 1974 Abortion Act permitted a woman to have an abortion at her request from 27 December 1974 by eliminating the restrictive clauses and cumbersome procedures present in the old Act. In that year the number of legal abortions jumped by 54.8 per cent to 11,105. Though the increase in legal abortions in government hospitals amounted to 33.1 per cent, the increase of 348.2 per cent in the number performed by private practitioners was much more dramatic. Apart from making legally induced abortion available to women on request, the new Act made it procedurally easy for doctors to perform abortions in the private clinics, thus introducing a new pattern whereby private doctors are able to play an enhanced role in influencing the level of legal abortions performed in Singapore.

The general trend in the incidence of abortions can be studied in terms of the abortion rate and the abortion ratio. The rate is defined as the number of abortions per thousand women in the reproductive ages from 15 to 44, while the ratio is expressed in terms of the number of abortions per thousand live-births. A fall in the abortion rate was recorded during the early years of the national family planning programme prior to the legalization of abortion in March 1970 as women switched to the use of readily available contraceptives as a means of birth control.[37] The rate fell consistently from 9.2 in 1965 to 6.7 in 1969. In the following year when abortion was legalized the rate jumped to 11.7 and oscillated slightly above this level until 1973.

In 1974 the rate rose sharply again to 18.1, and the only special influence responsible for this appears to be the Tiger Year in the Chinese calendar which coincided with this year. Among some Chinese the Tiger Year is not an auspicious year for bearing children and this may be the decisive factor that influenced the women to terminate their pregnancies by induced abortion rather than having a "Tiger" baby. This is partly substantiated by the halt in 1974 in the continuous decline in the proportion of abortees with 5 or more living children during the period 1970 to 1976 (see Table 4.1). The rise in this proportion from 18 per cent in 1973 to 23 per cent in 1974, declining again to 17 per cent the next year seems to suggest that some of these high parity women preferred to terminate their pregnancies rather than have Tiger children, particularly when they already had five living children. With the introduction of legal abortion on demand through the 1974 Abortion Act, the abortion rate rose sharply to 25.7 in 1975, and in the next two years it continued on an upward trend to 30.7 in 1976 and to a new high of 31.5 in 1977. The movement in the abortion rate particularly during the mid-seventies must be taken into consideration in evaluating the fertility trend in Chapter 8.

By and large, the abortion ratio followed the same path as the movement in the abortion rate. What is more interesting is the use of the abortion ratio for the purpose of international comparison of the level of legally induced abortion in Singapore which has one of the most liberalized laws concerning induced abortion. The legal abortion ratio of 321 per thousand live-births in 1975 was certainly not high as compared with 515 for Hungary, 485 for East Germany, 402 for Denmark, and 347 for Japan in the same year. However, the level of legal abortion appears to be comparable to countries like Sweden with 325 and Finland with 316, and somewhat higher than that of Czechoslovakia with 298 and Poland with 215 in the same year.[38] Since 1975 the abortion ratio in Singapore has continued on the upward trend, reaching the highest figure of 477.3 in 1977.

Notes

1. *White Paper on Family Planning*, Command 22 of 1965, presented to the Legislative Assembly on 27 September 1965 (Singapore Government Printer, 1965), p. 14.
2. In accordance with the recommendation of the *White Paper on Family Planning*, the emphasis of the national programme at the very beginning was on the IUD. But the complications and failure rate arising out of this method were so serious that the idea of pushing the IUD as the main method was abandoned and the pill was recommended instead. See *First Annual Report of the Singapore Family Planning and Population Board, 1966*, pp. 21–22.
3. K. Kanagaratnam, "Singapore: The National Family Planning Program", *Studies in Family Planning*, No. 28, April 1968, p. 6.
4. *Second Annual Report of the Singapore Family Planning and Population Board, 1967* (Singapore: Government Printing Office, 1968), pp. 24–25.
5. *Malay Mail*, 10 August 1967; and *Straits Times*, 11 August 1967.
6. *Eastern Sun*, 6 September 1967.
7. See, for example, the various issues of the *Straits Times* on 2 September 1967, 9 September 1967 and 13 September 1967.
8. *Eastern Sun*, 13 August 1967; and *Sunday Mail*, 13 August 1967.
9. *Straits Times*, 14 September 1967.
10. Quoted in the *Third Annual Report of the Singapore Family Planning and Population Board, 1968* (Singapore: Government Printing Office, 1969), pp. 27–28.
11. *Straits Times*, 6 December 1968; and *Eastern Sun*, 6 December 1968.
12. For more details, see *Report of Select Committee on the Abortion and Voluntary Sterilization Bills*, Part 6 of 1969 (Singapore: Government Printing Office, 1969).

13. *Straits Times*, 24 December 1969.
14. A full account of the debate is provided in *Parliamentary Debate Republic of Singapore Official Report, First Session of Second Parliament* (Singapore: Government Printing Office, 1970).
15. *Straits Times*, 30 December 1969. Those who spoke against the Bill were Mr P. Gowindasamy, MP for Anson, Mr Lawrence Sia, MP for Moulmein, Mr Ng Kah Ting, MP for Ponggol, Mr Ho See Beng, MP for Bras Basah, and Madam Chan Choy Siong, MP for Delta.
16. Ibid.
17. The lone abstainer was Mr Low Guan Onn, MP for River Valley, and among the absentees were the Prime Minister, Mr Lee Kuan Yew, Foreign Minister and Minister for Labour, Mr S. Rajaratnam, Minister for Science and Technology, Dr Toh Chin Chye, Minister for Social Affairs, Encik Othman Wok, and Minister for Communications, Mr Yong Nyuk Lin.
18. *The Abortion Act 1969*, No. 25 of 1969 (Singapore: Government Printer, 1969).
19. According to the *Straits Times*, 16 March 1970, the Health Minister announced the appointment of the following persons as founder members of the Board: Dr Ho Guan Lim, Director of Medical Services, as Chairman; Dr V. M. S. Thevathasan, Deputy Director of Medical Services (Health); Dr Yeoh Seang Aun, Deputy Director of Medical Services (Hospitals); Mr Lean Tye Hin, Senior Obstetrician and Gynaecologist; Dr Yap Meow Foo, Psychiatrist; Mr Lee Beng Guan, Director of Social Welfare; Mrs Thung Syn Neo, Lecturer, Department of Social Work, University of Singapore; Mrs Chen Yu Fong, Senior Almoner; Mrs T. Kulasekaram, Social Worker; Mrs Khoo Shu Fen, Principal of Hwa Yi School; and Dr Goh Poh Seng, Medical Practitioner.
20. *IPPF Medical Bulletin*, Vol. 5, No. 4, August 1971, p. 3.
21. The duration of pregnancy is defined in the 1969 Abortion Act as the period from the first day of last normal menstruation of the pregnant woman to the end of the twenty-fourth week or to the end of the sixteenth week, as the case may be.
22. For a fuller account, see S. B. Kwa, S. T. Quah and M. C. E. Cheng, "The Abortion Act, 1969 — A Review of the First Year's Experience", *Singapore Medical Journal* 12, no. 5 (October 1971): 250–55.
23. Section 16 of the Abortion Act 1969 stated: "This Act shall continue in force for a period of four years from the date of its coming into operation: provided that the Minister may, from time to time by notification in the *Gazette,* extend that period for a further period of not more than one year."
24. *Straits Times*, 7 November 1974.
25. Ibid. Those who spoke against the Bill were Mr Ivan Baptist, MP for Potong Pasir; Mr J. F. Conceicao, MP for Katong; Mr Ng Kah Ting, MP for Ponggol; and Mr Teong Eng Siong, MP for Sembawang.

26. *The Abortion Act, 1974*, No. 24 of 1974 (Singapore: Singapore National Printers, 1974).

27. Details of the qualifications are provided in *The Abortion Regulations, 1974* made by the Minister for Health and Home Affairs under section 12 of the 1974 Abortion Act and published in the *Government Gazette: Subsidiary Legislation Supplement*, No. 58, 27 December 1974, pp. 1116–17.

28. However, according to a report in the *New Nation*, 28 November 1975, some pregnant foreign women, especially Malaysians, came to Singapore to obtain quick and easy abortions from private clinics without signing any official document and without satisfying the Singapore citizenship or four-month residential requirement. The women, who could not obtain legal abortions in their own countries, might be asked to sign a note stating they had come for "vaginal bleeding".

29. For details of a comprehensive system of generating abortion statistics, see *Recommendations for Comparative Abortion Statistics in Countries Where Induced Abortion is Legalised*, prepared by Committee on Demographic Aspects of Abortion, International Union for the Scientific Study of Population, IUSSP Paper No. 7, 61 pp.

30. The current form in use was prescribed as Regulation 4 of the *Abortion Regulations, 1974*, published in the *Government Gazette: Subsidiary Legislation Supplement*, No. 58, 27 December 1974, p. 1119. The form collects data on name of the pregnant woman, date of birth, race, citizenship, marital status, education, total number of children born alive, and results of operation.

31. For details, see *Straits Times, 7* November 1974.

32. The statistics were kindly supplied by the Singapore Family Planning and Population Board.

33. For more details, sec Saw Swee-Hock, "Adolescent Marriage, Abortion and Parenthood", in *Adolescent Sexuality*, edited by S. S. Ratnam (Singapore: Singapore University Press, 1979).

34. *Straits Times,* 4 June 1978.

35. See S. S. Ratnam (ed.), *Adolescent Sexuality;* and *Straits Times*, 26 September 1977.

36. Christopher Tietze, *Induced Abortion: 1977 Supplementary*, Reports on Population/Family Planning, No. 14 (2nd edition), Supplement, December 1977, New York: Population Council.

37. The female population aged 15 to 44 for the non-census years 1971–76 are obtained from *Singapore: Population Estimates by Age Group, Ethnic Group and Sex* prepared by the Government Department of Statistics and those for the non-census years 1965–69 are from Saw Swee-Hock and Chiu Wing Kin, *Population Estimates of Singapore by Age Group, 1958–71* (Singapore: Institute of Economics and Business Studies, Nanyang University, 1976).

38. Christopher Tietze, *Induced Abortion*.

5

Voluntary Sterilization

Sterilization in the family planning context involves an operation upon the reproductive organs of a man or woman with a view to terminating permanently his or her capacity to produce a child. Female sterilization or tubal ligation of women for medical reasons has been performed in Singapore since the early post-war years though on a very limited scale. Since its inception in 1949 the Family Planning Association was quite often confronted by women seeking sterilization because of medical, social or economic reasons. As a matter of policy the Association could not accede to these requests for sterilization, but referred the more deserving cases to the Kandang Kerbau Hospital where each case was considered carefully on its own merits.[1] For instance, among the referred cases thirty women were sterilized in 1958 and twenty-seven in 1959. The position up to the late fifties is one where voluntary sterilization was performed discreetly, on a small number of women, without much publicity or public attention. Most of them were sterilized on medical grounds and only a handful on social or economic grounds provided they already had a large family of at least more than six children.

The idea of adopting voluntary sterilization as a means of population control was first openly advocated by Professor B. H. Sheares in an exclusive interview to the local press on 18 June 1959 after he had earlier presented his views in a paper delivered at the Conference of the International Planned Parenthood Federation at New Delhi during 14–21 February of the same year.[2] He reiterated his stand that the answer to the population control problem in Singapore lay in voluntary sterilization and not so much in contraception.[3] He was, however, careful to clarify that he was speaking only from an academic point of view and had no intention of influencing government policy or action. Nonetheless, the public statement of such an eminent academic in the newspapers could not but result in considerable public discussion on the pros and cons of using sterilization as an accepted method of population control. For a few months the daily papers continued the debate with opinions expressed by private citizens, organizations and government leaders.[4]

The most vehement opposition came from the Catholics; positive support was provided by the Family Planning Association; and a somewhat neutral position was adopted by the PAP Government at that time. In his first ministerial Press Conference held on 3 July 1959, the Minister for Health, Encik Ahmad bin Ibrahim, stated that the government had no objection to sterilization as a means of limiting family size. He added: "At this juncture, it will be purely a matter of individual freedom and not necessarily one of government approval."[5] On the same day Professor Sheares revealed that he had received some 135 requests for sterilization, but had not yet sterilized anyone on family limitation reasons though he had performed it before on medical or obstetric grounds.[6] It is interesting to note that Mrs Margaret Sanger, who happened to be visiting Hong Kong towards the end of June 1959, voiced her support in the British Colony for Sheares's idea of providing voluntary sterilization to women as a means of population control.

In the early sixties the government continued to permit female sterilization to be performed in Kandang Kerbau Hospital provided the woman had at least five children, but still the number of women undergoing this treatment in this hospital came to no more than a few hundred in a year.[7] Male sterilization or vasectomy has not been carried out at that time for the simple reason that it was not available in the hospital, quite apart from its unpopularity among men.[8] Furthermore, there were some legal problems encountered in the performance of sterilization since there was some doubt whether sterilization would constitute an offence of voluntarily causing grievous hurt under sections 87 and 320 of the Penal Code. In the meantime the government, conscious of the need to check the rapid rate of population growth, followed a policy of increasing relaxation of the grounds for female sterilization prior to the legalization of voluntary sterilization in March 1970.

MOVE TOWARDS LEGAL STERILIZATION

The review of the laws or guidelines in respect of sterilization was conducted simultaneously with that of the restrictive laws relating to induced abortion, but the former task was comparatively more straightforward and certainly less controversial in comparison with the furore generated by the legalization of induced abortion. In 1966 the Medical Committee of the SFPPB discussed the question of male and female sterilization, and came up with certain recommended guidelines for immediate implementation. It recommended the adoption of the criteria of at least four children and at least forty years of age.[9] However, not much headway was made because the number of sterilizations that could be performed was severely limited by the availability of beds for this service in Kandang Kerbau Hospital, and certain legal aspects of sterilization still required to be resolved before a clearer picture emerged.[10]

In 1967 the Medical Committee again discussed the problem of promoting sterilization and the criteria were further reduced to three children and thirty years of age. Though advised that the consent of the husband was not required in law for female sterilization, the Committee was of the opinion that it would be preferable to have this consent so as to avoid any possible embarrassment and matrimonial complications.[11] This relaxation, coupled with the availability of more beds in Kandang Kerbau Hospital resulting from a decrease in births, proved to be somewhat fruitful, and the number of women undergoing sterilization rose from 477 in 1966 to 653 in 1967. However, vasectomy made little progress as it was not popular with men though arrangements were made for the performance of this operation at one of the government hospitals. A more significant development during the year was the thorough review of the wide range of issues concerning sterilization conducted by the Medical Committee. The outcome of its deliberation was that legislation to give proper sanction to male and female sterilization and also to lay down the conditions for the performance of the operation was both necessary and desirable.[12] The views of the SFPPB regarding the legalization of sterilization were transmitted to the Ministry of Health for consideration, and the government agreed to take all the necessary steps to put sterilization on a proper footing so that it could be promoted as one of the methods of birth control.

On 3 December 1968 the Minister for Health, Mr Chua Sian Chin, introduced in Parliament for its first reading the Voluntary Sterilization Bill which was designed to permit voluntary sterilization subject to certain safeguards.[13] The announcement of the government's desire to legalize sterilization and the simultaneous release of the details of the Bill attracted little attention or comment from members of the House and the general public. The Bill passed through its first reading and could have gone through the required second and third readings without much difficulty had it not been for the controversial Abortion Bill. When Parliament decided to refer the Abortion Bill to the Select Committee, it was only natural that the Voluntary Sterilization Bill was also committed to the same committee.[14] After the Report of the Select Committee was studied by the government, the Voluntary Sterilization Bill, with some amendments, was presented to the House a year later on 24 December 1969 for its final passage. Only one member of the House spoke on the Bill which was passed on 29 December 1969 without any opposition and without a vote being called.[15]

LEGAL STERILIZATION

Under the Voluntary Sterilization Act, 1969, which came into force on 20 March 1970, a five-member Eugenics Board was constituted to provide the necessary authority to registered medical practitioners to perform male and female sterilization on medical, social and eugenics grounds in government hospitals and approved institutions.[16] The Board consisted of a District Judge as Chairman, two medical practitioners, one of whom was from the government service, and two others, one of whom was a professionally qualified social worker.[17] The prime function of the Board was to consider applications for voluntary sterilization under the provisions of the Act from both men and women, who had to appear for an interview before the Board.

Under section 5(2) of the Act, the Board could authorize treatment for sexual sterilization for any applicant of twenty-one years of age or over, if:

(a) the applicant applies to the Board in writing regarding treatment for sexual sterilization and giving consent to such treatment;
(b) such request is accompanied by a consent in writing of the wife or husband, if there is one, of the applicant; and
(c) the applicant is the father or mother, as the case may be, of three or more existing children.

As for a person under twenty-one years of age, the Board may authorize sterilization under section 5(3) if:

(a) the parent or parents, if they are living, or the guardian of that person, if there is no parent living, applies in writing to the Board requesting such treatment and certifies consent to such treatment;

(b) that person is afflicted with any hereditary form of illness that is recurrent, mental deficiency or epilepsy; and

(c) the Board considers that the treatment is in the best interest of that person and of society generally.

As for the legality of the operation, section 5(1) specifically stated that notwithstanding the provisions of any written law, but subject to the provisions of this Act, it would be lawful for a medical practitioner to carry out the treatment for sterilization on the authorization of the Board. Furthermore, section 13 stated that for avoidance of any doubt "it is hereby declared that any treatment for sexual sterilization authorised by the Board under this Act or permitted under section 6 of this Act shall not constitute a 'grievious hurt' under sections 87 and 320 of the Penal Code".

In order to allow the applicants to ponder over this decision very carefully, the treatment for sterilization could only be performed if the period of thirty days from the date of application had elapsed. During this period the applicants might at any time withdraw their request for such treatment. This waiting period of thirty days did not apply to pregnant women, with three or more existing children, in an approved institution providing treatment for termination of pregnancy under the Abortion Act or delivering a child. In such cases, sterilization could be performed immediately after such abortion or birth provided the provisions of the above paragraphs (a) and (b) of section 5(2) were complied with. In the more normal cases, the Board was required during the waiting period to interview the applicants and give them a full and reasonable medical explanation as to the meaning and consequences of the treatment, and they had in turn to certify that they clearly understood them.[18]

Certain necessary safeguards were incorporated in the Act. Every treatment for voluntary sterilization, except those under section 6 performed by a medical practitioner without the authorization of the Board but in consultation with another medical practitioner, had to be carried out in a government hospital or in an approved institution. Any facts or information relating to sterilization could not be disclosed by any person unless the applicant expressively gave his consent. Another important safeguard was that any person who compelled another person against his will to undergo sterilization was guilty of an offence under the Act and could be liable to five years' imprisonment and/or a fine of $5,000 on conviction. Finally, no person could be bound to participate in any sterilization if he had any objection on moral grounds.

The treatment for female sterilization involves a small incision in the abdomen or vagina to sever or tie the fallopian tubes through which the ovum passes from the ovary into the womb. The hospitalization period is about five days.[19] In male sterilization or vasectomy the operation cuts and seals a part of the tube through which the sperm proceeds from the testicle to the urethra. The operation is much simpler and hospitalization for days is not necessary. In both cases the operation itself costs $5, but hospital charges for female sterilization could range from less than $5 to over $30 per day. During the first six months the Eugenics Board received some 720 applications for sterilization, with about 95 per cent coming from women. About 80 per cent of the total applicants had a family income of less than $400 a month, and most of them had more than four children. Practically all the applications were approved by the Board. Nearly 70 per cent of the sterilizations were carried out in Kandang Kerbau Hospital and the others in Toa Payoh Hospital. A negligible number was performed in two approved private institutions: the Gleneagles Hospital and St. Mark's Hospital.[20]

FURTHER LIBERALIZATION OF THE STERILIZATION LAWS

The government's concern about the upsurge of the number of births and the crude birth rate in 1970 and 1971 led to a review of the whole question of population control measures. As part of this review, the working of the 1969 Voluntary Sterilization Act was examined in the light of the experience in the last two years or so. The outcome of this appraisal was that amendments to the Act were introduced in Parliament in March 1972 to make sterilization as a method of family planning readily available to men and women. In introducing the second reading of the amendment Bill, the Minister for Health stated that while the Abortion Act had more than fulfilled its objectives, the Sterilization Act had been less effective in the sense that the number of sterilizations performed was much below expectation on account of various constraints imposed by the Act. "This", he said, "was a pity since sterilization is the best method of family planning for those who have completed the number of children they wanted."[21] The Bill was passed by Parliament on 23 March 1972 and the Voluntary Sterilization (Amendment) Act, 1972, came into force on 12 May 1972.

The various amendments extended the conditions under which sterilization could be performed and allowed for a more liberal interpretation of the law. The principal changes were:

(a) The Eugenics Board is now empowered to authorize treatment for sterilization if an applicant has at least two living children instead of three as required previously.
(b) In addition, approval for sterilization may now be given to a person with only one living child under certain exceptional circumstances which may be medical, therapeutic, financial or social.
(c) Unmarried persons over 21 years of age and married persons of any age may now apply for sterilization if they are suffering from hereditary illness which is recurrent, mental illness, and mental deficiency or epilepsy. Previously only unmarried persons under 21 years suffering from the above diseases, except mental illness, could apply.
(d) It is no longer mandatory for applicants to be interviewed by the Eugenics Board to be briefed on the meaning and consequences of sterilization; it is left to the discretion of the Board.
(e) An applicant need wait only seven days, instead of thirty days, from the date of application to the Eugenics Board before treatment for sexual sterilization can be performed.

When the amendments came into force in May 1972, there was a marked rise in the number of applications for sterilization.[22] Another significant development in 1972 was the positive efforts taken to popularize vasectomy which until then had not made much headway. Increased publicity was given to sterilization in general and vasectomy in particular. More important still was the setting up of the Male Counselling/Vasectomy Clinic in the National Family Planning Centre in Dunearn Road on 21 June 1972.[23] This clinic functions every Wednesday evening from 8.00 p.m. to 10.00 p.m. and is serviced by a panel of eight surgeons and thirteen male medical counsellors. By the end of the year a total of 477 new patients had attended the clinic, and of these 279 came for vasectomy and 198 for counselling. The number of vasectomies performed showed a marked increase from August onwards on account of the Family Planning Campaign launched in July. From January 1973 a male doctor was appointed on a full-time basis to provide daily counselling services.

The determination to combat the rising trend in births also resulted in the introduction of incentives to promote sterilization; these measures will be examined in the next chapter.

STERILIZATION ON DEMAND

Both the Voluntary Sterilization and the Abortion Acts which came into force on 20 January 1970 were supposed to be temporary and subject to review five years later.[24] In view of the government's determination to have an effective overall population control programme and the satisfactory working of the Acts in the last five years, it was decided not only to continue with the two Acts but to liberalize them and make them permanent features of the laws of Singapore. Consequently, the new Voluntary Sterilization Act, 1974, which repealed the previous Act, was passed by Parliament on 6 November 1974 and came into force on 27 December 1974.[25]

Under the provisions of the new Act, sterilization may be obtained at the request of the persons and would be purely a matter between the persons concerned and their doctors approved for the purpose. Sterilization has been liberalized in the following manner as stipulated under section 3 of the Act:

(a) The decision to carry out treatment for voluntary sterilization rests entirely in the hands of registered medical practitioners. It is no longer necessary to obtain this authorization from the Eugenics Board which has been abolished forthwith.

(b) Sterilization is now available to persons without any children. Previously the person must have at least two living children or at least one under exceptional circumstances. The only requirement is the consent of the person if such a person is not married and is over 21 years of age, or if such a person is under 21 but married. The additional consent of the parent or guardian, if there is no parent, is required if the person is under 21 and unmarried. Curiously enough, those who are over 21 years and married have been left out, but we can assume that this category of persons should be placed in the same position as those over 21 years of age and not married.

(c) The interview of applicants at the discretion of the Eugenics Board is also dispensed with completely with the abolishment of the Board.

(d) The waiting period of seven days from the date of application before treatment for sterilization can be performed is also not mandatory now. The registered medical practitioners can now perform the operation any time after the date of application provided all the necessary formalities have been completed.

(e) The imposition of a fee of $5 no longer applies if the treatment is carried out in an approved institution, though it still applies if performed in a government hospital.

However, before treatment is carried out for voluntary sexual sterilization the registered medical practitioner must give to the person undergoing such treatment or to the person who gives consent on his behalf a full and reasonable explanation as to the meaning and consequences of such treatment and the person concerned or the person who gives consent on his behalf must certify that he clearly understands the consequences of such treatment. The medical practitioners who carry out treatment for sexual sterilization must hold prescribed qualifications or have acquired skill in such treatment over such period as may be prescribed. The regulations may prescribe different qualifications for medical practitioners who carry out treatment on females as distinct from males.

The safeguards existing in the repealed Act have been retained. Every treatment for voluntary sexual sterilization which does not consist solely of the use of drugs must be carried out in a government hospital or in an approved institution. Matters or treatment relating to sexual sterilization are privileged against disclosure. Compelling or inducing a person to undergo such treatment against his will is still prohibited. The right of a registered medical practitioner, nurse, and other related personnel to refuse to participate in any such treatment on grounds of conscience is preserved, as is the immunity of registered medical practitioners.

Another change in the existing law relates to the regulation-making power of the Minister. Power will be conferred upon the Minister to prescribe forms of consent to be given by a person undergoing treatment and to prescribe qualifications for registered medical practitioners or the period of time considered adequate to confer skill in such treatment as well as forms of certification to be given by registered medical practitioners under certain circumstances.

CHARACTERISTICS OF STERILIZED PERSONS

The legalization of sterilization has made it possible for the government to collect statistics from the prescribed forms completed by persons who have undergone the operation under the provisions of the Act. As in the case of abortion statistics, the Research and Evaluation Unit of the SFPPB has been responsible for the compilation of sterilization statistics from the completed forms submitted by the medical practitioners to the Director of Medical Services. A summary of the statistics is given in Tables 5.1 to 5.3.[26]

During the first year of the Act in 1970, Malay women were somewhat reluctant to come forward for sterilization as only 4 per cent of the sterilized women were Malays. This tendency persisted well into 1971, but appeared to have changed in 1972 when Malay women constituted some 7 per cent, due partly to the further liberalization of the laws in May that year. Since then the proportion remained at about 9-10 per cent but is still proportionately lower than the present racial composition of 15 per cent of the total population. The only possible reason for the lower participation of the Malays in the sterilization programme is their Muslim religion which condones family planning but does not permit sterilization.[27] It may be recalled that a higher proportion, some 15-17 per cent, of the new acceptors of the family planning programme were Malays. The proportion of the sterilized women belonging to the Chinese community has remained relatively high and fairly stable at about 83 per cent over the years, while the Indian proportion has fallen from 12 to 6 per cent during the whole period.

Until 1974 not a single woman under the age of 20 had been sterilized because the law was extremely strict with regard to persons aged 21 and below who could only be sterilized on the grounds of having an hereditary form of illness that was recurrent, or suffered from mental deficiency or epilepsy. Even for the second age group 20-24 the proportion remained very low over the years, generally between 6 and 9 per cent. Most of the changes occurred among the two middle age groups; the proportion in the 25-29 group increased from 28 per cent in 1970 to 32 per cent in 1977 and that in the 30-34 group fell from 40 to 34 per cent during the same period. By and large, the age composition of the sterilized women has not altered significantly, and the mean age has in fact been quite stationary at around 31 or 32 years.

The figures in Table 5.1 reveal that in the first three years not a single woman without any children was sterilized because of the strict law regarding the sterilization of persons without any children contained in the 1969 Act. Even after the further liberalization of the laws in 1972 and then again in 1975, less than 1 per cent of the sterilized women were nulliparous. Furthermore, sterilized women with only one child

TABLE 5.1

Per Cent Distribution of Sterilized Women by Race, Age, and Number of Living Children, 1970–77

Characteristics	1970	1971	1972	1973	1974	1975	1976	1977
Total Number	2,321	3,871	5,842	8,964	9,241	9,495	10,310	8,236
Race								
Chinese	83	87	83	83	82	83	83	82
Malays	4	2	7	9	10	10	9	10
Indians	12	9	8	7	7	5	6	6
Others	1	2	2	1	1	2	2	2
Age Group								
15–19	—	—	—	—	—	0	0	0
20–24	7	9	6	6	7	8	8	7
25–29	28	29	28	27	29	32	30	32
30–34	40	43	39	37	34	31	35	34
35–39	21	17	20	22	22	22	21	21
40–44	4	2	7	8	8	7	6	5
Mean	31.4	30.78	31.7	31.9	31.8	31.4	31.5	31.5
Number of Living Children								
0	—	—	—	0	0	0	0	0
1	1	—	2	3	4	1	2	1
2	22	35	15	16	20	14	18	20
3	41	51	24	28	28	35	39	41
4	18	6	19	20	20	23	21	22
5 or more	18	8	40	33	28	27	20	16
Mean	3.0	2.9	4.4	4.1	3.8	3.7	3.8	3.4

Note: The figures for 1970–72 refer to sterilization for socio-economic reasons only.

never exceeded 4 per cent in any one of the seven years. Sterilization is a drastic measure in that the sterility thereby achieved is permanent, with no assurance that the result can be reversed by a subsequent operation. It is only natural that the majority of the women who undergo sterilization would have at least two children. As a matter of fact, the further liberalization of the laws in May 1972 seemed to have greatly altered the parity pattern of the sterilized women in favour of those with larger families. For instance, the proportion with two children dropped from 35 per cent in 1971 to 15 per cent in 1972 and, more importantly, those with five or more children shot up from 8 per cent to 40 per cent. A more concise indicator is the mean number of children which rose sharply from 2.9 in 1971 to 4.4 in 1972. Thereafter, it fell to 4.1 in 1973 and settled down at around 3.8 during the next three years, but fell to 3.4 in 1977.

During the first year of legal sterilization some 80 per cent of the women who went for sterilization had very little education; 35 per cent had no education at all and 44 per cent had only primary education (see Table 5.2). The proportion with no education rose to the peak of 48 per cent in 1972 when the laws were further liberalized, and later fell back again to 33 per cent in 1976. The exact opposite was experienced by the proportion with primary education, falling to the low of 39 per cent in

TABLE 5.2
Per Cent Distribution of Sterilized Women by Education and Combined Income, 1970–76

Characteristics	1970	1971	1972	1973	1974	1975	1976
	Education						
No education	35	37	48	47	42	39	33
Primary	44	43	39	41	43	42	45
Secondary	18	17	12	11	14	17	20
Tertiary	2	2	1	1	1	1	1
Others	1	1	—	—	—	1	1
	Combined Income ($)						
Below 200	35	32	33	24	13	5	3
200–399	44	45	50	57	58	52	44
400–599	8	10	9	11	18	26	33
600–799	5	4	3	3	4	7	9
800–999	3	3	2	2	2	3	3
1,000–1,499	3	4	2	2	3	4	5
1,500 & above	2	2	1	1	2	3	3
Mean (S)	220	236	200	234	282	356	508

Note: The figures for 1970–72 refer to sterilization for socio-economic reasons only. The income figures for 1975 and 1976 refer to sterilizations performed in government institutions only.

1972 and thereafter rising to the high of 45 per cent at the end of the period. A somewhat similar trend was also experienced by the sterilized women with secondary education, their proportion going down from 18 per cent to 11 per cent in 1973 and then up to 20 per cent in 1976. On the whole, there was no significant change in the educational pattern of the sterilized women during these years.

In contrast, the figures given in the bottom of Table 5.2 indicate a definite shift in the pattern of the distribution of income among the sterilized women. The shift has been decidedly towards the higher income women as reflected in the steep fall in the proportion with less than $200 from 35 per cent to only 3 per cent and the equally sharp rise in the proportion with $400 to $599 from only 8 per cent to the peak of 33 per cent at the end of the period. The mean income of the sterilized women has risen from $220 to $508 during this seven-year period, partly a reflection of the rise in the per capita income of the general population in Singapore.

The typical profile of sterilized women in 1976 was as follows: 86 per cent were Singapore citizens and 85 per cent were not working, presumably performing home housework. About 81 per cent had practised birth control either at the time of sterilization or previous to that, and almost all of them, 97 per cent, were being sterilized for socio-economic reasons such as "financial difficulties" and "family completed". As high as 70 per cent had their sterilization performed during the post-partum period and another 19 per cent during the post-abortal period. As expected, the women generally resorted to sterilization at a younger age than the men, 31.3 years for the former and 35.5 for the latter. At the time of sterilization, the women had an average of 3.7 living children which was exactly the same as that for the men. Some 92 per cent of all sterilization operations were performed in government institutions.[28]

INCIDENCE OF STERILIZATION

Prior to the implementation of the Voluntary Sterilization Act in 1970, further progress was made in female sterilization in 1969. The continued efforts among high parity post-partum women, the additional availability of beds at the Kandang Kerbau Hospital, and the new source of beds for sterilization in the Toa Payoh Hospital led to a substantial rise in the number of female sterilizations from 1,054 in 1968 to 1,435 in 1969. On the other hand, male sterilization made little headway with only 3 performed in each of these two years.

The 1969 Voluntary Sterilization Act which defines clearly the procedures and conditions for sterilization was responsible for the perceptible rise in vasectomies to 51 and for the 62 per cent jump in tubal ligation to 2,321 in 1970. To a very limited extent the latter increase may also be attributed to the culdoscopic method of sterilization[29] made available at Kandang Kerbau Hospital from July 1970.[30] In the following year the number of female sterilizations rose to 3,871, an increase of 67 per cent. The liberalization of the sterilization laws in May 1972 and the introduction of incentives in August 1973 helped to maintain the increase at slightly more than 50 per cent in the next two years. The number of female sterilizations rose to 5,842 in 1972 and to 8,964 in 1973. The sixfold increase in vasectomies from 55 in 1971 to 347 in 1972 was solely due to the establishment of the Male Counselling/Vasectomy Clinic in the National Family Planning Centre as mentioned earlier.

Unlike abortions which a woman can have more than once, sterilization is subject to the saturation effect since persons undergoing sterilization would not appear again for the treatment. This partly accounts for the deceleration in the rate of increase from 1974 onwards. Unlike induced abortion, the number of sterilizations did not increase sharply in 1975 when the laws were liberalized in such a manner that sterilization was made available at the request of the men or women. However, the total number of sterilizations amounted to 9,567 in 1974, 9,948 in 1975, and reached the new high of 10,718 in 1976, after which it decreased by 20.0 per cent to 8,587 in the following year. The reduction in the number of sterilizations continued in 1978 since the number for the first nine months of the year was already down by 10.1 per cent to 5,779 as compared to the corresponding figure of 6,429 in the previous year.[31] Apart from the fact that no new incentives aimed at promoting sterilization have been introduced since 1975 when the last one on Primary One Registration came into force, the saturation effect is apparently beginning to become noticeable.[32] It should be emphasized that the effect of sterilization on births in any year should be viewed in terms of the cumulative number of sterilizations over the past years. Since 1965 some 64,836 persons have been sterilized, which means that this many number of couples have been removed from the risk of producing children.

TABLE 5.3
Number of Male and Female Sterilizations, 1965–77

Year	Female Sterilizations	Male Sterilizations	Total	Sterilization Ratio	Sterilization Rate
1965	542	—	542	9.7	1.5
1966	477	—	477	8.7	1.2
1967	653	—	653	12.9	1.6
1968	1,054	3	1,057	22.4	2.5
1969	1,435	3	1,438	32.3	3.3
1970	2,321	51	2,372	51.4	5.2
1971	3,871	99	3,970	84.1	8.4
1972	5,842	347	6,189	124.6	12.5
1973	8,964	374	9,338	193.5	18.3
1974	9,241	326	9,567	221.1	18.1
1975	9,495	453	9,948	249.0	18.2
1976	10,310	408	10,718	250.5	19.0
1977	8,236	351	8,587	223.8	14.8

One method of measuring the incidence of sterilization over the years is to compute the sterilization ratio which can be defined as the number of sterilizations per thousand live-births. The other index is the sterilization rate expressed in terms of the number of sterilizations per thousand women in the reproductive age group from 15 to 44. This gives an idea of the proportion of women removed from the risk of child-bearing. The computed ratios and rates are shown in the last two columns of Table 5.3.[33] The ratio increased from a negligible figure of 9.7 in 1965 to 51.4 in 1970, and finally to 250.5 in 1976. The same upward trend was exhibited by the sterilization rate which reached about 18.3 per thousand women in 1973, and thereafter remained stable at this level during the next three years. In 1976 it went up to 19.0 per thousand women aged 15 to 44, but descended swiftly to 14.8 in the following year.

Notes

1. *Ninth Annual Report of the Family Planning Association of Singapore, 1958* (Singapore: Malaya Publishing House Ltd., 1957), p. 22.

2. Professor B. H. Sheares, who was the Head of the Department of Obstetrics and Gynaecology, University of Singapore, at the time of the interview and also President of the Family Planning Association during 1960–62, has been President of the Republic of Singapore since 2 January 1971.
3. *Straits Times*, 19 June 1959: and *Singapore Tiger Standard*, 10 June 1959.
4. Among those whose views appeared in the newspapers were Sir Perry McNeice, Bishop H. B. Amstutz, Father J. Kearny, Mr Goh Hood Keng, Mrs Joanna Moore, Mrs Margaret Silcock, Dato K. M. Alsogoff, Dr Poh Soo Kai, Dr C. Marcus, and Dr V. M. S. Thevathasan.
5. *Straits Times*, 4 July 1959.
6. Ibid.
7. Wu San San, *Singapore Family Planning Programme (1966–70) and Its Implications on Fertility Decline — With Special Reference to Ethnic Groups*, Singapore Family Planning and Population Board Paper 19, p. 15.
8. K. Kanagaratnam, "Singapore: The National Family Planning Program", *Studies in Family Planning*, No. 28, April 1968, p. 5.
9. *First Annual Report of the Singapore Family Planning and Population Board, 1966*, p. 24.
10. Kanagaratnam, "Singapore: The National Family Planning Program", p. 5.
11. *Second Annual Report of the Singapore Family Planning and Population Board, 1967*, p. 23.
12. Ibid., p. 23.
13. *Straits Times*, 6 December 1968; and *Eastern Sun*, 6 December 1968. According to the press reports, the Voluntary Sterilization Bill, though not modelled on any existing legislation elsewhere, has benefited from legislation existing in Japan, Sweden and some of the states in the United States, particularly Virginia.
14. *Report of the Select Committee on the Abortion Bill and the Voluntary Sterilization Bill*, op. cit.
15. *Straits Times*, 30 December 1969.
16. *The Voluntary Sterilization Act, 1969*, No. 26 of 1969 (Singapore: Government Printer, 1969).
17. The Minister for Health, Mr Chua Sian Chin, announced on 15 March 1970 the appointment of Mrs Chee Tiang Chin, District Judge, as Chairman of the Board and, as members, Dr Yeoh Seang Aun, Deputy Director, Medical Services (Hospital); Dr (Miss) Oon Chiew Seng, Obstetrician and Gynaecologist; Mrs D. Muthuswamy, Social Worker; and Cik Salama Baharuddin, Nursing Sister. See *Straits Times*, 16 March 1970.
18. A comparison of the sterilization laws, including the Singapore Act, is given in *The World's Laws on Voluntary Sterilization for Family Planning Purposes in Sterilization, Population Report*, Series C–D, No. 2, April 1973, Washington:

Department of Medical and Public Affairs, George Washington University Medical Center.

19. See, for example, *Family Planning Handbook for Doctors* (London: International Planned Parenthood Federation, 1973); and *Sterilization and Abortion Procedures*, Proceedings of the First Meeting of the IGCC Expert Group Working Committee on Sterilization and Abortion, 3–5 January 1973, Penang, Kuala Lumpur: Inter-Governmental Coordinating Committee, Southeast Asia Regional Cooperation in Family and Population Planning.

20. For more information, see *Straits Times*, 25 September 1970.

21. *Parliamentary Debates Republic of Singapore Official Report, First Session of Second Parliament, Part III, Vol. 29* (Singapore: Government Printer, 1973).

22. *Straits Times*, 22 May 1972.

23. Margaret Loh, "The Singapore Family Planning and Population Programme with Special Reference to New Directions and Emphasis, 1973/74", *Singapore Public Health Bulletin*, No. 13, January 1974, p. 15.

24. Section 2 of the Voluntary Sterilization Act 1969 states: "This Act shall continue in force for a period of four years from the date of its coming into operation, provided that the Minister may, from time to time by notification in the *Gazette,* extend that period for a further period of not more than one year."

25. *The Voluntary Sterilization Act, 1974*, No. 25 of 1974 (Singapore: Singapore National Printers, 1974).

26. The sterilization statistics were kindly provided by the Research and Evaluation Unit of the SFPPB.

27. In his oral representation to the Select Committee, Tuan Haji Mohamed Sanusi Mahmood, Mufti, Special Committee of Majlis Ugama, stated, "As far as Islam is concerned, voluntary sterilization is not permitted. However, the prevention of conception such as family planning methods is condoned." *Report of the Select Committee on the Abortion Bill and the Voluntary Sterilization Bill*, p. B18.

28. *Eleventh Annual Report of the Singapore Family Planning and Population Board, 1976*, p. 38.

29. Culdoscopy is a simple and cheap method of female sterilization in which the fallopian tubes are reached through a vaginal rather than an abdominal incision. The operation leaves no external scar, requires only a local anaesthetic, calls for simple equipment, and can be performed in about ten minutes as an outpatient procedure.

30. Wan Fook Kee and Margaret Loh, *Second Five-Year Family Planning Programme, 1971–75*, Singapore Family Planning and Population Board Paper 16.

31. *Monthly Digest of Statistics*, Vol. XVII, No. 11, November 1978, Singapore: Department of Statistics.

32. See Chapter 6, pp 86–89.

33. See footnote 37 in Chapter 4.

6

Incentives and Disincentives

OVERVIEW

In providing every possible support, financial or otherwise, to the Family Planning Association in its attempt to assist women to plan their births and avoid having unwanted babies and to check the rapid rate of population increase in the early 1960s, the PAP Government was aware of the conflicting nature of some government policies with respect to the general concept of family planning and the promotion of a small family norm in particular. In his opening address to the Seventh Conference of IPPF held in Singapore on 10 February 1963, the Prime Minister, Mr Lee Kuan Yew, referred to the anomalies in certain government policies, carried over from the colonial period, seen from the point of view of population control. He stated,

> Even we, as a Government, find ourselves pursuing contradictory policies. On the one hand, we want to discourage large families. ... On the other, we have inherited and are still practising a system of values which gives the advantage to a man with a larger family. For instance, in public housing the number of points a man scores for priority in getting accommodation increases with the number of children he has got. So too with social welfare benefits, the bigger the family the bigger the relief and the same with income tax relief.[1]

However, these contradictory rules were not altered then as the Prime Minister felt that humanitarian values and sentiments had prevented the government from making any change.

It would appear that in the next few years the problem of these contradictory rules was constantly occupying the minds of the government leaders as the Prime Minister brought up this question once again in his National Day message on 9 August 1965. He said,

> We have to revise all our social values so that no one is required to have a large family in order to qualify for a Housing Board flat, for social relief and so on. Today, strange as it may seem, we are giving priority to people with large families, thereby encouraging people to have large families. This requires a revamping of all our social services, free primary schools, free hospitals and free maternity clinics regardless of how large the family is and the bigger social allowance given to the bigger families.[2]

The inclusion of this observation in the National Day message, traditionally reserved for matters of paramount importance, clearly signalled the government's intention of rectifying some of the anomalous rules in the not too distant future. Indeed, the next few years witnessed the modification of some of these rules in the area of maternity leave, accouchement fee and public housing.

Most of the changes were however instituted only in the early 1970s when the decline in the number of births and the crude birth rate faltered and even showed an upward trend. This reversal of birth trends in the context of an already fairly low fertility level forced the government to look beyond the family planning programme, legal abortion and liberalized sterilization for further measures that could help to counteract these adverse tendencies and promote the two-child family norm. In early 1972 various government rules were carefully scrutinized with regard to their implications in the area of population control, and those ascertained as incongruous were adjusted. By August 1972 the government announced the introduction of new incentives and disincentives relating to income tax and education, and the intensification of the earlier ones with regard to maternity leave, accouchement fees and public housing, most of which were to be effective after one year.[3] The mid-seventies have seen the further intensification of these measures and the introduction of a few new ones to encourage not only the two-child family concept but also sterilization which is regarded as the best method of birth control.

A whole series of incentive and disincentive measures with varying degrees of severity and effectiveness has become an integral part of the population control programme aimed at sustaining the two-child family norm first propagated in 1972 by the SFPPB. These measures, whether incorporated into law or remaining as administrative devices, directly affect the life of most couples in Singapore and appear to have played an important role in contributing to the final efforts towards the attainment of replacement fertility in 1975.

MATERNITY LEAVE

One of the old regulations inherited from the colonial government that tended to conflict with the idea of encouraging couples to have a small family was the one relating to maternity leave. The traditional practice was to give paid maternity leave to working women for a certain period before as well as after each confinement irrespective of the number of children they already had. The opportunity was taken to rectify this anomaly when the government decided in 1968 to introduce in Parliament the Employment Bill to regulate strikes and conditions of workers in the private sector. After a lengthy debate in the House, the Bill was passed on 31 July 1968. With effect from 15 August 1968, the day when the Employment Act 1968 came into force, a female worker was entitled under section 97(10) of the Act to paid maternity leave for four weeks before and four weeks after each confinement up to the third child only.[4] During this period she would receive from her employer the whole or part of her salary. In the second reading of the Bill, the Minister for Labour emphasized that the aim of the clause was to discourage rather than prohibit large families and to prevent the success of family planning being nullified.[5]

This disincentive measure, the first of a series to be introduced, continued in force until late 1973 when it was intensified as part of a wide range of measures announced a year in advance. On 24 October 1972 the Minister for Health, Mr Chua Sian Chin, gave notice during the debate on the President's statement of government policy to the newly elected third Parliament to the effect that further administrative measures in support of family planning in the realm of maternity leave, accouchement fees and public housing would be introduced to encourage the two-child family norm with effect from 1 August 1973.[6] In due course, paid maternity leave was to apply only to the first two confinements in the public sector through a Ministry of Finance directive and in the private sector through 'the Employment (Amendment) Act, 1973 with effect from 1 August 1973.[7] In moving the second reading of this amendment in Parliament, the Minister for Labour, Mr Ong Pang Boon, stated that the purpose was to encourage family planning in Singapore.

While the disincentive measure incorporated into the maternity leave regulation does not retrospectively penalize parents who already have more than three or two children as the case may be, its effectiveness has been confined to only those potential mothers who are working.

Statistics of live-births classified by economic activity status of mothers are not available, but it is commonly known that there are more married women who are not working than those who are. Data from the Labour Force Survey reveal that in 1977 only 92,237 or 27.9 per cent of the 330,266 married women aged 15 to 49 are economically active.[8] The policy appears to have worked smoothly without any major complications, apart from the savings in maternity leave pay enjoyed by employers in both the public and private sectors.

In the previous chapter we have examined the continuous liberalization of sterilization through various amendments of the law governing its performance. Convinced that it is a suitable and effective method of birth control, the government introduced a wide range of incentives designed to influence wives or husbands to undergo sterilization. The opportunity was taken to relate incentives to maternity leave entitlement. The government took the initiative by announcing that female employees in the civil service, not normally entitled to paid maternity leave because they already have two children, would be granted paid maternity leave prescribed by their doctors if they are sterilized after the delivery or abortion. In addition, the government also took the lead by granting seven days' unrecorded full-pay leave to male and female civil servants for the purpose of undergoing sterilization.[9] It should be borne in mind that these incentives can only have the effect of encouraging sterilization among civil servants and not the public at large.

ACCOUCHEMENT FEE

The second disincentive aimed at discouraging large families is an administrative measure incorporated in the accouchement fee charged in government maternity hospitals. For many years the fee was fixed at a standard flat rate, and from 1 April 1969 it was raised to $50 for the fourth or subsequent child, with the $10 for the first three children remaining the same.[10] This two-tier system was rather mild and did not discourage parents from having a third child. In the following year it was accordingly amended to $10 for the first child, $20 for the second, $50 for the third, and $100 for the fourth or subsequent child. However, it was subsequently ascertained that these rates were a deterrent only to the lowest income groups.

TABLE 6.1
Accouchement Fees with Effect from 1 August 1973

Birth Order	Class A	Class B	Class C
1st child	$250	$100	$50
2nd child	$300	$150	$75
3rd child	$350	$200	$100
4th child	$400	$250	$200
5th child & subsequent children	$400	$300	$250

The government maternity hospitals have always been divided into classes and this was taken into consideration in the next review of the disincentive measure. On 24 October 1972 the Minister for Health announced in Parliament that with effect from 1 August 1973 a more comprehensive system would be introduced whereby different progressions of the charges with advancing parity were affixed to the three different classes.[11] The revised accouchement fees were as shown in Table 6.1.

The desire to reduce fertility further led to the introduction of tougher measures on 18 July 1975 when the fees were raised once again (see Table 6.2). The first child fee appears to be low for Class C in comparison with those for Classes B and A, but the increase in fees over birth order is much more accelerated for Class C. The reason for this is to impose a greater penalty on the lowest income group parents who tend to have more children though they can ill afford them. Moreover, the very fact that this measure involves a financial penalty means that its

TABLE 6.2
Accouchement Fees Revised on 18 July 1975

Birth Order	Class A	Class B	Class C
1st child	$300	$120	$60
2nd child	$360	$180	$90
3rd child	$420	$240	$120
4th child	$480	$300	$240
5th child & subsequent children	$480	$360	$300

impact is greater among the poorer classes. Apart from having no retrospective effect, the measure does have a strong and wide influence since some 83 per cent of the total live-births in Singapore are delivered in government maternity hospitals every year. From the government point of view, the system has the additional advantage of generating more revenue to meet the rising cost of running these hospitals.

Incentives to sterilization have also been incorporated in the system of accouchement fees in government maternity hospitals. In August 1973 the government announced that the fees, which have been made progressively higher with birth order, for patients in Classes B and C wards would be waived if either the husband or wife undergoes sterilization within six months of the delivery of the birth. In addition, ward charges for these Class C patients would be remitted on application after sterilization.[12] If the patient is not sterilized but her husband undergoes vasectomy within one month after the wife has delivered her last child, the accouchement fees incurred by the wife would be waived. These positive measures will no doubt have an effect in promoting sterilization among poorer couples.

PERSONAL INCOME TAX

For many years the prevailing system of income tax in Singapore provided relief to child dependants. In October 1972 the tax relief for families with more than three children was revised by an amendment to the Income Tax Act.[13] Under this amendment two situations are distinguished. Taxpayers who had more than three children on or before 1 August 1973 were given a tax relief of $750 for the first child, $500 for the second and third, $300 for the fourth and fifth. For those with less than four children after 1 August 1973 the tax relief was fixed at $750 for both the first and second child and $500 for the third. No deduction would therefore be allowed for any child born on or after this date if he was the fourth or subsequent child. Other conditions were, first, that the child concerned should be unmarried, and, second, that he was under sixteen years of age or receiving full-time education at any university, college, school or other educational institution or serving under articles or indentures with a view to qualifying in a trade or profession or if he was unable to maintain himself by reason of physical or mental infirmity.

The disincentive measure was announced about eleven months prior to its implementation so that mothers planning for their fourth or higher order child at the time of announcement might be aware of the penalties in advance. By comparison with the measures incorporated in maternity leave and accouchement fee, the tax relief measure has a wider and more lasting influence because it applies to all taxpayers with children and penalizes those affected every year in their tax returns instead of just once.

PUBLIC HOUSING

Some of the previous government rules in the area of public housing had a tendency to encourage parents to produce more rather than fewer children. In its search for suitable population policies in the late 1960s, the government therefore scrutinized the rules governing the provision of subsidized flats by the Housing and Development Board (HDB). One of these rules stipulated that to qualify for these flats the minimum household size should be five, thus barring couples without any children or with only one to two children from applying for these flats.[14] In 1968 the HDB made an important concession whereby such couples became eligible for these flats although it meant that more flats would have to be built by the Board. The previous rule tended to encourage couples to have children, and as quickly as possible, in order to qualify for these flats. A further relaxation was introduced in 1972 when two or more spinsters, one of whom must be forty years or older, may apply to rent or buy the flats provided they satisfy all other existing conditions.[15]

In allocating the flats on a points system to those on the waiting list, the HDB had been giving preference to larger families on the basis of greater need. This might have encouraged applicants on the waiting list to have more children in order to accumulate more points. In accordance with the announcement by the Minister for Health in Parliament on 24 October 1972, the allocation procedure was altered with effect from 1 August 1973 so that families regardless of size would have equal priority in the acquisition of HDB flats. At the same time the rule with respect to sub-letting was revised to allow only families with not more than three children to sub-let rooms in their HDB and Jurong Town Corporation flats under certain conditions. Prior to this ruling, sub-letting of any kind was strictly forbidden, and the penalty, whether the flat was rented or purchased, was eviction. The new measure, providing an opportunity to the flat dwellers to derive extra income, has had the effect of encouraging some families to stop at three children. On the whole, the population policies built into the regulations governing subsidized public housing should have some impact on family size since about 60 per cent of the total population in 1977 resided in these flats, and the demand for these flats is still immense, with some 62,000 applicants on the waiting list.[16]

PRIMARY SCHOOL REGISTRATION

The excessive demand for Primary One places in certain schools because of the keen desire of some parents to send their children to premier schools necessitated the introduction of some kind of priority system in the annual registration of children who attain the age of six on 1 January the following year. The registration exercise, first introduced in 1972 and carried out around August of each year, is divided into three phases. Phase One is for children with brothers or sisters studying in the same schools. Phase Two is for children whose parents, brothers or sisters are former students, members of school advisory committees, school management committees or school staff, whose elder brothers or sisters are studying in affiliated schools, or who are the only children in the family. Phase Three is for all other children.

As part of its search for a more comprehensive population control programme, the government decided to take advantage of the Primary One registration to introduce new incentive and disincentive measures. For the August 1973 registration exercise, the Ministry of Education ruled that in line with family planning policy priority for registration under Phase One and Phase Two would be given only up to the third child in the family. However, the fourth child would be accorded the same priority as the first three children if he was the last child in the family.

The Primary One registration was also utilized by the government to advance the cause of sterilization. In the 1974 registration exercise, children of parents, one of whom had undergone sterilization, were accorded some priority irrespective of birth order or age of parents. This incentive was reinforced in the 1975 registration exercise when first priority in priority (A) under Phase Two was given to children, one of whose parents was sterilized. This was still independent of the age of parents and the number of children such parents might already have, and this has created certain problems. As a result of criticism two modifications were introduced in the 1976 registration exercise whereby priority was accorded only to children of parents who were sterilized before the age of forty, and even in such cases greater priority would be given to children who are the first or second child only.[17] In 1977 another change was made to the effect that these children would not be accorded first priority in priority (A) under Phase Two, and, unlike the previous year, would be given equal priority with all other cases in priority (A).[18]

The details of the registration procedure released by the Ministry of Education for implementation in the August 1977 registration, and which continued to be used in the August 1978 exercise, are as follows:[19]

Phase One

For children with brothers and/or sisters studying in the same school.

Phase Two

(A) For children who are either the first or second child of parents one of whom has been sterilized after the birth of the first or second child provided such sterilization was done before the age of forty. Also for children whose parents, brothers or sisters are: old boys or girls who completed their entire primary schooling in those schools; members of the school advisory or school management committees or staff of those schools; old boys or girls who underwent part of their primary or secondary schooling in those schools.

(B) For children whose parents have direct connections with those schools.

(C) For children who are the only child in the family; and for boys whose elder sisters are studying in girls' schools or girls whose elder brothers are studying in boys' schools which are affiliated.

(D) For children who are the third or subsequent child of parents one of whom has been sterilized provided such sterilization was carried out before the age of forty.

Phase Three

For children who are either not eligible for or not successful in Phase One and/or Phase Two.

It should be noted that under this system of registration children who are the only child are given greater preference than previously as they are accorded priority (C) under Phase Two. Furthermore, priority for registration in other cases under Phase One as well as Phase Two is accorded to the third child only. The only exception is priority (D) under Phase Two which is accorded to not only children who are the third child in the family but also to those who are the fourth or subsequent child of parents one of whom has been sterilized before the age of forty. On the other hand, if the children of such sterilized parents are either the first or second child, they move up to priority (A) under Phase Two and would stand a very good chance of getting admittance to the desired schools.

Unlike other measures, the adjustment of the priority system in the Primary One registration to incorporate the population policy of promoting smaller families incurred some criticism. For one thing, the measure penalizes parents retrospectively since it applies to parents who had their children many years ago when such a rule did not exist. Parents affected by this measure have to send their fourth and subsequent children to less desired schools, apart from the daily trouble of sending them to different schools from their first three children. Among all the measures, this measure appears to be the only one that imposes a penalty on the children directly by depriving them of being with their brothers/sisters in the same school, and all the inconveniences that go with it. But the measure does act as a deterrent to some couples thinking of having a fourth or higher parity children.

The immediate outcome of giving priority to children whose parents were sterilized was that in 1975 there was a conspicuous rush by the parents, more often than not the mother, to undergo sterilization in order to take advantage of this new ruling. Besides, those who had been sterilized before the announcement and did not bother to obtain a letter of certification, quickly applied for the certificates.[20] In subsequent years children of many sterilized parents who normally would have to register under Phase Three, moved into Phase Two to priority (D) or even to priority (A) and succeeded in entering the premier schools. The incentive for sterilization is undoubtedly strong for parents who place great emphasis on sending their children to the "right" schools.

In as much as it was intended to promote sterilization, the incentive measure incorporated in the educational system had some measure of success though with more than a fair share of problems and criticisms.[21] In the 1975 registration exercise many children of old boys or girls, staff and parents who had direct connections with the schools were not given places in the good schools of their choice. Instead, these schools, particularly the mission schools, found they had a sizeable number of pupils who were complete "strangers" to the schools but were admitted on the basis of their parents having been sterilized. Some of these mission schools were compelled to open additional classes in order to absorb the children who were pushed out by those with sterilized parents. The 1975 rule also appeared to have discriminated against parents with only one or two children as compared with those with a large number just because they have been sterilized. The amendments introduced in the 1976 registration exercise in respect of the age of parents and parity mitigated the problems somewhat and gave some relief to the popular mission schools.[22] But still some parents who were sterilized in early 1976 at an age above forty years complained that they had lower priority now for their children and were cheated. The slight amendment introduced in 1977 to give equal chances to children of sterilized parents with only one or two children together with other children in priority (A) under Phase Two would relieve further the problems encountered by the popular schools.

The main difficulty was encountered by the Catholic schools which objected to the original or modified measure because they maintain that the granting of privileges to sterilized parents is against their religious beliefs.[23] This objection from the Catholic schools was also raised by some members of Parliament in the House on a few occasions, questioning the necessity of insisting that the Catholic schools should give priority to children of sterilized parents against their moral principles.[24] An inherent defect of the system is that by comparison the majority of the poor and/ or uneducated parents with large-sized families would not bother about the quality of their children's education. This indifference tends to render the incentive policy somewhat ineffective in so far as trying to reduce the family size of these people is concerned. From the egalitarian point of view, however, the policy provides an opportunity to the children of poor parents, one of whom is sterilized but with no connection or influence in the select schools or the community in general, to enter these superior schools.

WORK PERMIT

Foreigners working in Singapore and earning less than $750 are issued with work permits by the Work Permit Office of the Ministry of Labour.

Since 1 July 1973, to try and minimize social problems arising from the influx of young workers from neighbouring countries, work permit holders have been required to obtain approval from the Commissioner of Employment before they can marry Singapore citizens if permanent residence or Singapore citizenship is sought.[25] Those who have worked in Singapore for more than five years or who have certain skills are usually granted permission. The Registrar of Marriages has in fact adopted the policy of not issuing marriage licences in such cases unless the required approval is shown, though there is no enactment to this effect. There were some 1,400 marriages between citizens and work permit holders in 1974.[26]

However, more than a year after the rule came into existence, there were repeated appeals from work permit holders whose original applications to marry were rejected. These were young people who did not meet the set criteria but were now expecting an offspring out of wedlock. In January 1976 the government relented and introduced a rule whereby this category of work permit holders would be given permission to marry, together with all the attendant benefits, if both partners give a written undertaking that both would undergo sterilization after the birth of the second child.[27] Failure to observe this rule in due course might result in the forfeiture of certain privileges such as withdrawal of work permit, non-renewal of permit, and loss of medical, educational and housing benefits. This incentive for sterilization is different in that it was introduced because of very special circumstances and also in that sterilization is not required immediately but for a future period some months later. The government ruling was repeatedly aimed at, among other things, conferring legitimacy on children born out of wedlock.

The effect of this measure to promote sterilization is rather limited as it applies not to the general population but to a very limited group. This measure appears to be subject to the most misunderstanding or misinterpretation if the complexities underlying it are not appreciated. Some criticisms were levelled at this policy. Even a newspaper editorial remarked in January 1976 that "making sterilization after the second child a condition of marriage between Singaporeans and work permit holders seems unnecessarily harsh",[28] but the same newspaper admitted in March 1977 that that statement was made without the background information later made available in Parliament.[29] The important point to note is that the sterilization condition is not required of work permit holders who are not expecting a child at the time of applying for permission to marry Singapore citizens.

Notes

1. "Welcome Speech by Mr Lee Kuan Yew", *Proceedings of the Seventh Conference of the International Planned Parenthood Federation*, p. 27.
2. Quoted in George G. Thomson and T. E. Smith, "Singapore: Family Planning in an Urban Environment", in *The Politics of Family Planning in the Third World*, edited by T. E. Smith (London: George Allen & Unwin, 1973), p. 252.
3. *Eleventh Annual Report of the Singapore Family Planning and Population Board, 1976* (Singapore: Secura Singapore, 1977). On p. 2 the Report states, "New directions in the form of expanded and intensified disincentive and incentive policies related to family planning and population were announced in 1972 to give the National Programme fresh impetus."
4. *The Employment Act, 1968*, No. 122 of 1968, Singapore: Government Printer, 1968.
5. Thomson and Smith, "Singapore: Family Planning", p. 252.
6. *Straits Times*, 25 October 1972.
7. *The Employment (Amendment) Act, 1973* (Singapore: Government Printer, 1973).
8. *Report on the Labour Force Survey of Singapore, 1977*, p. 31.
9. *Singapore*, Population Profiles 1 (New York: United Nations Fund for Population Activities, n.d.).
10. *Fourth Annual Report of the Singapore Family Planning and Population Board, 1969*, p. 3.
11. *Straits Times*, 25 October 1972.
12. Margaret Loh, "The Singapore Family Planning and Population Programme with Special Reference to New Directions and Emphasis, 1973/74", *Singapore Public Health Bulletin*, No. 13, January 1974.
13. *Income Tax (Amendment) Act, 1973* (Singapore: Government Printer, 1973).
14. *Population and Trends* (Singapore: Ministry of Health, 1977), p. 34.
15. Ibid., p. 34.
16. *HDB Annual Report, 1 April 1977 to 31 March 1978*, p. 5.
17. *Straits Times*, 18 July 1976. This issue of the newspaper gives the details released by the Ministry of Education with regard to Primary One registration from 26 July to 21 August 1976.
18. *Straits Times*, 23 August 1977.
19. *Straits Times*, 28 July 1977.
20. *Sunday Nation*, 17 August 1975.

21. Some of these problems and criticisms are reported in *Sunday Nation*, 17 August 1975; *New Nation*, 4 November 1975; *New Nation*, 13 August 1976; *Straits Times*, 13 August 1976.

22. *New Nation*, 19 August 1976.

23. *New Nation*, 22 March 1976. It was reported that in a letter read in all Catholic churches over the week-end, the Archbishop M. Olcomedy said, "At no time has the Catholic church, either directly or indirectly, approved the granting of privileges on admission to a child, one of whose parents is known to be sterilized. This is a matter of conscience."

24. It was reported in the *Straits Times*, 24 March 1976, that Mr Ng Kah Ting, MP for Ponggol, raised the matter in Parliament on 23 March 1976, and in the *Straits Times*, 17 February 1977, that Mr Sia Khoon Seong, MP for Moulmein, also touched on this matter in the House on 16 February 1977.

25. *Straits Times*, 24 June 1973.

26. *New Nation*, 27 January 1976.

27. *New Nation*, 24 January 1976; and *Straits Times*, 25 January 1976.

28. Editorial entitled "A condition that's not needed" in *New Nation*, 27 January 1976.

29. Editorial entitled "Hobson's choice for MPs" in *New Nation*, 17 March 1977. This is the commentary on the clarification given by Mr Ong Pang Boon, Minister for Labour, in reply to a question raised by Mr Ho See Beng, MP for Khe Bong, in respect of a work permit holder who was asked to leave Singapore because her Singaporean husband refused to keep his promise to be sterilized after the second child.

7

Knowledge, Attitudes, and Practice

In this chapter the knowledge, attitudes, and practice of married women in respect of family planning, abortion, sterilization, and government population policies will be examined. The source of data for this study is the First National Survey on Family Planning conducted in 1973 on a sample basis. By means of a two-stage stratified sample design, a slightly less than 1 per cent sample of 2,167 married women aged fifteen to forty-four were selected for the survey which was conducted from 7 to 29 September 1973. During this period, 2,078 of the selected women were successfully interviewed and the remaining 89 were refusals and non-contact cases, giving a response rate of 96 per cent which is quite satisfactory as compared to similar surveys conducted in other countries. During the data processing stage a few completed questionnaires had to be rejected for various reasons and the number finally accepted for tabulation amounted to 2,076. A wealth of information pertaining to these 2,076 married women was published in the report, but only the more important features that are relevant to this study will be discussed here.[1]

FAMILY PLANNING

In the survey the respondents were asked the number of birth control methods they had heard about but need not necessarily know how to use. Some 97.4 per cent of the 2,076 married women replied that they have heard of at least one contraceptive method. This is a very satisfactory figure as compared to the corresponding proportion of 94.7 per cent in Japan (1973)[2] and 84.5 per cent in Peninsular Malaysia (1970).[3] The almost universal knowledge of contraceptive methods among Singapore women is not surprising in view of the continuous clinical, information and educational activities of the Family Planning Association since 1949 and subsequently the SFPPB since 1966. In addition, there is the high literacy rate and excellent mass communications channels in a small compact cosmopolitan community.

The detailed figures in Table 7.1 show that contraceptive knowledge has indeed permeated all strata of the community. The married women in each of the three main races experienced equally high levels of contraceptive knowledge, above 97 per cent, and so did the married women in each of the three age groups. More revealing features are brought out by the figures according to education; here the proportion reached 100 per cent for married women with tertiary education. It decreased very slowly the lower the educational level, but then even those without any formal education experienced contraceptive knowledge

TABLE 7.1

Proportion of Married Women Who Had Heard of and Who Knew How to Use at Least One Contraceptive Method by Race, Age, and Education, 1973

Characteristics	Heard of at Least One Method	Know How to Use at Least One Method
Total	97.8	87.7
Race		
Chinese	97.4	87.6
Malays	98.4	88.4
Indians	98.7	84.2
Age Group		
15–24	97.7	87.4
25–34	98.5	90.5
35–44	97.0	84.3
Education		
No formal education	97.3	84.8
Primary	98.3	87.4
Secondary	97.8	91.4
Post-secondary	97.1	97.1
Tertiary	100.0	100.0

of as high as 97.3 per cent. Additional evidence of the high level of contraceptive knowledge may be seen in the proportion of married women who have heard of specific methods of birth control. The proportions approached 94.9 per cent for the pill, 80.7 per cent for the condom, and 50.7 per cent for the IUD.

The ability to use contraceptive methods is also quite high among the married women, as can also be observed in Table 7.1. Some 87.7 per cent replied that they knew how to use one or more methods of birth control. Among the three main races, the Malay women had the highest proportion (88.4 per cent), and the Indian women the lowest proportion (84.2 per cent), with the Chinese women occupying an intermediate position (87.6 per cent). These differentials are small and without much significance; the more important point is that the proportions are extremely high and satisfactory, indicating the extensive ability of all the races to practise birth control.

The ability to use contraceptive methods was greatest among married women in the 25–34 age group, followed by those in the 15–24 age group and finally the 35–44 age group. One plausible explanation is that the older women, apart from having less formal education, are approaching the end of their reproductive age span and have less incentive to learn how to use contraceptives. The youngest women did not have their desired number of children yet and gave less thought to birth control. Only those in the 25–34 age group probably had their desired number of children and are eager to acquire the knowledge to practise birth control. Of the married women 84.8 per cent without any formal education knew how to practise birth control, and this proportion increased with the advance of education until it reached 100 per cent among those with tertiary education. By and large, better educated women have greater access to sources of information, greater ability to learn, and a higher level of expectation which results in substitution away from children to other sources of satisfaction.

In the survey the respondents were asked whether they approve of married couples doing or using something to prevent pregnancy. The principal aim of this question was to ascertain the married women's attitude towards the general idea of family limitation and child spacing rather than their attitude towards specific methods. Thus in the phrasing of the question the terms "birth control" and "contraceptives" were not employed. The answers were grouped under "Approve", "It depends", "Disapprove", "Indifferent", and "Don't know". Of the married women

69.1 per cent approved of family planning, 18.8 per cent said "it depends" and 11.4 per cent disapproved. Surprisingly, the group giving their approval did not exceed 69.1 per cent, which is somewhat low when viewed in terms of local conditions prevailing then and also viewed in terms of other countries. For instance, the corresponding proportions were 87.0 per cent in Japan (1973) and 77.9 per cent in Peninsular Malaysia (1970).

As a matter of fact, the detailed figures provided in Table 7.2 indicate that the objections came mainly from the Chinese with only 66.3 per cent of the married women who approved of family planning. A much higher proportion of the other two races gave their approval: 77.5 per cent in the case of the Malays and 72.4 per cent for the Indians. Age and education do not seem to have had a direct bearing on the proportion giving their approval. The proportion was about 68 per cent for married women in the 25–34 age group and in the 35–44 age group, while 73.8 per cent of the youngest women approved of family planning. This is a

TABLE 7.2

Proportion of Married Women Who Approved of Family Planning and Average Ideal Number of Children by Race, Age, and Education, 1973

Characteristics	Per Cent who Approved of Family Planning	Average Ideal Number of Children
Total	69.1	3.06
	Race	
Chinese	66.3	3.02
Malays	77.5	3.44
Indians	72.4	2.73
	Age Group	
15–24	73.8	2.70
25–34	68.0	3.15
35–44	68.7	4.22
	Education	
No formal education	69.9	3.31
Primary	69.2	3.08
Secondary	67.7	2.65
Post Secondary	67.7	2.63
Tertiary	70.4	2.33

reflection of the conservative attitudes of the older women as opposed to the more modern and broad-minded view of the young women. No definite pattern emerges from the proportions for the five educational groups, the figures lying within the narrow range of 67.7 and 70.4 per cent. The highest proportion of 70.4 per cent is for those with tertiary education but this is not much higher than the 69.9 per cent for those with no formal education at all. Education is thus a negligible factor in the approval or otherwise of the married women of family planning in general. The findings of the survey confirm the favourable attitudes towards family planning among all sections of the community.

An attempt was made in the survey to gather information on the attitude of the respondents towards the ideal number of children for married couples. The answers to this question are best analysed in terms of the average number of children; the computed averages are given in Table 7.2. The ideal average number of children was computed as 3.06 which exceeded the two-child family norm first promoted by SFPPB in 1972, a year before the survey. This overall average was distorted by wide variations among the age groups. For the oldest age group, the average was as high as 4.22, and dropped to 3.15 for the 25–34 age group and finally to 2.70 for the youngest age group. The large average desired by the older women poses a problem, but fortunately they have passed their childbearing prime. This is a good sign for the future in the sense that at least the young women of Singapore are more in favour of a smaller family size. There is also some relationship between the attitude towards the average number of children and educational attainment, though not as pronounced as age. The average amounted to 2.33 for those with tertiary education, and tends to increase slowly to 3.31 for those with no formal education. The findings seem to suggest that, unlike attitudes towards family planning approval, attitudes towards ideal number of children were influenced by the educational attainment of the respondents.

Apart from attitudes and knowledge, the survey collected information on the practice of birth control among the respondents. The extent of birth control practice has a direct influence on the level of fertility prevailing in the country. The results given in Table 7.3 indicate that 77.0 per cent of the married women have practised birth control at one time or another. This is slightly lower than the corresponding figure of 81.3 per cent in Japan (1973), but higher than the 68 per cent in Taiwan (1973) and the 28.7 per cent in Peninsular Malaysia (1970). A more meaningful

TABLE 7.3

Proportion of Married Women Currently Practising, Who Practised Before, and Who Never Practised Contraception, by Race, Age, and Education, 1973

Characteristics	Currently Practising	Practised Before	Never Practised
Total	60.1	16.9	23.0
Race			
Chinese	63.6	17.2	19.2
Malays	48.7	16.4	34.9
Indians	51.9	14.6	33.5
Age Group			
15–24	51.8	17.1	31.1
25–34	63.9	17.6	18.5
35–44	58.8	15.9	25.3
Education			
No formal education	56.7	18.7	24.6
Primary	61.5	15.6	22.9
Secondary	63.0	16.1	20.9
Post-secondary	64.7	8.8	26.5
Tertiary	59.3	29.6	11.1

picture may be gained by a comparison of the proportion still practising birth control at the time of the interview. Some 60.1 per cent of the married women were practising birth control at the time of interview in September 1973, a very satisfactory level if one considers that the proportion in Japan in the same year was 59.3 per cent.

Marked differences in the level of contraceptive practice among the races are revealed by the figures given in Table 7.3. The proportion of current users of contraception was 63.6 per cent for the Chinese women which was higher than the proportion of about 50 per cent for both the Malay and the Indian women. Among the three age groups, the highest level of current contraceptive practice was experienced by those in the middle age group — 25–34 years — and the lowest in the youngest age group. Women who are in their prime years of reproduction and have their desired number of children will generally be more inclined to practise family planning. The young women are less inclined to practise birth control for family limitation, and if they do practise, they would do so for reasons of child spacing. On the other hand, many of the old women will not practise birth control because they are nearing the end of their reproductive period and feel there is less need to do so. There seems to be only a slight relationship between education and current practice of birth control. The proportion of current users amounted to 56.7 per cent for women with no formal education, and rising very slowly with greater education to 64.7 per cent for those with post-secondary education, but dropping again to 59.3 per cent for those with tertiary education.

The figures in the last column of Table 7.3 refer to those who have never practised any form of birth control and represent what is commonly known as the "hard-core" group. This group has been the focus of attention from the SFPPB in recent years in its search for further means of increasing family planning acceptors to reduce fertility to replacement level. The so-called hard-core group consisted of some 23.0 per cent of the married women at the time of the survey in 1973, which was somewhat higher than the 15.1 per cent in Japan in the same year. A reduction in the proportion of this group of married women within the reproductive ages of 15 to 44 through acceptance of family planning or sterilization would undoubtedly have an impact on fertility levels in the future. It would be useful to examine in greater detail the characteristics of this category of married women.

The proportion of never-users was only 19.2 per cent among the Chinese women as compared to 34.9 per cent and 33.5 per cent for Malay women and Indian women respectively. There is thus a greater possibility of increasing family planning acceptance among women in the Malay and Indian communities. With regard to the variable age, a perceptibly higher proportion of married women between the ages of 15 and 24 had never practised contraception on account of their desire to start a family at an early stage of their married life. This may be substantiated by the finding that some 59 per cent of the never-users preferred the interval between marriage and the first child to be shorter than one and a-half years. After starting a family, the married women would want to practise birth control to space their subsequent children and later to limit their number of children. Consequently, the proportion of never-users dipped sharply from 31.1 per cent to 18.5 per cent in the middle age group.

No definite pattern is being exhibited by the figures according to educational levels. For instance, the proportion of never-users was higher for married women with a post-secondary education (26.5 per cent) than for those with no education at all (24.6 per cent). It should be emphasized that not all married women who have never practised contraception can be regarded as hard-core in the sense that they have many children and are deliberately closing their minds to the need for family planning. Some of these married women, or their husbands, were infertile cases. The survey data in fact show that the never-users were low parity women with a mean number of 1.3 male children and also 1.3 female children.

Information on the method of contraception used by the respondents currently practising birth control provides an idea of the different methods employed by the general population. The most popular method was the pill which was used by 36 per cent of the married women, followed by the condom (28 per cent) and IUD (6 per cent). However, the percentages of new acceptors within the national programme choosing pills and condoms came to 56 per cent and 41 per cent respectively. This is nothing but a reflection of the subsidized contraceptives offered for sale by the SFPPB. The popularity ranking of pill, condom and IUD was the same for the Chinese and the Malays, but more Indians preferred the condom to the pill.

Data on the source of contraceptive supplies for those who practised family planning were also collected in the survey. Most of the users obtained their contraceptive supplies from the SFPPB clinics, while those who have never attended these clinics procured their supplies from their private practitioners. The next source in order of importance were the roadside stalls which, as to be expected, were frequented mainly by those with little education and low income.

ABORTION

The laws concerning abortion were liberalized by the Abortion Act which came into force on 20 March 1970 amidst considerable debate about, among other things, the moral and medical implications of legalizing abortion. By the time of the survey, the Act had been in operation for some three and a-half years and the opportunity was taken to gather detailed information on the respondents' knowledge, attitudes, and practice of abortion. One of the first things to be ascertained from the respondents was whether they were aware that induced abortion is legal in Singapore. Surprisingly, only 55.3 per cent knew that it was legal. The other group who had no knowledge of legal abortion at all might encounter certain complications in resorting to the traditional source of abortion which carries with it greater dangers of impairing the health of the mothers.

Only minor variations in the awareness of legal abortion existed among the three main races, as can be seen in Table 7.4. The highest level of awareness amounting to 59.5 per cent was experienced by the Indian women, which was not much higher than the 58.7 per cent for the Malay women and 54.1 per cent for the Chinese women. Even lesser differentials are revealed by the figures according to age groups. On the other hand, there is a strong positive correlation between awareness of legal abortion and educational attainment, but only up to a point. Some 44.9 per cent of married women with no formal education were aware that induced abortion was legal, and this percentage rose to 53.5 per cent for those with primary education and then to 75.9 per cent for those with secondary education. Thereafter, it did not matter whether they

TABLE 7.4
Percentage of Married Women Who Knew Abortion Was Legal and Who Knew Where to Obtain Legal Abortion, 1973

Characteristics	Know Abortion is Legal	Know Where to Obtain Legal Abortion
Total	55.3	43.9
Race		
Chinese	54.1	42.9
Malays	58.7	46.6
Indians	59.5	49.4
Age Group		
15–24	55.0	41.4
25–34	56.0	45.0
35–44	54.5	43.6
Education		
No formal education	44.9	35.4
Primary	53.5	42.6
Secondary	75.9	60.3
Post-secondary	67.6	61.8
Tertiary	74.1	55.6

had education up to post-secondary or tertiary level since the percentages did not continue on an upward trend.

At the time of the survey legal abortion could be obtained from certain designated places such as government MCH/ Family clinics, the National Family Planning Centre, government outpatient clinics, government hospitals, and registered medical practitioners. The respondents were asked whether they knew of any place for obtaining legal abortion if they wanted one, and the number of positive answers came to 43.9 per cent. One may regard this as satisfactory considering that this percentage was not much lower than the 55.3 per cent who were aware of legal abortion. The variables of race, age, and education appear to reveal the same pattern in their knowledge about places of obtaining abortion as in the case of awareness of legal abortion. However, the findings suggest that there is still scope for information and educational activities on the part of the SFPPB in focusing attention on the legality of abortion and the places where it can be obtained.

A question of whether the respondents approved of induced abortion in general was also included in the survey, and the answers have been tabulated in the same five categories as those for approval of family planning. The proportion of respondents who approved of induced abortion was quite low — 23.1 per cent — as against the 52.0 per cent who disapproved, and 22.1 per cent said "it depends", 0.6 per cent were indifferent and 2.2 per cent said they "don't know".

Perhaps the most significant finding refers to the unequivocal disapproval of induced abortion by some 52 per cent of the married women, which was undoubtedly high as compared with the corresponding figure of 12.7 per cent in Japan in the same year. It would appear that notwithstanding the legalization of abortion some three and a-half years ago, the married women in Singapore still look upon induced abortion as not such a desirable method of terminating unwanted pregnancies. They would prefer to practise birth control in the first place, which explains the comparatively low legal abortion rate of 12.3 per thousand women aged 15 to 44 in 1974 as compared to 65.8 in Bulgaria in 1974, 44.6 in Hungary in 1974, 53.3 in South Korea in 1973, and 25.4 in Japan in 1974.[4] As observed earlier, a satisfactorily high proportion of not less than 60 per cent of married women were practising birth control.

Attitudes towards induced abortion vary somewhat among the three main races. Table 7.5 shows that the extent of approval of induced abortion was the lowest among Chinese women (22.4 per cent) and

TABLE 7.5

Percentage of Married Women Who Approved of Induced Abortion and Who Were Willing to Undergo Abortion, 1973

Characteristics	Approved of Induced Abortion	Willing to Undergo Abortion
Total	23.1	17.2
Race		
Chinese	22.4	17.8
Malays	24.8	13.5
Indians	29.1	22.2
Age Group		
15–24	20.4	15.2
25–34	21.3	17.5
35–44	26.3	17.6
Education		
No formal education	23.2	13.6
Primary	22.8	17.5
Secondary	22.6	22.3
Post-secondary	26.5	26.5
Tertiary	33.3	18.5

highest among Indian women (29.1 per cent). No clear-cut pattern emerged from the figures for education, except that the married women with tertiary education exhibited a conspicuously high degree of approval. Those without any formal education approved of abortion to essentially the same degree as those with primary or secondary education. Perhaps uneducated women could never have been drawn into the complexity of the moral issues underlying most of the objections to abortion.

Data with some practical implications are those indicating whether the respondents were willing to subject themselves to legal abortion in the future. The figures are laid out in the second column of Table 7.5. With one exception, the proportion willing to undergo legal abortion was lower than that which approved of induced abortion. Only 17.2 per cent of the married women were prepared to submit to legal abortion. Those willing to undergo legal abortion were further asked under what conditions they would do so. Of these 70.7 per cent cited "enough children", 13.2 per cent "too close to previous pregnancy", and 0.9 per cent "unsuitable timing of pregnancy". In comparison with the other two races the Malay women were less inclined to undergo legal abortion.

The findings concerning approval of induced abortion and willingness to undergo abortion have some influence on the extent of the practice of abortion. In view of the somewhat unfavourable conditions concerning these two aspects of abortion, it would be hardly surprising that only about 6 per cent of the married women have ever had an abortion. The possibility that this figure was underestimated cannot be discounted completely in view of the sensitive nature of the subject which might prevent the respondents from telling the whole truth. In any case, at the time of interview in 1973, in Japan the corresponding percentage of women who had experienced abortion was 38.8.

STERILIZATION

As mentioned previously, the Voluntary Sterilization Act came into force on the same day as the Abortion Act on 20 March 1970. The official view of the Singapore Government towards sterilization is that it is a safe and effective method of birth control, and various measures have therefore been instituted to promote it. It was deemed appropriate to collect information on the respondents' knowledge, attitudes, and practice of sterilization in the survey. It was shown that 94.5 per cent of the respondents had heard of female sterilization, but only 50.1 per cent had heard of male sterilization. Among the former group of respondents, 84.4 per cent knew at least one place where female sterilization could be performed, while among the latter group only 13.8 per cent knew where male sterilization could be performed. It is only natural that the married women should know more about female than male sterilization because they are directly involved, physically and mentally, in the former operation. A more noteworthy finding refers to the far higher level of knowledge about sterilization than about abortion.

The detailed figures according to the characteristics of respondents are given in Table 7.6. Knowledge of female sterilization was extremely high and fairly even among all subgroups of married women with respect to race, age and education generally, being above 91 per cent in every case. Wide differences are noticeable in the case of knowledge of male sterilization. First of all, knowledge of male sterilization was positively correlated with education. The proportion was only 33.6 per cent for married women without any formal education but increased

TABLE 7.6
Percentage of Married Women Who Had Heard of Male Sterilization and Female Sterilization and Who Knew Where to Obtain Male Sterilization and Female Sterilization, 1973

Characteristics	Heard of Male Sterilization	Heard of Female Sterilization	Knew a Place for Male Sterilization	Knew a Place for Female Sterilization
Total	50.1	94.5	13.8	84.4
Race				
Chinese	52.4	95.6	13.7	86.6
Malays	36.2	91.2	9.0	78.8
Indians	48.1	91.1	11.4	79.7
Age Group				
15–24	51.8	91.6	10.7	75.1
25–34	55.5	95.7	16.8	88.0
35–44	43.1	94.1	11.4	83.7
Education				
No formal education	33.6	92.0	6.3	81.8
Primary	49.1	95.2	10.3	85.0
Secondary	77.4	96.5	29.5	87.6
Post-secondary	82.4	94.1	32.4	88.2
Tertiary	96.3	100.0	70.4	81.5

steeply with greater education to touch the high of 96.3 per cent for those with tertiary education. Similarly, knowledge of where to obtain male sterilization was positively correlated with education.

An attempt was made in the survey to ascertain the source of information about female sterilization among the respondents who had heard of this method. The dominant source of information can be traced to relatives, friends and neighbours, amounting to 57.7 per cent. This was followed by family planning clinics (11.6 per cent), family planning staff (10.7 per cent), maternity hospitals (9.9 per cent) and private doctors' clinics (2.2 per cent). Among those who were aware of female sterilization, they were asked whether they knew of the various methods of operation. 43.7 per cent of this group of women knew about abdominal ligation but only 1.7 per cent was aware of vaginal ligation.

Unlike information on attitudes towards family planning and abortion which was solicited from all respondents, data on attitudes towards sterilization were only obtained from the 1,041 respondents who had heard of both female and male sterilization. This inherent difference in the three sets of data should be borne in mind in interpreting the figures shown in the first column of Table 7.7. Among this group of 1,041 women, 80.9 per cent approved of sterilization, 9.3 per cent said "it depends", 1.0 per cent were either indifferent or "don't know", but only 8.3 per cent objected to sterilization. Another useful finding is that among those who had not been sterilized, a sizeable proportion of 38.9 per cent indicated their willingness to undergo the operation in the future. In contrast to abortion, there was very little resistance to sterilization as the majority of the women were in favour of sterilization and a good number of those not yet sterilized were prepared to do so after having their desired family size. This suggests that conditions in Singapore are quite conducive to the idea of sterilization being propagated as one of the methods of population control.

The practice of family planning and abortion does not exert the same kind of impact on the level of fertility as the practice of sterilization. The latter constitutes a permanent solution and reduces permanently the number of women exposed to the risk of childbearing. Nearly 12.4 per cent of the married women had been sterilized as compared to the 6 per cent noted earlier for abortion. With regard to the reasons for sterilization, 87.6 per cent of the sterilized women cited "enough children" as the reason. The other minor reasons were: 5.8 per cent, medical reasons; and, for 0.8 per cent, waiver of the accouchement fee.

TABLE 7.7

Percentage of Married Women Who Had Heard of Female and Male Sterilization and Who Approved of Sterilization and Who Were Willing to Undergo Sterilization, 1973

Characteristics	Approved of Sterilization	Willing to undergo Sterilization
Total	80.9	38.9
	Race	
Chinese	83.2	45.1
Malays	74.5	20.4
Indians	81.6	33.5
	Age Group	
15–24	84.4	54.7
25–34	80.2	48.5
35–44	80.7	21.1
	Education	
No formal education	83.3	29.6
Primary	80.8	41.3
Secondary	81.1	49.9
Post-secondary	64.3	55.9
Tertiary	76.9	33.3

GOVERNMENT POPULATION POLICIES

In the previous chapter we have examined the various social incentives and disincentives introduced by the government to promote the two-child family norm with a view to achieving zero population growth in the long run. Information on the respondents' knowledge and attitudes towards these measures was solicited in the survey so as to provide us with some data by which to assess their effectiveness. The compilation of this kind of data is unique to the Singapore survey and is never carried out in knowledge, attitudes, and practice (KAP) surveys conducted in other countries.

One of the questions attempted to ascertain whether the respondents knew how many children the government recommends that every married couple should have, and it was found that 75.2 per cent of the married women knew of the exact number of children recommended by the government. Only 16.8 per cent admitted they were unaware of the two-child family advocated by the government, while the remaining 8.0 per cent were non-commital with "don't know" replies. The fairly satisfactory level of knowledge about the two-child concept may be attributed to the information and educational activities of the SFPPB and the incentive and disincentive policies aimed at promoting the two-child family.

The detailed figures given in Table 7.8 reveal some variation in awareness of the two-child concept among the three races. This awareness was far higher among the Indian women (84.2 per cent) than among the

TABLE 7.8

Percentage of Married Women Who Were Aware of the Two-Child Family Recommended by Government and Who Agreed That Two Was Just Right, 1973

Characteristics	Aware of Two-child Family	Two-child Family is "Just Right"
Total	75.2	51.5
Race		
Chinese	75.5	49.9
Malays	70.4	41.8
Indians	84.2	77.9
Age Group		
15–24	79.9	62.2
25–34	77.4	53.1
35–44	70.6	45.4
Education		
No formal education	64.0	39.9
Primary	78.0	51.7
Secondary	87.9	68.7
Post-secondary	94.2	73.5
Tertiary	81.5	74.1
Combined Income ($)		
Less than 200	64.0	43.2
200–399	74.8	48.6
400–599	79.7	53.6
600–799	84.4	53.0
800–999	86.8	77.4
1,000 & above	87.5	74.9

Chinese women (75.5 per cent) or Malay women (70.4 per cent). With regard to age, the younger married women have a greater awareness of the two-child family, and this has some impact in terms of influencing future fertility trends. In general, this awareness was lower among the less educated poorer classes.

To probe deeper into the two-child family concept, the respondents were asked whether this number was too many, too few or just right. The replies to this question seem to be divided evenly among the respondents, though the balance was slightly tipped in favour of the "just right" category. The two-child family was described as too few by 46.1 per cent of the respondents, while 2.3 per cent were unsure and 0.1 per cent (one respondent) regarded it as too many. The fairly high 51.5 per cent who thought it was just right may be viewed with some satisfaction since the government's advocation of this concept had been initiated only a year previously.

Apart from being most aware of the two-child family, the Indian women again clearly stood out ahead of the other women in exhibiting a favourable attitude towards the adequacy of two children per family. The proportion of Indian women giving "just right" answers was 77.9 per cent, in contrast to the low of 41.8 per cent and 49.9 per cent of the Malay and the Chinese women respectively. This is in agreement with an earlier finding on the opinion of the average ideal number of children for married couples among the three races; here the lowest average was provided by Indian women and the largest by Malay women.

The results by age appear to be promising in terms of future fertility levels. No less than 62.2 per cent of the young women in the 15–24 age group regarded two children as adequate, and this proportion declined progressively with the advance of age. Less hopeful results emerged from the figures tabulated by educational and income classifications. By and large, the married women with a lower educational attainment or lower combined income of husband and wife had a tendency to regard two children as inadequate. This tendency appears to be quite strong as can be observed from the pronounced progression of the percentages shown in Table 7.7.

The respondents were requested to name the measures taken by the government to discourage people from having too many children. By the time of the survey in September 1973 the incentives and disincentives introduced were in the areas of accouchement fee, HDB flat allocations, paid maternity leave, income tax relief and primary one registration. The married women were most knowledgeable about the accouchement fee policy (92.4 per cent), followed by primary one registration (80.7 per cent), and HDB flat allocation (69.2 per cent). They were far less knowledgeable about income tax relief (41.6 per cent) and paid maternity leave (38.3 per cent), which could possibly be due to the fact that those who did not work would be less likely to be aware of the two measures, apart from income tax being a technical matter more familiar to their husbands.

In the survey information on the reaction of the respondents towards the incentive and disincentive policies introduced lately by the government was collected. More specifically, they were required to state whether the measures had affected or would affect them personally in their decision regarding the number of children they wanted. It should be noted that the question was framed in such a manner that the answers would incorporate a combination of two types of effect, the actual one which had already influenced the women and the potential one which the women felt would affect them in the future. In the opinion of the women, the measure which had the greatest impact on their decision concerning family size was the accouchement fee with 42.4 per cent. Primary One registration with 39.1 per cent came a close second. The other three measures appeared to have exerted a much lower degree of influence, 25.8 per cent for HDB flat allocation, 14.3 per cent for income tax relief and 11.0 per cent for paid maternity leave. In the main the effectiveness of the five policies varied in accordance with the personal background of the respondents.

A close examination of the detailed figures tabulated according to the personal characteristics of the married women reveals some interesting features. Without any exception, the effectiveness of each of these measures was reported to be greatest among Malay women and the least among Chinese women, with an intermediate influence among Indian women. In general the younger women were more affected by these measures, in particular accouchement fee and paid maternity leave, because proportionately more of them would be giving births. Since most of these measures involve financial penalties for those with larger families, we should expect the combined income of husband and wife to have considerable influence on the effectiveness of these measures. Among all income groups, those with the lowest income of less than $200 reported that they were most affected by these measures, excluding income tax relief. Since some of them did not pay any income tax at all

TABLE 7.9

Percentage of Women Who Thought Government Population Policies Had Affected or Would Affect Their Own or Other People's Family Size, 1973

Population Policy	Affect own Family Size	Affect other People's Family Size
Accouchement fee	42.4	70.3
Primary one registration	39.1	63.6
HDB flat allocation	25.8	51.3
Income tax relief	14.3	25.1
Paid maternity leave	11.0	30.7

as their annual income was below the taxable minimum, income tax relief would have less effect on them than on those in the higher taxable income bracket. As to be expected, the effect of accouchement fee was closely related to the income levels of the women, with the proportion reporting it had an effect decreasing from 55.1 per cent for the less than $200 group to 26.6 per cent for the $1,000 and above group.

A complementary question asked the respondents to state whether they thought the measures had affected or would affect many people in their decision regarding the number of children they wanted. A summary of the results are also given in Table 7.9. The most interesting finding is that the women believed that the measures would have a far greater effect on other people than on themselves. However, the actual difference was not similar for every measure. In the case of paid maternity leave, the women seemed to think that the extent of the effect would be about three times more for other people than for themselves. For HDB flat allocations it was about twice, and much less than twice in the case of the other three measures. On the whole, one may say that the incentive and disincentive policies have affected and will continue to affect the number of children that married couples have in Singapore in the future.

Notes

1. Wan Fook Kee and Saw Swee-Hock, *Report of the First National Survey of Family Planning in Singapore* (Singapore: Singapore Family Planning and Population Board and National Statistical Commission, 1974).

2. *Summary of Twelfth National Survey on Family Planning*, Series No. 24, Tokyo: The Population Problems Research Council, The Mainichi Newspaper, 1975. It should be noted that the figures for Japan quoted in the rest of this chapter are also taken from this particular publication.

3. *West Malaysia: Interim Report on Family Survey, 1910*, Kuala Lumpur: Department of Statistics, 1971. It should be noted that this publication is the source for all the other figures for Peninsular Malaysia mentioned in the rest of the chapter.

4. Christopher Tietze and Marjorie Cooper Murstein, *Induced Abortion: 1975 Factbook*, Reports on Population/Family Planning, No. 14 (2nd edition), December 1975 (New York: Population Council, 1975).

8

Rapid Fertility Decline

Having examined at great length the nature of the population control programme with its various components introduced at different times in response to prevailing demographic trends and economic conditions, we will now proceed to investigate the levels and trends in fertility during the post-war period up to 1977, paying particular attention to the more interesting developments that have taken place in the seventies. In this task we have been greatly assisted by the availability of accurate and comprehensive birth statistics[1] generated from the efficient vital registration system in Singapore. For one thing, the coverage of birth statistics is known to have attained near 100 per cent completeness, and from 1953 these data have been made available according to the date of occurrence of live-births. Data on live-births by age of mother have been made available progressively in greater detail since 1943, with birth order statistics first published in 1967.

Our study of fertility levels and trends is based largely on the total fertility rate though the crude birth rate is also used. The crude birth rate, defined as the total number of live-births occurring during one calendar year per thousand population living in the middle of the same year, is easy to compute and understand, but it suffers from some inherent defects. It is distorted by differences in population structure and is not suited for assessing fertility differences over time or among various groups of the population. The total fertility rate is the average number of children that would be born per woman in a group of women if all women survived to the end of their reproductive years and bore children at each age in accordance with the age-specific fertility schedule for women of various ages. Computation of this rate requires data on the number of births during the year tabulated by the age of the mother and on the total female population at mid-year of the same year by five-year age groups. The total fertility rate, which is independent of the effect of the sex and age composition of the population, is a satisfactory measure for analysing fertility trends and differentials.

LONG-TERM GENERAL TRENDS

After World War II the number of births in Singapore rose year after year, from 43,045 in 1947 to the peak level of 62,495 in 1958. The crude birth rate remained exceptionally high, above 45 per thousand population, up to 1954, after which it began to fall. An interesting question naturally arises whether the latter phenomenon marks the beginning of a change in the level of fertility downwards. There is evidence to suggest that the drop in the crude birth rate, which attracted considerable attention at that time among those connected with the private family planning programme, was engendered entirely by a reduction in the proportion of women in the reproductive ages brought about by the entry of a relatively smaller number of women than usual into the reproductive age range. This smaller cohort of women, resulting from the low birth rate and high infant mortality during the war years 1941–45, would by 1957 have consisted of women within the ages of 13 to 16. This, coupled with the increasing proportion of women born after this cohort, has caused the ratio of women of reproductive age to the total population to be lowered from 23.0 per cent in 1947 to 21.7 per cent in 1957. That the level of fertility has not been reduced at all may be seen in the figures for the total fertility rate shown in Table 8.1; the rate has in fact remained stubbornly high at above the 6.00 level and even showed a gentle upward trend towards 1957 (see Figure 8.1).

The extremely high fertility prevailing during the first post-war decade or so may be attributed to attitudes and beliefs which were deeply embedded in the cultural and religious tradition of the people. First, compared with regions of low fertility, there was in Singapore the interaction of the lower mean age at first marriage of women; the high marriage rate, and the larger proportion ultimately married. At that time women were expected to marry early; marriage was universal; and celibacy found little social acceptance among the people. Second, the average size of a family was very near seven children which was partly a manifestation of the tradition of desiring large families among practically all the races. Among the many and varied factors favouring large families

TABLE 8.1

Births, Crude Birth Rate and Total Fertility Rate, 1947–77

Year	Number of Births	Crude Birth Rate	Total Fertility Rate	Per Cent Annual Change		
				Births	CBR	TFR
1947	43,045	45.9	6.55	—	—	—
1948	44,450	46.3	*	+3.3	+0.9	—
1949	46,169	47.2	*	+3.9	+1.9	—
1950	46,371	45.4	*	+0.4	−3.8	—
1951	48,116	45.0	*	+3.8	−0.9	—
1952	51,196	45.4	6.30	+6.4	+0.9	—
1953	54,548	45.8	*	+6.6	+0.9	—
1954	57,029	45.7	*	+4.6	−0.2	—
1955	57,812	44.3	*	+1.4	−3.1	—
1956	60,892	44.4	6.54	+5.3	+2.3	—
1957	61,757	42.7	6.56	+1.4	−3.8	+0.3
1958	62,495	41.1	6.39	+1.2	−3.8	−2.6
1959	62,464	39.4	6.14	−0.5	−4.1	−3.9
1960	61,775	37.5	5.80	−1.1	−4.8	−5.5
1961	59,930	35.2	5.46	−3.0	−6.1	−5.9
1962	58,977	33.7	5.26	−1.6	−4.3	−3.7
1963	59,530	33.2	5.17	+0.9	−1.5	−1.7
1964	58,217	31.6	4.95	−2.2	−9.6	−4.3
1965	55,725	29.5	4.62	−4.3	−6.7	−6.7
1966	54,680	28.3	4.42	−1.9	−4.1	−4.3
1967	50,560	25.6	3.95	−7.5	−9.5	−10.6
1968	47,241	23.5	3.50	−6.6	−8.2	−11.4
1969	44,561	21.8	3.15	−5.7	−7.2	−10.0
1970	45,934	22.1	3.10	+3.1	+1.4	−1.6
1971	47,088	22.3	3.06	+2.5	+0.9	−1.3
1972	49,678	23.1	3.07	+5.9	+3.6	+0.3
1973	48,269	22.1	2.81	−3.2	−4.5	−8.5
1974	43,268	19.5	2.37	−10.4	−11.8	−15.7
1975	39,948	17.8	2.08	−8.0	−9.2	−12.2
1976	42,783	18.8	2.11	+6.6	+5.6	+1.4
1977	38,364	16.6	1.82	−11.5	−11.7	−13.7

Note: * Not available.

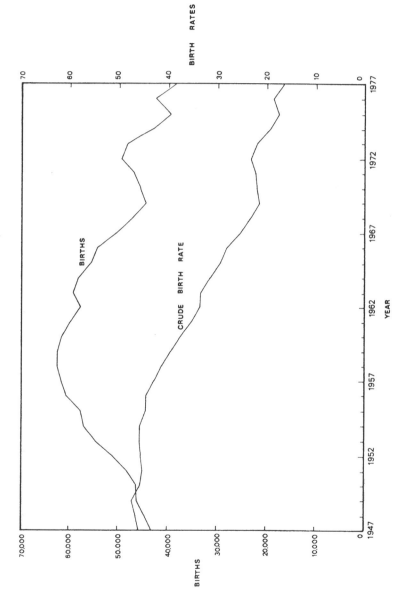

FIGURE 8.1

Births and Crude Birth Rates, 1947–77

were the desire for male heirs, deep-rooted religious injunctions, and the Asian form of extended family system and kinship. Last, the people in general did not practise family planning to such a significant extent as to influence fertility level. The idea of reducing mortality level through medical and public health measures had long been accepted by the people, but the notion of taking concrete steps to space as well as to limit the number of children ultimately produced was something new and revolutionary in the minds of the public at that time.

While the decade up to 1957 was dominated by a very high level of fertility that remained fairly stable, the period following was equally noteworthy for the sudden drop in the fertility level. As can be observed from the total fertility rate, the decline of fertility began in 1958, some ten years after family planning services were made available by the Family Planning Association. The fall of 2.6 per cent in that year was sustained at the modest rate of less than 6 per cent per annum in most years until 1965. However, the 29.6 per cent decline accomplished during this whole nine-year period was quite satisfactory as compared with the first nine years of decline amounting to 18.3 per cent in Taiwan[2] during the period 1951–59 and 11.6 per cent in Peninsular Malaysia[3] during the period 1956–64. During the second year of the national programme in 1967 the decline gathered momentum with a fall of 10.6 per cent, and continued to do so at an accelerated rate during the next two years when a fall of 11.4 per cent took place in one particular year.

The next few years saw the fertility decline slackening dramatically to 1.6 per cent in 1970 and to 1.3 per cent in 1971, and subsequently coming to a complete halt in 1972 when a small rise of 0.3 per cent was recorded. The only possible explanation for these adverse trends is that the women, who had earlier become acceptors of family planning during the first three years of the national programme to space their children, were now beginning to produce the postponed births. The rise in 1972 after some fourteen years of continuous decline was, as noted earlier, viewed with some anxiety and concern by the government and led to the tightening of old incentive and disincentive measures and the introduction of new ones to reinforce the overall population control programme.

The fertility rise in 1972 was also interpreted to mean that the total fertility rate of 3.07 had probably reached rock bottom and that any further substantial fall would be rather unlikely. To the pleasant surprise of many observers, fertility not only resumed its downward path in 1973 but fell by a big margin of 8.5 per cent.[4] Though this decline was not as precipituous as that experienced in 1968 and 1969, its significance in the context of the prevailing low fertility level can hardly be over-emphasized. This noteworthy achievement was soon eclipsed by the spectacular decline of 15.7 per cent in 1974, followed by another impressive fall of 12.2 per cent in the following year, pushing fertility below the replacement level of 2.08. It is estimated that according to current mortality experience, the total fertility rate will be around 2.15 when the net reproduction is exactly 1.000. The small rise of 1.4 per cent in 1976 followed by the huge drop of 13.7 per cent in 1977 may be considered a clear indication that the future course of fertility will be one of oscillation below the replacement level. The factors determining the recent trends will be discussed later.

As the fertility descent took place continuously after 1957, the number of births fell from its peak in 1958 to a low of 44,561 in 1969. Subsequently, another short upswing in the number of births took place: from 45,934 in 1970 to 47,088 in 1971 and 49,678 in 1972. The number of births then took a down-turn again to 48,269 in 1973 and continued to fall steeply to 39,948 in 1975, but in the very next year it rose again to 42,783. The latest year 1977 witnessed a sharp descent to 38,364, the lowest ever recorded during the whole post-war period. As can be observed in Table 8.1, the crude birth rate followed the same path in recent years, moving down to a low of 21.8 per thousand population in 1969, then moving up until 1972, and then down again in the next three years to touch the low of 17.8 in 1975. Thereafter, it rose to 18.8 in 1976 but fell to the all-time low of 16.6 in 1977.

The pattern of fertility declines over the various reproductive age groups at five-year intervals in the last three decades as shown in Table 8.2 will now be considered. In calculating the age-specific fertility rates the relatively small number of births to women under 15 and above 49 years has been included in the 15–19 age group and 45–49 age group respectively.[5] It has been established that among the countries of the world there are three basic types of age patterns of fertility: the early-peak type in which fertility is highest at ages 20–24 years, the late-peak type in which peak fertility occurs at ages 25–29, and the broad-peak type characterized by maximum and nearly uniform fertility levels in age groups 20–24 and 25–29.[6] The figures show that the age pattern of fertility in Singapore resembled that of the broad-peak type prior to the commencement of fertility decline, after which it shifted to the late-peak

TABLE 8.2
Age-Specific Fertility Rates, 1947–77

Age Group	1947	1952	1957	1962	1967	1972	1977
				Rates			
15–19	101.8	88.0	78.0	53.2	35.7	25.7	13.7
20–24	314.1	330.7	302.5	250.7	194.9	137.9	92.4
25–29	333.8	347.1	354.5	295.4	245.5	218.9	142.3
30–34	269.7	271.2	289.4	233.3	166.4	139.2	87.2
35–39	196.3	193.5	194.8	158.1	95.7	65.4	28.7
40–44	83.3	81.7	81.3	65.6	42.7	20.8	6.7
45–49	10.6	10.1	11.3	9.2	7.6	3.0	0.8
				Percentage Change			
15–19		–13.6	–11.4	–31.8	–32.9	–28.0	–46.7
20–24		+5.3	–8.5	–17.1	–22.3	–29.3	–33.0
25–29		+4.0	+2.1	–16.7	–16.9	10.8	–35.0
30–34		+0.6	+6.7	–19.4	–28.7	–16.4	–37.4
35–39		–1.4	+0.7	–18.8	–39.5	–31.7	–56.1
40–44		–1.9	–0.5	–19.3	–34.9	–51.3	–67.8
45–49		–4.7	+11.9	–18.6	–17.4	–60.5	–73.3

type and has remained so ever since, notwithstanding the profound changes in the rates.

Prior to the commencement of fertility decline in 1958, there was a minor shift in the pattern of fertility over the age groups. During the first five-year period 1947–52, a small increase in fertility rates was recorded by the three quinary age groups between 20 and 34 and an equally minor decrease was recorded by the three groups above the age of 34. A more interesting change refers to the pronounced drop of 13.6 per cent registered in the teenage group 15–19. This tendency continued into the next period 1952–57 when this youngest age group again experienced the largest decrease, amounting to 11.4 per cent. A decline was also recorded in two other age groups, while a rise was recorded in four age groups. By and large, these are still minor shifts in the pattern that did not affect the overall level of fertility and are comparatively less significant than the new developments that have emerged since 1957.

The detailed annual rates for the first few years of fertility decline following 1957 indicate that during this initial phase each group within

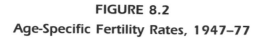

FIGURE 8.2
Age-Specific Fertility Rates, 1947–77

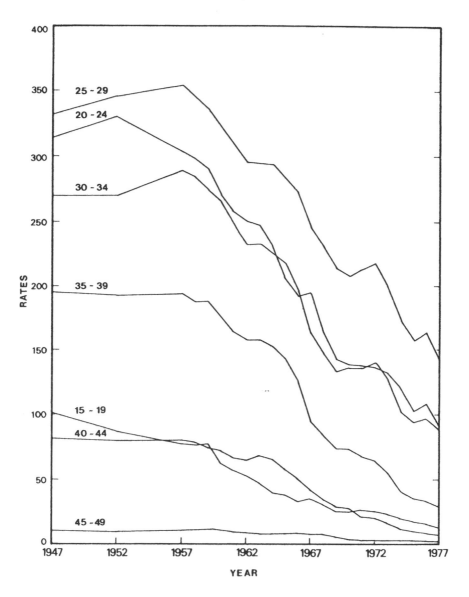

the reproductive age range began to record a reduction at different times and sustaining this decline at different speeds.[7] However, during the first five-year period of decline from 1957 to 1962 a fairly uniform decrease of 17 to 19 per cent was recorded by all the age groups from 20 and over. As for the teenage group of 15-19, a relatively much steeper fall of some 32 per cent was experienced. The greater reduction at the youngest age group and the lesser but almost same extent of decline at the other age groups appear to be different from the pattern observed in Western Europe[8] and Taiwan[9] where the decreases have been concentrated among women at the older age groups. Considerable significance may be attached to this difference in the initial path towards lower fertility. The women who were having fewer children at a young age are likely to have fewer children when they become older, thus affecting fertility of the older age groups in due course. Moreover, the almost equal decreases at the second age group upwards would mean that the population will grow less in the long run because of the increasing average length of the new generation.

The more pronounced decline experienced by women in the youngest age group, coupled with the large decline they had experienced prior to the onset of overall fertility decline in 1958, suggests that the fertility decline in Singapore, in the absence of illegitimate births, was triggered off mainly by a rise in the average age at marriage. According to population census data, the median age at first marriage of women has increased from 19.8 years for the cohort marrying during 1946–50 to 20.2 for the cohort marrying during 1951–55, 21.4 for the cohort marrying during 1956–60, and 22.5 for the cohort marrying during 1961–65.[10] According to data from the registration of marriages, the average age at first marriage of women rose from 22.2 years in 1961 to 23.0 in 1965, after which it remained fairly stable between 23.1 to 23.3 years right up to 1976.[11] The trend towards later marriage was caused by, among other things, women attaining higher levels of education and participating in increasing proportion in the labour force. The minimum age for marriage for both bride and groom under the *Women's Charter* was raised from 16 to 18 years with effect from September 1961, and a few years later in 1966 the minimum age for girls marrying under the Muslim law was raised from 15 to 16.

The levelling off of the rise of marriage age and the extensive use of birth control to limit family size since 1966 caused the pattern of fertility declines to take on a new direction whereby the older women were experiencing larger reductions. Even during the period 1962–67 the women in the two age groups between 35 and 44 had experienced a reduction of 40 per cent and 35 per cent respectively, engendered by a preference for smaller families. The swing towards larger decreases at the older ages not only continued but became progressively more pronounced after 1967 when the emphasis of the population control programme was aimed at the high parity women who were to be found at the older age groups. Indeed, during the period 1967–72 the greatest reduction of 60.5 per cent was recorded by the oldest age group 45–49 and the second largest of 51.3 per cent by the second oldest age group. The relatively larger reductions in these two oldest age groups were not only maintained but reinforced during the latest period 1972–77.

Another aspect of the post-war changes in fertility at various ages may be illustrated by considering the relative contribution of each age group to gross total fertility. This contribution is measured by adding the fertility rates for each age group and determining the percentage of the rate for each age group to the total. These percentages are presented in Table 8.3 for four specified calendar years.

The relative contribution of women in the youngest age group has been lessened continuously during the period under consideration, falling from 7.8 to 3.7 per cent during the last three decades. As for the women

TABLE 8.3
Relative Contribution of Each Age Group
to Gross Total Fertility, 1947–77

Age Group	1947	1957	1967	1977
15–19	7.8	5.9	4.5	3.7
20–24	24.0	23.1	24.7	24.8
25–29	25.5	27.0	31.1	38.3
30–34	20.6	22.1	21.1	23.4
35–39	15.0	14.8	12.1	7.7
40–44	6.4	6.2	5.4	1.8
45–49	0.8	0.9	1.0	0.2
Total	100.0	100.0	100.0	100.0

in the second age group 20–24, their relative contribution diminished slightly from the initial level of 24.0 per cent during the first decade prior to the commencement of overall fertility decline in 1958, but rose gently during the second decade, and levelled off towards 1977 when it stood at 24.8 per cent. The situation near the end of the childbearing period was quite different. The women aged 45 to 49 have recorded a minor rise in their relative contribution during the first two decades and on the contrary, a very sharp fall in the last decade to the negligible level of 0.2 per cent in 1977. An equally marked reduction in the relative contribution was also recorded by women aged 40 to 44 in the last decade, but this downward movement had started, though at a very slow pace, by 1947. A somewhat similar path was experienced by women in the 35–39 age group. The relative contribution to gross total fertility by women in the 30–34 age group rose from 20.6 per cent in 1947 to 22.1 per cent in 1957, dipped down to 21.1 per cent in 1967 and rose again to 23.4 per cent by the end of the period. By far the most notable change is the persistent rise in the relative contribution of women aged 25 to 29 from 25.5 per cent in 1947 to 38.3 in 1977, with a much larger rise occurring in the last decade.

The changes in the relative contribution of women at various ages have resulted in the initial greater spread of the total fertility becoming more concentrated in essentially the three age groups between 20 and 34. Compared with the 70.1 per cent in 1947, these three groups contributed no less than 86.5 per cent of the total fertility at present, with women between the ages of 25 and 29 alone accounting for more than a third of the total fertility. It should be emphasized that this concentration of fertility within the peak reproductive years has taken place during the entire period of fertility decline when a reduction was experienced by all the age groups, and was only brought about by the greater reduction at the young age groups during the initial phase of decline and subsequently by the much greater reduction at the older age groups during the later phase. The concentration of fertility in an increasingly narrow portion of the reproductive period that was observed to have occurred in Singapore is one of the major characteristics of declining fertility in a country. The position where childbearing takes place over a much shorter segment of the reproductive age span is typical of a country like Singapore where fertility is at replacement level.

EFFECT OF THE CHANGING AGE COMPOSITION

Before embarking on a detailed analysis of fertility trends in recent times, we will examine the distorting influence exerted by the changing proportion of women in the reproductive ages on the recent crude birth rates. The increase in the number of babies born after World War II up to 1958 is now reflected in the number of women at present in the reproductive age groups. The proportion of women aged 15 to 49 to the total population has increased yearly from 23.2 per cent in 1969 to 27.4 per cent in 1977. The detailed figures are given in Table 8.4. To measure the effect of this change in the age structure on the crude birth rate, we have computed the standardized birth rate for the years 1970 to 1977 using the estimated 1969 female population as the standard population.

Table 8.5 shows that in 1970 and 1971 the increasing proportion and distribution of women within the reproductive ages has negated the effects of the modest fertility decline on the crude birth rate. The standardized birth rate registered a decline of 1.8 per cent in 1970 and 0.9 per cent in 1971 compared with the increase of 1.4 per cent and 0.9 per cent respectively in the crude birth rate. This serves to confirm what we already know from the fall in the total fertility rate — that the rise in the crude birth rate, and incidentally the rise in the number of births, was entirely a function of the age structure of the female population of reproductive age in these two years.

TABLE 8.4
Proportion of Women Aged 15–49, 1969–77

Year	Total Population	Female Aged 15–49	Per Cent Females
1969	2,042,500	473,200	23.2
1970	2,074,507	493,541	23.8
1971	2,110,400	512,300	24.3
1972	2,147,400	533,100	24.8
1973	2,185,100	552,800	25.3
1974	2,219,100	572,700	25.8
1975	2,249,900	593,200	26.4
1976	2,278,200	612,600	26.9
1977	2,308,200	631,300	27.4

TABLE 8.5
Crude Birth Rate, Standardized Birth Rate, and
Total Fertility Rate, 1969–77

Year	Crude Birth Rate	Standardized Birth Rate	Total Fertility Rate
		Rates	
1969	21.8	21.8	3.15
1970	22.1	21.4	3.10
1971	22.3	21.2	3.06
1972	23.1	21.3	3.07
1973	22.1	19.7	2.81
1974	19.5	16.9	2.37
1975	17.8	14.9	2.08
1976	18.8	15.2	2.11
1977	16.6	13.2	1.82
		Annual Per Cent Change	
1969	—	—	—
1970	+1.4	-1.8	-1.6
1971	+0.9	-0.9	-1.3
1972	+3.9	+0.5	+0.3
1973	-4.5	-7.5	-8.5
1974	-11.8	-14.2	-15.7
1975	-8.7	-11.8	-12.2
1976	+5.6	+2.0	+1.4
1977	-11.7	-13.2	-13.7

More interesting facts are revealed by the data for 1972 when the total fertility rate rose by 0.3 per cent for the first time after fourteen years of decline. If the age distribution of women aged 15 to 49 in 1969 had remained constant up to 1972, the crude birth rate in 1972 would have been 21.3 instead of 23.1, an increase of 0.5 per cent instead of 3.6 per cent over that of 1971. We can thus conclude that 86 per cent of the total rise in the crude birth rate recorded in 1972 was due to changes in the age structure of the female population of reproductive age and only 14 per cent was caused by a rise in fertility of individual women.[12]

During 1973, 1974 and 1975, the standardized birth rate was reduced by 7.5 per cent, 14.2 per cent, and 11.8 per cent respectively as compared with the corresponding decline of 4.5 per cent, 11.8 per cent and 8.7 per cent of the crude birth rate. In these three years there was a fall of 8.5 per cent, 15.7 per cent and 12.2 per cent in the total fertility rate. These comparisons demonstrate that the drop in the crude birth rate in these three years was caused entirely by a fall in fertility, and was in fact lessened by a rise in the proportion of women of childbearing age.

In 1976 there was again an upsurge in the crude birth rate but this time the total fertility rate also increased, the former by 5.6 per cent and the latter by 1.4 per cent. However, the standardized birth rate increased by 2.0 per cent. From these changes it is evident that 64 per cent of the total rise in the crude birth rate registered in 1976 may be attributed to changes in the age structure of the female population of reproductive age and 36 per cent was due to the rise in fertility of individual women. The decline of 11.7 per cent in the crude birth rate and 13.2 per cent in the standardized birth rate in 1977 may be taken to mean that the drop in the crude birth rate was brought about entirely by a fall in fertility.

CHANGES BY AGE

The next question is how the various reproductive age groups contributed to the annual fertility decline in recent years. The information concerning age-specific fertility rates in Table 8.6 shows that women in all but one age group contributed to the decline in 1970 and 1971. In the former year the fertility reduction was less than 3 per cent in the first three younger age groups, but became more sizeable in the early 40s (9.2 per cent) and late 40s (14.5 per cent). The greater reduction at the older age groups became more pronounced in 1971 when the two oldest age groups recorded a fall of 17.6 per cent and 25.5 per cent. The slight increase in fertility in 1972 was caused by a rise in the two most fertile age groups from 25 to 34, with still greater reduction experienced by women at the older ages.

Women in all age groups (15–49) contributed to the 1973 fertility decline of 8.1 per cent, the greater role however being played by the older age groups. In the two youngest age groups the reduction in the rates is less than 5 per cent, and in the next two age groups it is around 8 per cent. It becomes progressively greater among the older women until the last age group 45–49 where a 20 per cent drop in the rate was recorded. The record drop of 15.9 per cent in fertility in 1974 was also contributed by women in all the reproductive age groups, but again with

TABLE 8.6
Age-Specific Fertility Rates, 1969–77

Age Group	1969	1970	1971	1972	1973	1974	1975	1976	1977
					Rates				
15–19	27.3	26.1	25.8	25.7	24.5	21.0	17.1	16.5	13.7
20–24	143.2	139.0	138.3	137.9	132.2	120.9	104.1	109.5	92.4
25–29	214.5	208.8	214.9	218.9	200.9	174.1	157.1	163.6	142.3
30–34	133.4	138.0	137.2	139.2	128.2	103.2	95.6	97.6	87.2
35–39	74.8	74.5	68.0	65.4	56.7	42.2	35.8	33.5	28.7
40–44	29.4	26.7	22.0	20.8	17.3	12.6	10.0	8.0	6.7
45–49	5.5	4.7	3.5	3.0	2.4	1.9	1.2	0.8	0.8
				Annual Per Cent Change					
15–19		-2.9	-1.1	-0.4	-4.7	-13.9	-18.6	-3.5	-17.0
20–24		-2.9	-5.0	-0.3	-4.1	-8.9	-13.9	+5.2	-15.6
25–29		-2.6	+2.9	+1.9	-8.2	-13.3	-9.8	+4.1	-13.0
30–34		+3.4	-0.6	+1.5	-7.9	-19.6	-7.4	+2.1	-10.7
35–39		-0.4	-8.7	-3.8	-13.3	-25.7	-15.2	-6.4	-14.3
40–44		-9.2	-17.6	-5.5	-16.8	-27.2	-20.6	-20.0	-16.3
45–49		-14.5	-25.5	-14.3	-20.0	-20.8	-36.8	-33.3	0.0

a greater decline experienced by the older women. By and large, this pattern of decline among the age groups was again registered in 1975 when fertility fell by 9.2 per cent to reach replacement level. The 1.9 per cent rise in fertility in 1976 was caused by women between the prime reproductive ages of 20 and 34, but even so a substantial reduction in the rates was recorded by women in their 40s. This pattern of reduction is in sharp contrast to that experienced during the early years of fertility decline in the late 1950s and early 1960s. Then the younger age groups recorded a greater reduction which was primarily due to the rise in the average age of women at marriage. The greater reduction experienced by older women seems to suggest that the desire to limit family size even further has been the principal factor causing the already low fertility rates to continue to fall further. In the year 1977, when fertility plummeted by 13.5 per cent to far below replacement level, all the age groups recorded a fall in the rates but no longer with a greater reduction at the older age groups. The reduction of the rate for the oldest age group 45–49 came to a halt in 1977 when the rate was reduced to a negligible level of 0.8. Even for the second oldest age group the rate is now only 6.7.

CHANGES AMONG MARRIED WOMEN

We will now examine the recent trends in age-specific fertility rates among currently married women. In computing these rates the birth data used are the same as those employed to derive the age-specific fertility rates of women of all marital status, but the denominator requires a different set of data, i.e., currently married women tabulated by similar quinary age groups. The latter figures for 1970 are readily obtainable from the 1970 Population Census[13] and those for 1974 to 1977 are obtained from the estimated figures derived from the Annual Labour Survey.[14] The figures for 1969 and 1971 to 1973 are estimated, firstly, by a linear interpolation of the age-specific proportions currently married for 1970 and 1974 and a linear extrapolation of these proportions to 1969, and, secondly, by applying these interpolated and extrapolated proportions to the relevant total female population by quinary age groups. With the two sets of prerequisite data, the rates are computed and presented in Table 8.7. It should be pointed out that in the computation of the rates we have assumed that all the births are legitimate, an assumption necessitated by the non-availability of births broken down into legitimate and illegitimate groups. However, no significant errors would be introduced by this procedure because it is generally known that illegitimate births in Singapore are negligible.

The fertility rates of married women in the youngest age group 15–19 increased steadily from 539.3 in 1969 to 619.2 in 1973, after which it dipped down in the following year and soon recovered again to 616.0 in 1975, and then shot up to 708.5 in 1976. In the second age group the rate increased slowly from 396.9 to 421.3 in the first four years, decreased in the next three years to 355.4 in 1975, and then increased again to 380.2 in 1976. A somewhat similar trend was experienced by the married women in their late 20s (25–29).

In the 30–34 age group the married women registered little change in fertility for the first four years but a definite downward trend in the next three years, with a small rise in 1976. The married women in the last three age groups experienced a continuous decline in fertility during the whole period, but with one important difference in that the speed of decline accelerated over the years with advancing age towards the end of

TABLE 8.7
Age-Specific Marital Fertility Rates, 1969–77

Age Group	1969	1970	1971	1972	1973	1974	1975	1976	1977
					Rates				
15–19	539.3	546.4	570.5	606.9	619.2	530.6	616.0	708.5	576.8
20–24	396.9	397.6	408.5	421.3	417.9	381.7	355.4	380.2	374.4
25–29	274.4	274.0	289.2	302.4	285.2	248.2	222.1	257.9	231.9
30–34	152.2	157.1	155.9	157.7	144.9	120.6	109.2	110.7	104.9
35–39	83.7	83.0	75.5	72.3	62.4	47.5	39.7	39.5	30.9
40–44	34.1	30.7	25.0	23.4	19.3	13.3	10.5	8.7	6.8
45–49	6.9	5.7	4.2	3.6	2.9	2.2	1.4	0.9	0.9
					Annual Per Cent Change				
15–19		+1.3	+4.4	+6.4	+2.0	−14.3	+16.1	+15.0	−18.6
20–24		+0.2	+2.7	+3.1	−0.8	−8.7	−6.9	+7.0	−1.5
25–29		−0.1	+5.5	+4.6	−5.7	−13.0	−10.5	+16.1	−10.1
30–34		+3.2	−0.8	+1.2	−8.1	−16.8	−9.5	+1.4	−5.2
35–39		−8.4	−9.0	−4.2	−13.7	−23.9	−16.4	−0.5	−21.8
40–44		−10.0	−18.6	−6.4	−17.5	−31.1	−21.1	−17.1	−21.8
45–49		−17.4	−26.3	−14.3	−19.4	−24.1	−36.4	−35.7	0.0

the childbearing period. This was apparently responsible for the similar tendencies exhibited by the age-specific fertility rates of women of all marital status noted earlier and was in turn related to the proportionately greater decline in the higher birth order rates among these older women.

CHANGES BY PARITY

To throw more light on this matter, the analysis needs to be supplemented by examining the changes in fertility rates by birth order or parity.[15] For this purpose, the gross total fertility rates by birth order is examined. The gross total fertility rate of a given birth order is obtained by adding the age-specific fertility rates for births of that order calculated for quinary age groups. This form of measurement is superior to the general fertility rate by birth order because it isolates the influence of the changes in the age composition of women within the reproductive age range, and it thus serves our purpose better in view of the recent changes in the age structure of Singapore women.

Trends in the gross total fertility rates by birth order for women aged 15 to 49 are shown in Figure 8.3 where the rates are depicted in the usual arithmetic scale in order to indicate the relative importance of each order. On such a scale, it appears that the largest fluctuations occurred in the first order rates, and the magnitude of the fluctuations tend to diminish as the order of birth increased. This is a correct impression in terms of absolute amounts of change. It is quite clear from the figure that during the accelerated decline in fertility in 1968 and 1969, the total fertility rates for every order fell during these years. The pattern of changes for the rest of the period was not quite so simple and clear-cut.

According to the figures for the annual percentage change given in Table 8.8, there was a rise in the rates for the first to third orders and a fall for the sixth order and above during the years 1970 to 1972. The extent of the increase recorded by the first to third orders in these years was quite modest, generally much less than 7 per cent. On the other hand, the declines were of greater magnitude for most of the birth orders from sixth and above. The slackening in the speed of decline in overall fertility in 1970 was related to the rise in the rates for the first to fourth orders after declining in the previous year. In 1970 the reduction came to 5.1 per cent for the fifth order and became progressively greater with higher birth orders until it reached 15.9 per cent for the order ten and above. This pattern was repeated in 1971 with more often than not a larger reduction taking place in the higher birth orders. The slight upward trend in overall fertility in 1972 was caused by a steeper rise in the rates for the first three orders, a rise again in the rate for the fourth order after declining in the previous year, and a rise for the first time in recent years in the rate for the fifth order. This could be partly due to the appearance of births previously postponed by women who were practising family planning to space their children.

In 1973 when the overall fertility rate resumed its downward trend, the fall in the rates not only became more substantial at these higher birth orders but also penetrated the second and third orders again. By 1974 when the post-war record of a 15.9 per cent reduction of overall fertility was registered, even the first order underwent a decline though by a small margin of 0.7 per cent, and equally significant is the accelerated decline experienced by the second to fourth orders as compared with the previous year. In the fifth and sixth orders the reduction was almost

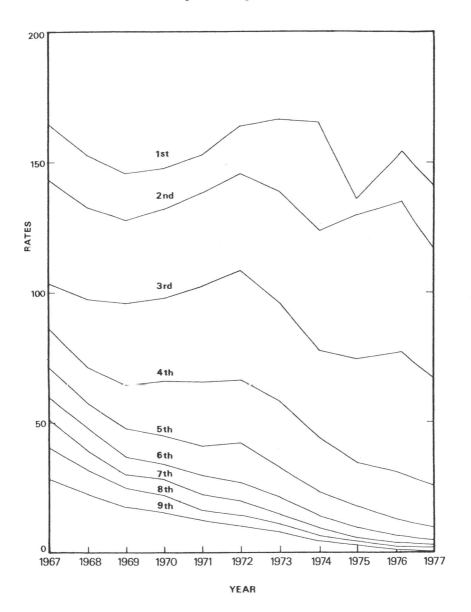

FIGURE 8.3
Gross Total Fertility Rates by Birth Order, 1967–77

TABLE 8.8
Gross Total Fertility Rates by Birth Order, 1969–77

Birth Order	1969	1970	1971	1972	1973	1974	1975	1976	1977
					Rates				
1	146.1	148.0	153.2	164.2	166.8	165.6	136.5	154.5	141.9
2	128.9	132.2	138.0	146.0	139.0	124.4	130.0	135.5	117.1
3	96.4	98.3	102.6	107.9	95.6	77.5	74.6	77.6	66.3
4	64.6	65.8	65.4	66.4	57.7	43.7	34.9	31.3	25.3
5	47.5	45.1	40.6	42.2	32.4	23.0	18.2	12.8	9.0
6	37.0	34.1	29.4	27.2	21.0	13.7	9.8	6.5	4.3
7	30.0	28.5	22.7	19.8	14.7	8.8	5.7	3.8	2.7
8	25.1	22.0	16.3	14.8	10.9	6.5	4.0	2.4	2.0
9	17.8	15.7	12.5	10.2	7.9	4.3	2.9	1.6	1.4
10 & over	31.5	26.5	20.0	18.7	13.0	7.9	4.7	2.8	2.2
					Annual Per Cent Change				
1		+1.8	+3.5	+7.2	+1.6	−0.7	−17.6	+13.2	−8.2
2		+2.6	+4.4	+5.8	−4.8	−10.5	+4.5	+4.1	−13.6
3		+2.0	+4.4	+5.2	−11.4	−18.9	−3.7	+4.0	−14.6
4		+1.9	−0.6	+1.5	−13.1	−24.3	−20.1	−10.3	−19.2
5		−5.1	−8.9	+3.9	−23.2	−29.0	−20.9	−29.7	−29.7
6		−7.8	−13.8	−7.5	−22.8	−34.8	−28.5	−33.7	−33.8
7		−5.0	−20.4	−12.8	−25.8	−40.1	−35.2	−33.3	−28.9
8		−12.4	−25.9	−9.2	−26.4	−40.4	−38.5	−40.0	−16.7
9		−11.8	−20.4	−18.4	−22.5	−45.6	−32.6	−44.8	−12.5
10 & over		−15.9	−24.5	−6.5	−30.5	−39.2	−40.1	−40.4	−21.4

30 per cent, and for the seventh order upwards it was extremely pronounced, generally exceeding 40 per cent.

The fall of the total fertility rate to below the replacement fertility level in 1975 may be attributed solely to the spectacular decline of 17.6 per cent recorded by the first birth order since the declines in the other birth orders were not as large as those experienced in the previous year. This dip in the rate for the first order is more vividly illustrated in Figure 8.3, and is directly related to the steep rise in the proportion of nulliparous women undergoing abortion from 7 per cent in 1974 to 20 per cent in 1975 (see Table 4.1). In 1976 when the overall fertility rate rose again, the rate in the first order rose by an equally large jump of 13.2 per cent, with a moderate rise of some 4 per cent in the second and third orders. The rates in the other higher orders continued to experience substantial reductions as in the previous years. The severe incentive and disincentive measures introduced in the early 1970s to encourage the two-child family norm have continuously exerted a positive effect upon decline in the fourth and higher orders during the years between 1973 and 1976. The last few years have therefore witnessed women of larger families taking great precautions, through contraception, sterilization or abortion, to control their fertility for the purpose of limiting their family size.

Though the declines have been greater at the higher parity levels, their impact on overall fertility would be less because of the lower rates in the higher orders. The movements in the rates in the lower orders as determined by the annual marriage rate and child-spacing behaviour will be the major factors influencing the short-term annual fluctuations in the gross reproduction rate in the future. The greater speed of decline at the higher parity appeared to have come to an end in 1977 when fertility tumbled down to the well below replacement level of 0.896.

It should be emphasized that the rates discussed above do not reflect the probability of births of different orders occurring. The changes in the rates are to a great extent a reflection of changes in the distribution of mothers by the number of children previously born. Clearly births of order x can occur only among women having $(x-1)$ children. Therefore, the number of first births should be related to the number of women who have never given birth to a child, second births to women who have given birth to one child, and so on. This implies that changes found in the fertility rates for births of the first order were obviously influenced to a large extent by fluctuations in the annual number of newly-married couples.

CHANGES BY RACE

In attempting to probe deeper into the dynamics of fertility trends, it is worth looking at the fertility changes among the different races that make up the Singapore population, which as of mid-1977 was 76.2 per cent Chinese, 15.0 per cent Malays, 6.8 per cent Indians, and 2.0 per cent minority races. It should be borne in mind that in view of the numerical predominance of the Chinese, a change in the level of Chinese fertility would by comparison have a greater impact on the national fertility level. Table 8.9 shows that in 1970 a fall in the Malay and Indian

TABLE 8.9
Total Fertility Rate for the Three Main Races, 1969–77

Race	1969	1970	1971	1972	1973	1974	1975	1976	1977
					Rates				
Chinese	3.00	3.03	3.01	3.03	2.80	2.34	2.07	2.15	1.81
Malays	3.65	3.50	3.31	3.33	2.91	2.48	2.14	1.91	1.88
Indians	3.96	3.19	3.18	3.16	2.64	2.32	1.96	1.85	1.69
					Annual Percentage Change				
Chinese		+1.0	−0.7	+0.7	−7.6	−16.4	−11.5	+3.9	−15.8
Malays		−4.1	−5.4	+0.6	−12.6	−14.8	−13.7	−10.7	−1.6
Indians		−19.4	−0.3	−0.6	−16.5	−12.1	−15.5	−5.6	−8.6

fertility contributed to the slight decline in national fertility of about 1.4 per cent, notwithstanding the minor rise in Chinese fertility. In 1971 all three main races contributed to the fertility decline, though a largest reduction was recorded by the Malays. The unusual rise in overall fertility in 1972 was brought about by a rise in Chinese and Malay fertility.

In 1973 all three main races contributed to the resumption of the fertility decline, with the Indians and the Malays experiencing the more rapid decline. Indian fertility fell by 16.5 per cent and Malay fertility by 12.6 per cent, while Chinese fertility fell by only 7.6 per cent. A complete reversal of this relative speed of decline is underlined by the figures for 1974 when fertility decreased by some 15.7 per cent. By far the greatest contribution to this decline was brought about by the Chinese whose fertility was sharply curtailed by 16.4 per cent on account of Chinese women trying to avoid Tiger babies. Next was Malay fertility which fell by 14.8 per cent and Indian fertility by 12.1 per cent. In 1975 the fertility decline of the Malays and the Indians was so substantial that their fertility went well below the replacement level, and even so this decline continued unabated into the next two years, 1976 and 1977. The rise in national fertility during 1976 was caused entirely by an increase in Chinese fertility in the face of opposite trends observed among the other two races. The Chinese women like to have babies during the Dragon year which coincided with 1976, and this also explains the pronounced fall in Chinese fertility in the following year since those who purposely planned for a Dragon baby would not be producing another child in 1977.

At the beginning of the period 1969 to 1972 the Chinese were clearly experiencing much lower fertility and the Malays the highest fertility, with Indian fertility nearer to that of the latter. From 1973 the relative position was altered, with the Indians recording the lowest fertility and the Malays the highest, with the Chinese fertility occupying an intermediate level. The diminution of the differentials among these three races during these years is a continuation of the process initiated soon after World War II.[16] This process has practically run its course now that all the three races are experiencing below replacement fertility, which in itself constitutes a significant result that may have some relevance to other countries with sizeable Malay or Indian population. By and large, the differentials among the three races are not only insignificant but they may alter position quite easily in the years to come.

CAUSES OF FERTILITY CHANGES

The spectacular performance achieved by Singapore in the area of fertility decline in the last two decades before the mid-seventies may be traced to a combination of factors, some of which are interdependent. In the first place, the commencement of fertility decline in 1958 was triggered off by the rising age at first marriage of women and reinforced by the fall in the proportion of women ultimately married. Secondly, there was the catalytic role played by the private family planning programme which had been providing not only clinical services to new and old acceptors but also educational and motivational activities to create the general acceptance of family planning for almost ten years prior to the descent of fertility in 1958. The Association recruited 27,128 new acceptors from November 1949 to the end of 1958 and 60,793 from January 1959 to October 1968. Thirdly, from 1966 onwards the downward movement of fertility was accelerated by the introduction of the national family planning programme which managed to recruit some 156,556 new acceptors during the First Five-Year Plan 1966–70 and 89,501 during the Second Plan 1971–75.

In the seventies when the number of new acceptors had reached a saturation point of about 16,000–19,000 per year, and when fertility fell by a negligible amount in 1970 and 1971 and even rose in 1972, the fertility decline after 1972 was sustained and further accelerated by what we sometimes referred to as measures beyond family planning.[17] The first of these designed to put more force into the population control programme refers to the progressive liberalization of the laws concerning abortion to make it available to women on request. During the period 1970–77 some 59,359 legal abortions were performed, apart from the 23,791 so-called spontaneous abortions which were not carried out under the Abortion Act. This termination of pregnancies obviously resulted in a reduction in that number of births, assuming that none resulted in still-births.

The second measure is the legalization of sterilization, which led to no less than 60,689 women and men being sterilized during the period 1970–77. In this connection, we must bear in mind the cumulative effect of sterilization exerting an ever-growing influence on the fertility level in these years and in the future. Finally, there are the incentive and disincentive measures in the areas of maternity leave, accouchement fees, income tax, housing, education and work permits. These measures, aimed at promoting the two-child family by discouraging high order births, have succeeded in making reductions in births of order three and above the most important factor in fertility decline in the last few years.[18] They have also encouraged sterilization to some extent. Singapore is indeed a good example of a country which has resorted to a comprehensive range of beyond family planning measures to push fertility down to a point, i.e. replacement level, which traditional family planning alone cannot possibly hope to achieve.

We must not forget the interaction of cultural, social and economic forces that came into play during the whole process of fertility decline since 1958. These are the cultural and social variables expressed in terms of modernization, higher levels of education, changing attitudes towards the value of children and family size, the breakdown of the extended family system, and the increasing scarcity of domestic help. Consideration should also be given to the impact of rapid economic progress through mainly industrialization leading to, among other things, a higher standard of living and greater economic participation of women in the labour force. The labour force participation rate of women has increased from 18.0 per cent in 1957 to 25.7 per cent in 1970, and still further to 32.5 per cent in 1977. The influence of this tendency of women on fertility decline lies in the much greater rise in the age-specific participation rates at the prime reproductive ages of women, which has the effect of encouraging single women to postpone marriage or remain permanently unmarried and inducing married women to space or terminate childbearing so as to continue to work.

Finally, the style of government and politics in Singapore is one of the key factors in the whole complex process of fertility decline. One can single out the political determination of the PAP Government in its concerted and well-orchestrated effort to accelerate fertility decline as a means of checking the rate of population growth.

Apart from the above factors that determine long-term trends, there are some special circumstances which have contributed to annual fluctuations in recent times. A case in point is the all-time record drop of 15.7 per cent in fertility in 1974. In July 1973, as noted earlier, the government introduced a new regulation whereby immigrant workers with work permits earning less than $750 per month must seek the permission of the Commissioner of Employment to marry Singapore citizens. Those who were refused permission, and there were quite a number, might otherwise have produced children in 1974. Another very special influence concerns the Chinese calendar year of the Tiger coinciding with the major part of 1974 and, according to Chinese tradition, the Tiger year is not a propitious time for having babies.[19] In the past this belief had a noticeable effect on the number of births, as on the two previous occasions in 1950 and 1962, and must have had some effect on the number of births in 1974.[20] Though such a belief might be less widely held nowadays, Chinese women of today are not only better equipped to plan their births but can avoid having Tiger babies by resorting to casily available abortion, which did increase by a large percentage in 1974, particularly among women with five or more children, as observed in Chapter 4. It is known that in times of extreme economic difficulties some parents may have second thoughts about having their first child or subsequent children because of the extra financial burden. It is possible that the recession in Singapore, with all its attendant ill effects such as retrenchment and lower economic expectations, resulted in the postponement of some births in 1974.

The further reduction of 12.2 per cent in 1975, after the record decline in the previous year, which resulted in fertility falling to below replacement level, can be associated with only one possible special influence. This is the upsurge in the number of abortions from 9,571 in 1974 to 14,034 in 1975 made possible by the complete liberalization of abortion through the enforcement of the new Abortion Act in December

1974. As noted earlier, the sharp rise in the proportion of nulliparous women undergoing abortion to 20 per cent in 1975 from its previous year's of 7 per cent caused the total fertility rate in the first order to tumble by the all-time record of 17.6 per cent. After the pronounced fall in 1974 and 1975 when fertility descended below replacement level, it is only to be expected that there would be a brake on this downtrend sooner or later, hence the slight rise of 1.4 per cent in 1976. Still there appears to be a special influence operating during that year and this may be traced to the Chinese calendar year of the Dragon which is traditionally believed to be an auspicious year to have children.[21] Indeed, in 1976 there was an upsurge in Chinese fertility of some 3.9 per cent in contrast with the maintenance of fertility decline among the Malays and the Indians. It was also reported that the Dragon year was partly responsible for some extra births in Taiwan.[22] The second largest reduction in the fertility rate amounting to 13.7 per cent in 1977 was probably caused by the fact that the Chinese who wanted more children would have planned to have them in the Dragon year instead of in the normal year 1977. The steeper decline of 15.8 per cent among the Chinese than among the other two races substantiates this hypothesis.

FUTURE TRENDS

The relentless effort of the Singapore Government in implementing its population control programme in the context of rapid modernization and industrialization has paid handsome dividends, judged in terms of the completion of fertility transition from the high plateau of the mid-fifties to replacement level in 1975. Singapore has now joined the exclusive group of countries experiencing the lowest fertility level in the world and, more important still, has the distinction of becoming the second country in Asia to attain replacement level. This achievement within a comparatively short span of eighteen years is probably unprecedented in the demographic history of any country. For instance, in Japan it took almost three decades for fertility, which first began to descend in the mid-twenties, to reach the replacement level in 1956.[23]

    If the experience of Japan and the European countries which have had recorded replacement fertility is anything to go by, the future path of fertility in Singapore will be one of persistent oscillation below the line of replacement level, with slight annual ups and downs as determined by short-term influences. It goes without saying that any relaxation of the population control programme in the future will cause fertility to ascend by an amount depending on the extent of the relaxation. This would not be completely out of the question. The fall in fertility to well below replacement level, coupled with the record post-war low of 38,364 births in 1977, should be taken as a fair warning that a careful review of the present population control programme might be necessary and timely in order to ensure that fertility will be consistent with the demographic goal of maintaining it at replacement level and not to allow it to fall far below replacement point for long periods of time in the future.[24] Otherwise, considerable disruptions in the social and economic systems would be caused by persistent sharp drop in the number of births, apart from the fact that in the long-run the population would after a point of time start to diminish. If the programme is to be relaxed, it would be advisable to dismantle some of its harsher aspects, particularly those related to the incentive and disincentive measures.

Notes

1. See the series of yearly *Report on the Registration of Birth and Death, and Marriages*.
2. *1973 Taiwan Demographic Fact Book* (Taipei: Ministry of the Interior, 1974).
3. Saw Swee-Hock, "Recent Fertility Declines in Malaya", in *Population Problems in the Pacific: New Dimensions in Pacific Demography*, edited by Minoru Tachi and Minoru Muramatsu (Tokyo. The Eleventh Pacific Science Congress, 1966), p. 104.
4. Saw Swee-Hock, "Singapore: Resumption of Rapid Fertility Decline in 1973", *Studies in Family Planning* 6, no. 6 (June 1975).
5. The sources of data for the female population by quinary age group for the non-census years used in this chapter are Saw Swee-Hock and Chiu Wing Kin, *Population Estimates of Singapore by Age Group, 1958–1971* (Singapore: Institute of Economics and Business Studies, Nanyang University, 1976), and *Singapore: Population Estimates by Age Group, Ethnic Group and Sex*.
6. United Nations, *Conditions and Trends of Fertility in the World*, Population Bulletin No. 7, ST/SO A/Series N/7 (New York: United Nations Department of Economic & Social Affairs, 1976).
7. For more details, see Saw Swee-Hock, *Singapore Population in Transition* (Philadelphia: University of Pennsylvania Press, 1970), pp. 75–77.
8. United Nations, *Recent Trends in Fertility in Industrialized Countries*, ST/SOA/ Series A/27 (New York: United Nations Department of Economic and Social Affairs, 1968).

9. *1973 Taiwan Demographic Fact Book*, p. 69.

10. P. Arumainathan, *Singapore: Report on the Census of Population 1970*, Vol. I (Singapore: Department of Statistics, 1973), p. 66.

11. *Report on the Registration of Births and Deaths, and Marriages*. The average age is computed from all marriages solemnized and registered under the *Muslim Ordinance, 1957* and the *Women's Charter, 1961:* prior to the introduction of the latter ordinance on 15 September 1961, registration of marriages in Singapore was not complete.

12. These figures are derived by expressing 3.1 and 0.5 as percentages of 3.6.

13. Arumainathan, Vol. II.

14. See Table 3 in *Report on the Labour Force Survey of Singapore*, for the years 1974 to 1977.

15. Statistics of livebirths classified by birth orders and age of mothers were first made available for the year 1967.

16. See, for instance, Saw Swee-Hock, *Singapore Population in Transition*, p. 84.

17. See, for example, Kingsley Davis, "Population Policy: Will the Current Programs Succeed?", *Science*, Vol. 58; and Bernard Berelson, "Beyond Family Planning", *Studies in Family Planning*, No. 38, February 1969.

18. See also John E. Anderson, Mark C. E. Cheng and Wan Fook Kee, "A Component Analysis of Recent Fertility Decline in Singapore", *Studies in Family Planning*, Vol. 8, No. 11, November 1977.

19. A detailed account of the Chinese animal year may be obtained in Saw Swee-Hock, "Errors in Chinese Age Statistics", *Demography*, vol. 4, no. 2, 1967.

20. Saw Swee-Hock, "Singapore: Resumption of Rapid Fertility Decline in 1973", p. 169.

21. The association between the year of the Dragon and the rise in births in 1976 was mentioned by Mr Lee Kuan Yew, the Prime Minister, in his Chinese New Year message given in February 1977. See *Straits Times*, 18 February 1977. The *Eleventh Annual Report of the Singapore Family Planning and Population Board, 1976* also states on page 15, "It appears probable that those Chinese who married in 1974 and 1975 might have delayed child-bearing until 1976 in order to have a 'Dragon' baby."

22. Dr Wang Chin-Mao, Director of National Health Administration, reported in the Legislative Yuan (Parliament) that the births in Taiwan have gone up in 1976 which would be attributed, at least in part, to the Chinese belief that children born in the Dragon year are destined for greatness. See *Straits Times*, 16 March 1977.

23. See Irene B. Taeuber, *The Population of Japan* (Princeton: Princeton University Press, 1958); and Population Problems Research Council, Mainichi Newspapers, *Family Planning in Japan* (Tokyo: Japan Organisation for International Cooperation in Family Planning, 1972).

24. Professor S. S. Ratnam, former Head of the Department of Obstetrics and Gynaecology, University of Singapore, and former President of the Family Planning Association, has also called for a review of the population policies. See his article entitled "Population Control — A Decade of Independence", in *Singapore — A Decade of Independence*, edited by Charles Ng and T. P. B. Manon (Singapore: Alumni International Singapore, 1975), pp. 70–76.

Part Two

Pronatalist Period

9

Uplifting Fertility of Better-Educated Women

INTRODUCTION

After the attainment of replacement fertility in 1975, no changes to the national population control programme were made until the mid-eighties when measures designed to encourage the better-educated women to produce more babies and the lesser-educated to bear fewer babies were introduced. These measures were meant to influence the quality rather than the quantity of the future population to ensure an adequate supply of talented people for the small island state. The genesis of the shift towards the qualitative aspect of the population can be traced to the traditional address delivered by the Prime Minister, Mr Lee Kuan Yew, at the National Day Rally attended by a gathering of People's Action Party members and other specially-invited guests on 14 August 1983. Appendix A reproduces the full text of his speech.

Touching on the prevailing problems and issues confronting Singapore, he talked at considerable length about the differences in fertility according to the educational level of mothers as reflected in the 1980 Population Census data. He also cited the findings, particularly those of Thomas Bouchard of the University of Minnesota, which seem to indicate that the intelligence of a child is determined more by nature (about 80 per cent) than by nurture (about 20 per cent). He expressed his concern about the lopsided pattern of procreation in Singapore where the better-educated mothers are bearing too few children, which will eventually have the undesirable effect of lowering the quality of the population in the long run. He emphasized the need to change "our policies, and try to reshape our demographic configuration so that our better-educated women will have more children to be adequately represented in the next generation".[1]

The Prime Minister's remarks on the above population issue in the much-heralded National Day Rally beamed live over television and reported prominently in the newspapers provoked a great debate among the general public.[2] The debate centred on the validity of the hypothesis that the intelligence of the children is determined by the educational level of their mothers and that intelligence is dependent more on nature than nurture. As to be expected, there was no consensus among the people regarding these somewhat controversial and emotional issues. After several months of public discussion on the lopsided procreational pattern of women, the government introduced several measures in early 1984 to address this undesirable reproductive behaviour of the population.

GRADUATE MARRIAGE MATCHMAKING

When the Prime Minister discussed the need to improve the qualitative aspect of the population, he drew attention to the large proportion of single graduate women as shown in the 1980 Population Census. Highly-educated women should be encouraged to get married and produce intelligent children. The government therefore established the Social Development Unit (SDU) in the Public Service Division of the Ministry of Finance in July 1984 to provide matching services to single graduate officers, male and female, in government departments, statutory boards, and government-linked companies. The setting up of this special organization was not announced publicly and its activities during the initial years were conducted discretely. The somewhat low profile was adopted in view of the sensitivity of government involvement in graduate matchmaking and the need to protect the privacy of the graduate participants.

It was about a year later in March 1985 that some information about SDU was published in the newspaper. On 7 March 1985, the *Straits Times* included a report of the answers given by Dr Tony Tan, Minister for Finance, to questions raised in Parliament about the work of SDU.[3] On the same day, another newspaper had a feature article about the SDU with some information provided by the Director, Dr Aileen Aw. Thereafter, information about the activities of the SDU has been made more available to the public through the mass media.

The activities of the SDU are focused on getting the male and female single graduate officers to come together through appropriate events such as talks, courses, workshops, dances, parties, local outings, overseas trips and computer matchmaking services. In recent years, more innovative activities such as speed dating, personal advertisement on internet, and joining a meet-new-friends website have been introduced.[4] In the late nineties, the SDU was transferred to the Ministry of Community Development and Sports, which has been assuming a greater role in promoting pro-family activities.

Over the years the work of the SDU has met with increasing success. Two years after its launch in 1984, the SDU managed to match only 350 graduates or 3.5 per cent among a total membership of about 7,000. A few years ago in 1999 only 2,789 members got married. Nowadays, the success rate is much higher — some 4,050 graduates or 15 per cent of the total membership of about 26,000 in 2003.[5] After so many years in existence, the SDU can now function more openly as there is now a greater acceptance of government getting involved in matchmaking. The work of the SDU in assisting single graduates to marry and produce children is an integral part of the strategy to ensure the procreation of talented children by highly-educated women.

ENHANCED CHILD RELIEF

On 2 March 1984, the Minister for Finance, Dr Tony Tan, announced the introduction of the second pronatalist measure targeted at better-educated women in his presentation of the 1984 Budget to Parliament.[6] There was in existence at that time the enhanced child relief for specially qualified women in the income tax return meant to induce these highly-educated women to re-enter or remain in the workforce. Providing financial incentives to these women was important so as not to waste the scarce human resources in Singapore. Under the then existing rule, the specially qualified women were eligible to claim an additional 5 per cent of their annual earned income for each of their first three children, apart from the normal child relief of $750 for the first two children and $500 for the third child which all working women regardless of educational level could claim. A new incentive designed to encourage better-educated women to produce more children was built into the enhanced child relief scheme.

The scheme was therefore amended to raise the enhanced child relief for specially-educated women to 5 per cent of their earned income for the first child, 10 per cent for the second child, and 15 per cent for the third child. There was, however, the maximum of $10,000 as the limit they could claim for each child. Furthermore, the eligibility for this improved enhanced child relief was widened from the original group of specially-qualified women to women with at least 5 passes at Ordinary Level in the General Certificate of Education (GCE) examination. In making this scheme more generous, the Minister for Finance concluded "that a somewhat more liberal scheme can be justified not only to influence all better-educated married women to continue to work, but, more important to encourage them, hopefully, to have a second, if not a third child. This will go a little way toward correcting the present lopsided pattern of procreation in Singapore which is a cause for concern."[7]

The amended enhanced child relief scheme came into effect for the income earned by the better-educated working mothers in 1984 and filed in the 1985 Year of Assessment. The modified scheme certainly reinforced the original aim of encouraging married women to enter, re-enter or remain in the workforce in the context of the tight labour market prevailing in Singapore. It was argued that this measure might not be able to persuade a significant number of better-educated working women to produce more children since money is not the primary determinant of their reproductive behaviour. There are more important factors such as availability of good domestic servants, convenient infant and childcare centres, and conflicting demands at home and at work that may play a greater role in determining whether the better-educated working women will produce more children. The enhanced child relief was further improved in 1989, but was eventually replaced by the working mother's child relief with effect from the 2005 Year of Assessment.

PRIMARY SCHOOL REGISTRATION

The third pronatalist measure favouring better-educated married women was built into the old scheme of registering Primary One pupils in the middle of each year for admission in January of the following year. The primary school registration system was introduced years ago in 1972 to provide a transparent and orderly system of primary school admission in the context of excessive demand for places in particularly the more popular schools. As observed in Chapter 6, the government wanted to strengthen the population control programme and took the opportunity to incorporate antinatalist measures linked to the birth order of the child with the sterilization of parents in the 1973 registration exercise.

The modification of the system to incorporate the special kind of pronatalist policy in early 1984 again drew considerable public discussion mainly on the grounds that it was unfair to give children of better-educated mothers an advantage over the lesser-educated mothers, regardless of whether the intelligence of the children is linked to the educational level of the mothers. The priority scheme of primary school registration and the 1984 changes to incorporate the new policy are laid out in Table 9.1.[8]

The above modifications to factor in the special pronatalist incentives into the priority school registration system resulted in an increase in the number of stages for the various groups to register. The whole registration exercise in 1984 had to start much earlier, on 2 May. Some 157 children belonging to graduate mothers were accorded priority under the modified system, and the vast majority of the 40,000 or so children were still registered according to their schools of choice.[9] The outcome did not appear to be very satisfactory. Only a small number of children of graduate mothers benefitted from the new pronatalist measure. Worse still, a great deal of unhappiness and resentment seemed to have been generated among both the better-educated as well as the lesser-educated. This general discontent was manifested in the public expression of unfavourable comments in the letters to the press, the election rally speeches made during the 1984 general election, and, to some extent, the protest votes in the election results.

It did not come as a surprise that the Minister for Education, Dr Tony Tan, informed the Schools Council meeting held on 2 February 1985 that his Ministry had started to review the implementation of the special pronatalist measure introduced in the previous year's registration exercise.[10] The reversal of this very unpopular scheme was announced by him in Parliament on 25 March 1985. He was obliged to say:

> The crucial issue is whether graduate mothers will be induced to have more children simply because this will give them priority in registering their children for Primary One or pre-primary. The response from graduate mothers would indicate that the premise is unlikely to be true. In view of the animosity and resentment which the priority scheme has aroused in Singapore, both graduate and non-graduate, and as the scheme is not likely in my view to produce the desired results, I see no good reason for continuing the scheme.[11]

TABLE 9.1
Old and New Systems of Primary One Registration

Old System	New System
Category I: Children who are citizens or permanent residents	Category I: No Change
Phase 1 For a second child who has an elder brother or sister studying in the same school	*Phase 1* (A) For a child whose mother has at least 3 children and has an acceptable university degree or approved professional qualification. (B) For a second child whose brother or sister is studying in the school of his choice. *OR* For a child whose mother has only 2 children and has an acceptable university degree or an approved professional qualification. *OR* For a child whose mother or father has been sterilized before 24 January 1984 after the birth of the first child and whose mother has an acceptable university degree or an approved professional qualification. *OR*

Phase 2

(A) For a child one of whose parents has been sterilized after the birth of the first or second child.

OR

For a first or second child one of whose parents received his/her education in the same school or is a member of the school advisory or management committee or a staff.

OR

For a second child whose elder brother or sister received his/her education in the same school.

For a child whose mother has been medically certified to be unable to produce any more children and has an acceptable university degree or an approved professional qualification.

Phase 2

(A) For a child one of whose parents has been sterilized after the birth of the first or second child and neither parent has any 'O' level passes.

OR

For a child one of whose parents has been sterilized before 24 January 1984 after the birth of the first or the second child.

OR

For a child from a three-child family, one of whose parents has at least one 'A' level pass or the equivalent.

OR

For a first or second child who has a parent or sibling directly connected with the school.

continued on next page

TABLE 9.1 — cont'd

Old System	New System
(B) For a first or second child one of whose parents is directly connected with the school.	(B) For a child from a two-child or three-child family, one of whose parents has at least three 'O' level passes or the equivalent.
(C) For a child who is from a one-child or two-child family. OR For a second child whose elder brother or sister is studying in an affiliated school.	(C) No change.
(D) For a child one of whose parents has been sterilized before the age of 40 and after the birth of the third or subsequent child.	(D) No change.
Phase 3 For a child who is either not eligible for, or not successful in Phase 1 and/or Phase 2.	*Phase 3* No change.
Category II: Children who are neither citizens nor permanent residents.	Category II: No change.
Phase 4 (A) For a child whose parents are citizens or permanent residents.	*Phase 4* (A) For a child with at least one parent who is a citizen or permanent resident.
(B) For a child whose parents are neither citizens nor permanent residents.	(B) No change.

The final decision was made in a meeting of Parliament held on 14 May 1985 when the Minister for Education declared that the government had decided to discontinue the graduate mother priority scheme and to revert to the 1982 registration guidelines. However, he had to assure Parliament that the previous commitment under the graduate mother scheme would be honoured. Children born during the short period between 24 September 1984 and 14 March 1986 to graduate mothers who had responded to take advantage of the scheme would continue to enjoy the priority scheme. The old 1982 registration scheme with no priority for children of graduate mothers was reinstated on 15 July 1985 when the primary school registration exercise for the 1986 school year commenced. It follows that this pronatalist measure built into only one primary school registration exercise had a negligible influence in bringing about more babies produced by graduate mothers.

STERILIZATION CASH INCENTIVES

In contrast to the above three pronatalist measures designed to induce better-educated mothers to bear more children, two antinatalist eugenic measures were introduced to discourage the poor and lesser-educated mothers from having many children.[12] The premise underlying these measures is that these mothers would produce less talented children, thus diluting the talent pool for the country. The first measure announced on 2 January 1984 took the form of a $10,000 cash grant given under the following conditions:

1. The mother must be under thirty years and be sterilized or ligated after the first child.
2. Neither of the parents should have any Ordinary Level passes in the General Certificate Examination.
3. The combined monthly family income must not exceed $1,500.
4. Neither the wife nor the husband should be earning more than $750.
5. Both spouses must be Singapore citizens or permanent residents.

Married women who had been sterilized or ligated before 1 June 1984 were not eligible for the cash grant.[13] If the mothers, having fulfilled the above conditions and accepted the cash grant, produced another child, then they would have to pay back the $10,000 plus 10 per cent compound interest a year.

Under the sterilization cash incentive scheme the government would pay the $10,000 cash grant into the married woman's Central Provident Fund (CPF) account. If she did not have one, an account would be opened for her regardless of whether she had worked before. The money deposited in her account would earn the usual CPF interest rate, and she was only allowed to withdraw the $10,000 plus earned interest at the retirement age of 55. This arrangement might not be attractive enough to many married women from very poor households because they needed the money now rather than many years later when they reach 55 years of age.

An alternative arrangement for the utilization of the cash grant was therefore offered to the married women who agreed to undergo sterilization. Instead of having to put the $10,000 into their CPF account, they were permitted to use the cash grant to purchase a Housing and Development Board (HDB) apartment under certain conditions as specified below:

1. The apartment must be registered in the name of the married woman who had been sterilized.
2. If she decided to use additional funds from her husband's CPF savings, the apartment could be purchased under their joint names.
3. If option 2 is chosen and subsequently they divorced, the wife could retain the apartment provided she met the HDB home ownership criteria.
4. Furthermore, she would have to repay into her ex-husband's CPF account whatever sum he had contributed to the purchase of the apartment. If she did not have the money to do so, the HDB could assist her by offering her a loan to be repaid in her good time.

In the mid-eighties, the $10,000 cash grant constituted about one-third of the price of a three-room HDB apartment. The grant could also facilitate the 20 per cent downpayment needed to purchase the apartment. This alternative arrangement for married women served to give the uneducated and low-income families a chance to own an apartment which they might not be able to do on their own limited savings. Of course, the prime aim underlying the cash grant was to discourage the low-income and lowly-educated mothers from having more than two children. Indeed, the statement issued from the Prime Minister's Office reinforced this:

Unless we break this low education, large family cycle, we will have a small but insignificant minority of our people permanently trapped in poverty sub-culture, whilst the rest of the population will move even further up the economic and social ladder.[14]

At the time of introducing the sterilization cash incentive scheme in the mid-eighties, it was estimated that some 35,000 married women would be eligible to participate in the scheme. It was believed that the arrangement, especially the second alternative, would be attractive to these women wishing to own an HDB apartment. There was, however, no big rush among the women to take advantage of the new incentive. Some eight months following the implementation of the scheme, the National Registration Department, responsible for administering the scheme, mentioned that a total of 57 couples have submitted their applications and 47 couples, with the wife sterilized, have qualified.[15] This special antinatalist policy was stopped some years ago.

HOSPITAL ACCOUCHEMENT FEES

When the government announced the sterilization cash incentive scheme on 2 June 1984, it gave advance notice about its intention to modify the existing antinatalist policy incorporated in accouchement fees in government hospital. Some eight months later on 7 February 1985, the Ministry of Health issued a press statement giving the detailed changes to the accouchement fees.[16] In short, the fees for four ward classes were raised for the third and subsequent order of birth, with those for the first two children remaining the same. These changes, laid out in Table 9.2, came into effect from 1 March 1985.

It can be observed from Table 9.2 that for Class C wards catering primarily to the poorer and lesser-educated women, the accouchement fees were raised from $300 to $400 for the third child, from $500 to $600 for the fourth child, and from $600 to $1,000 for the fifth and subsequent children. In sharp contrast, the fees for Class A wards patronized by the richer and better-educated women remained at the old level for the third and fourth children. For fifth and subsequent children, the fees were only raised by a relatively small sum from $850 to $1,000. Similarly, the fees for Class B1 wards remained unaltered for the third and the fourth children, and were increased from $700 to $1,000 for the fifth and subsequent children. In the second lower class wards, i.e. Class B2, the

TABLE 9.2

**Changes in Accouchement Fees in Government Hospitals
with effect from 1 March 1985**

Birth Order		Class A	Class B1	Class B2	Class C
1st child	No Change	$350	$200	$150	$100
2nd child	No Change	$400	$250	$200	$150
3rd child	Old	$550	$400	$350	$300
	New	Same	Same	$400	$400
4th child	Old	$750	$600	$550	$500
	New	Same	Same	$600	$600
5th	Old	$850	$700	$650	$600
or					
subsequent child	New	$1,000	$1,000	$1,000	$1,000

fees were widely raised from $350 to $400 for the third child, from $550 to $600 for the fourth child, and from $650 to $1,000 for the fifth and subsequent children.

The above changes have resulted in the mothers paying the same fees of $1,000 in the four wards for the fifth and subsequent children. In the case of the fourth child, the changes had resulted in fees of $600 for Class C, in Class B2 and Class B1, and $750 for Class A. For the third child, the fees were made the same for the three lower classes ($400) and slightly higher for Class A ($550). The new schedule of accouchement fees is quite different from the old system which charged lower fees for the lower class wards. The overall objective of the revised fees was to modify the original antinatalist measure meant to discourage high parity births from all segments of the society into one that imposes a greater financial penalty on the poorer and lesser-educated women for delivering their higher order births in government hospitals. The underlying intention is to discourage the lesser-educated mothers from producing too many children.

CONCLUSION

The year 1984 ushered in a new phase in the demographic history of Singapore when for the first time the government attempted to influence the qualitative aspect of the population. It is somewhat difficult to state with any degree of certainty whether the measures had yielded the desired results.[17] In any case, the pronatalist measure built into the primary school registration exercise was in operation for only one year. The graduate marriage matchmaking operated by the Social Development Unit has recorded some reasonable success, but there are no data to indicate the number of children produced by these better-educated women. The enhanced child relief scheme has certainly lightened the financial burden of better-educated in bearing and taking care of their children.

On the other hand, there are the two antinatalist measures targetted at the lesser-educated women, which would have the effect of reducing the number of births produced by them. It is worth noting that in almost every population, the fertility pattern according to the educational attainment of mothers is one where fertility level falls naturally from lesser-educated mothers to the better-educated. This fertility pattern is taken for granted in most countries and no attempt is being made to reverse this pattern on the grounds of improving the qualitative aspect of the population. What is worse is that this obsession with ensuring an adequate pool of talented persons has not been abandoned in subsequent years when measures were introduced to persuade the general population to produce more children. This serves as an obstacle to the total abolishment of the old antinatalist policies and the introduction of complete pronatalist policies.

Notes

1. Lee Kuan Yew, "National Day Rally Speech", 14 August 1983. See Appendix A.
2. See the various issues of the *Straits Times, Sunday Times, Singapore Monitor* and *Sunday Monitor*, and also *Asian Wall Street Journal*, 25 January 1984 and *Asiaweek*, 2 March 1984 and 22 June 1984.
3. The information was given by the Minister for Finance in Parliament on 6 March 1985 in response to questions put by Members of Parliament. See *Straits Times*, 7 March 1985.
4. The activities are published in the bi-monthly magazine, *Take Flight*, Social Development Unit.
5. *Straits Times*, 30 August 2004.
6. *1984 Budget Statement*, Singapore Government Press Release, Ministry of Culture, 1984.
7. Ibid.
8. *Straits Times*, 24 January 1984.

9. Statement by Dr Tay Eng Soon, Minister of State for Education, and Parliament, and reported in the *Straits Times*, 30 August 1984.

10. The announcement was made in the Schools Council Meeting held on 2 February 1985, and reported in the *Sunday Times*, 30 June 1984.

11. *Straits Times*, 26 March 1985.

12. Statement issued by the Prime Minister's Office on 2 June 1984, and published in *Sunday Times*, 3 June 1984 and *Sunday Monitor*, 14 June 1984.

13. *Straits Times*, 10 June 1984.

14. *Sunday Times*, 3 June 1984.

15. Ibid.

16. Statement issued by the Ministry of Health, and published in the *Straits Times*, 8 February 1985.

17. Saw Swee-Hock, "Singapore: New Population Policies for More Balanced Procreation", *Contemporary Southeast Asia* 7, no. 2 (September 1985).

10

Relaxing Old Antinatalist Policies

NEED FOR CHANGE

It may be recalled that the population control programme was implemented in the mid-sixties. Its specific objective was to lower the level of fertility so as to reduce the rate of population growth. This was part of the national development strategy to raise the standard of living of the people. As it became increasingly obvious that this objective would be achieved by the mid-seventies, attention was focused on the wider issue of the maximum size of the population that Singapore could accommodate in the future. The extremely small land area with no endowed natural resources must necessarily imply that Singapore cannot allow the population to grow indefinitely into an unmanageable size that can threaten the very existence of the island Republic. This led to the government declaring in 1974 that the national demographic goal thereafter was to stabilize the population in the future.[1]

In order to achieve this long-term demographic goal, it was essential to fulfil two conditions concerning fertility in accordance with stationary population theory. The first condition requires the lowering of fertility to the replacement level of total fertility rate (TFR) equivalent to 2.1, and the second condition entails the maintenance of fertility at this level indefinitely. In Singapore the first condition was realized in 1975 when fertility fell for the first time to replacement level. But the second condition has never been fulfilled because, instead of proceeding henceforth along a horizontal path, fertility has oscillated well below this point for about a decade or so before any changes to the strong antinatalist programme were made.

It would appear that at that time the immediate target of working towards fertility moving down to replacement level was generally recognized as a necessary condition for achieving the long-term goal of a stationary population. However, there is some evidence to suggest that there was a failure to appreciate the importance of holding fertility at this level indefinitely in the future beyond 1975. It was this lack of understanding of the absolute necessity to ensure the fulfillment of the second condition in the context of a stationary population theory that below replacement fertility has been allowed to persist in Singapore.

The need to hold replacement fertility constant beyond 1975 was first mentioned in the 1977 *Report of the Singapore Family Planning and Population Board*. The report stated, "With Replacement Level attained in 1975, the broad policy of the National Family Planning and Population Board Programme during the Third Five-Year Plan is to maintain fertility at this level".[2] The objective of the 1976–80 plan was merely repeated every year in the annual report of the Board right up to 1982. But then no action was taken to eliminate the existing strong antinatalist programme in order to give fertility a chance to move back to replacement level.

In fact, the very low fertility recorded a few years before 1975 should have already sent a clear signal to the government that in a short time fertility would reach replacement level, and it was time to take action immediately to abolish all the antinatalist measures. It should have been quite obvious that the continuation of these measures would surely depress fertility to well below replacement level, and indeed that was what actually happened. These measures were left untouched for more than a decade. We must not forget the group of social and economic factors favouring small family norms that will always continue to exert a powerful influence on the reproductive behaviour of Singapore women. The presence of these factors will inhibit any major rise in fertility even if the government were to adopt a non-interventionalist policy by abolishing all antinatalist measures.

The need for changes in the fertility policy of Singapore was made known on numerous occasions. The importance of making policy changes was first made public by the author in a paper delivered in December 1979 at a seminar on "Singapore Towards the Year 2000" organized by the National Academy of Science and the Singapore Science Centre. After presenting some facts and figures, the author made the following statement:

> ...the persistence of fertility well below replacement level during the past four years, and most probably in the next few years, should be taken as a fair warning of the need to conduct a thorough review of our

population policies relating to induced abortion, voluntary sterilization, and incentive and disincentive measures.[3]

This public call to review and abolish the strong antinatalist policies was repeated in his book on *Population Control for Zero Growth in Singapore*, completed in 1979 and published in early 1980.[4]

It was not until the mid-eighties that the government began to pay serious attention to the sustained movement of fertility below replacement level and the undesirable consequences that would emerge from this trend. In December 1984 the government established a high-level Inter-Ministerial Population Committee, consisting of mainly Permanent Secretaries and the author who was then Professor of Statistics at the National University of Singapore. The Committee was charged with the responsibility of conducting a thorough review of the population control programme and to make recommendations accordingly. While the Committee was quietly deliberating on the various aspects of the subject matter, there were some public discussions in the press. The author published two articles in the *Sunday Times* on 15 June and 6 July 1986, setting out in simple layman's language the problems attendant on the below-replacement fertility in Singapore, and the need to reverse the fertility policy (see Appendices B and C).[5] To be sure, these articles were followed by further discussions in the press.

On 24 July 1986, the Acting Minister for Health, Mr Yeo Cheow Tong, belatedly announced in a letter to the *Straits Times* that the government was in the process of reviewing the fertility policy through the Inter-Ministerial Population Committee, and called for suggestions from the public. This was followed by the First Deputy Prime Minister, Mr Goh Chok Tong, discussing the population issue in his address, "The Second Long March" to Nanyang Technological Institute undergraduates on 3 August 1986 (see Appendix D). Soon after that, the Chairman of the Inter-Ministerial Population Committee, Dr Kwa Soon Bee, gave some information on 17 August 1986 on certain possible measures being considered by his Committee. The open discussions and various dialogue sessions between government officials and the public continued during the rest of 1986 and in early 1987.

The recommendations of the Inter-Ministerial Population Committee were submitted to the government in January 1987. On 1 March 1987, the First Deputy Prime Minister, Mr Goh Chok Tong, held a press conference to announce the changes to the population policies and programmes.[6] Some details of the changes pertaining to taxation were announced by the Minister for Finance, Mr Richard Hu, in his Budget Statement to Parliament held on 4 March 1982.[7] Details of the other changes were provided in due course in press statements issued by the relevant government ministries. The rationale of these changes was to persuade mothers to produce more children by relaxing some of the existing antinatalist measures and introducing new pronatalist measures.

But the desire to enhance the qualitative aspect of the population was not completely abandoned since some of the changes still left the modified policies linked to the educational attainment of the mothers or family income. This is reflected in the adoption of the new slogan of "Have Three or More If You Can Afford It". Furthermore, the old antinatalist measures were not eliminated. They were rendered less severe by removing the disincentive from, or extending the incentive to, the third child and sometimes to the fourth child to permit for some additional births. There was still the concern that a complete elimination of the antinatalist measures might lead to excessive births among certain segments of the population, such as the poor and lesser-educated group.

ABORTION

The laws governing legalized abortion on demand have never been amended to make it more difficult for women to undergo abortion despite the sustained fertility below replacement level. What was introduced was compulsory counselling by doctors before and after abortion, and even so this applied to only women with not more than two children and with at least some secondary education. This compulsory counselling was put into effect from 1 October 1987 and must be provided by all doctors authorized to perform abortions in government and private hospitals. Hopefully, this will provide all the essential facts concerning abortion to the women to give them a chance to change their mind and proceed with the pregnancy. For those who decide to opt for an abortion, counselling is provided once again after the operation with the hope of preventing them from seeking repeat abortions in the future.

Since the legalization of induced abortion in 1970, the incidence of abortion has been increasing rapidly. By the year 1986, there were 23,035 abortions as compared with 38,379 births in the same year, giving an abortion ratio of 600 abortions per thousand live-births. For sure, this extremely high incidence of abortion contributed significantly to the low below-replacement fertility of 1.42 in 1986.[8] The introduction of compulsory counselling before and after abortion cannot be very effective, especially among the private doctors who derive income from performing legal abortions. What is required are certain changes to the more liberal sections of the Abortion Act through legislation.

STERILIZATION

As observed earlier, sterilization has been one of the major components of the population control programme, and some incentives have been put in place to encourage married women and men to undergo sterilization. For example, public sector employees were given one week's unrecorded leave immediately after undergoing tubal ligation or vasectomy. This leave was amended from 1 April 1987 to make it unavailable to those with one or more passes at Ordinary Level in the GCE examination regardless of how many children they have.[9] The intention of this change was to discourage government employees, except the lowly-educated ones, from going for sterilization and hence to continue to produce children in the future.

There was also the old antinatalist policy intended to encourage women or their husbands to undergo sterilization by offering them lower accouchement fees in government hospitals. For B2 and C Class wards, the fees would be waived if the women patient or her husband underwent sterilization within six weeks of the delivery of the baby. A modification of this scheme was put into effect on 1 April 1987 when the women warded in these lower class wards could only have the fees waived if she or her husband went for the sterilization operation after having the third or higher order births.[10] The change was meant to stop discouraging couples with only one or two children from having more children. Notwithstanding this change, the original antinatalist character of the policy still remained but to a lesser extent because the fee waiver incentive is no longer available to couples producing their fourth or subsequent children.

Another change in the area of sterilization was connected with the primary school registration system. As noted earlier, the scheme was liberalized somewhat by extending priority to the third child in Phase 2C. The original intention of persuading married women or their husbands to undergo sterilization was also modified. Phase 2D in the overall priority arrangement was meant for a child, one of whose parents had been sterilized before the age of forty and after the birth of the third or subsequent children. The second condition was altered from the third or subsequent children to the fourth or subsequent children.[11] The implication of this modification was that the parents could proceed to produce a fourth child without losing priority in the registration exercise under Phase 2D.

The final measure aimed at limiting sterilization among couples was the introduction of compulsory pre-sterilization counselling in 1987 for women and men with only one or two children. It was noted earlier that voluntary sterilization in Singapore is available on demand by women and men, even among those with only one or two children. The compulsory counselling may change the mind of those women and men with fewer than three children, and hopefully additional children might be forthcoming in the future. The additional second or third child can of course enjoy the various financial and other benefits provided under the different incentive schemes.

PUBLIC HOUSING

An old Housing and Development Board rule required young couples to pay a 20 per cent downpayment for the purchase of an apartment. With effect from 28 August 2000, the rule was relaxed to permit the downpayment to be made in two stages, 10 per cent when the couple sign the agreement and the other 10 per cent when they took possession of the apartment. This was to apply as of 1 October 2000 to couples buying a four-room apartment for the first time. The husband or wife must be between 21 and 30 years of age. This relaxation of the HDB rule was meant to facilitate young couples to marry and start a family as soon as possible.

USE OF MEDISAVE

Medisave is a compulsory savings scheme introduced in April 1984 as an integral part of the Central Provident Fund (CPF). The scheme has been designed to help Singaporeans build up sufficient savings for their hospitalization expenses, especially in their old age. Under the scheme, every employee contributes 6–8 per cent, depending on his/her age group, of his/her monthly salary to a special Medisave account. The savings can be withdrawn to pay the hospital bills of the account holder and his/her immediate family members.

The Medisave scheme could previously be employed to pay for medical expenses incurred in childbirth for the first two children only. This facility was extended on 1 March 1987 to allow payment of delivery and hospital charges for the third child from the Medisave account. This liberalization of the old antinatalist policy makes it easier for couples to have their third child by allowing them to use their savings in the Central Provident Fund (CPF) through the Medisave scheme.

THIRD CHILD MATERNITY LEAVE

The antinatalist policy introduced in the early seventies restricts paid maternity leave to eight weeks for the first two children in accordance with the Employment Act.[12] Unpaid maternity leave of eight weeks is still available to mothers regardless of the birth order. The relaxation of this old antinatalist policy was announced by the Prime Minister, Mr Goh Chok Tong, in his address delivered in the National Day Rally held on 20 August 2000.

In discussing the issue of paid maternity leave for the third child, he said,

> We must create a total environment conducive to raising a family. Our policy is to have three children or more if you can afford it .... We have to do something, even while recognizing that getting married and having children are personal decisions ... Many Singaporeans have said that the lack of paid maternity leave for the third child is an obstacle to having their third child. The Government will help reduce the obstacle to you being so.[13]

The key issue in giving paid maternity leave for the third child was the question of who is going to pay for the salary bearing in mind the necessity not to overburden the employers with additional costs.

Instead of taking unpaid maternity leave, working mothers could take eight weeks of paid maternity leave when they give birth to their third child with effect from 1 April 2001. Their employers are not required to incur any expenses because the government will pay the cost of the maternity leave for the third child, subject to a maximum of $20,000. A system was put in place whereby the employers would continue to pay the usual salary to the working mothers, and claim for reimbursement from the Ministry of Community Development and Sports, responsible for the administration of this scheme.[14]

To be eligible for the scheme, mothers who are employed or self-employed must fulfil certain conditions. The child's mother must be lawfully married to the child's father at the time of birth, the child must be a Singapore citizen, and the child must be the third live-birth of the mother. Stepchildren or adopted children are not eligible for the scheme and cannot be employed to reckon the birth order of the children in the family. To qualify for the scheme, the mother must have worked with the employer for at least 180 days prior to the birth of the child. There are, however, no eligibility criteria linked to the age or educational qualification of the working mothers.

If the working mother already has a first child and produces a pair of twins, she can only claim either the second or third child maternity leave, but not both. If she is already entitled to the second child maternity leave paid by the employer under the Employment Act, she will not be allowed to claim for the new third child maternity leave scheme. If a third child was born before the implementation date of 1 April 2001, she could only claim for the period of the maternity leave consumed on or after 1 April 2001. The amount receivable will be pro-rated according to the actual duration of the leave period covered by the scheme.

To enable the employer to pay the mother the usual payroll while she is on the third child maternity leave, she must submit a declaration form (Form ML1) to her employer at least one week prior to commencing her maternity leave. The employer will in turn submit a claim form (Form ML2) to the Ministry of Community Development and Sports after the completion of the eight-week maternity leave, and this must be done within one month. The reimbursement of the amount paid to her will be deposited into the employer's bank account within three weeks for Internet submission and four weeks for manual submission.

An important advantage of the scheme is that it allows self-employed mothers to participate in the scheme in order to compensate them for the loss of earnings during their maternity leave. They must not be actively engaged in their trade, business, profession or vocation during the maternity leave period and must have suffered a loss of income before they can submit their claim. They must submit the completed Form ML3 to the Ministry of Community Development and Sports, together with a six-month income and expenditure statement for the period preceding the maternity leave, the latest available year-end income and expenditure account declared for taxation, and certification of Registration of Business Company. Upon approval of the application, they will be reimbursed an amount equivalent to the average monthly net income earned in the 180 days before the maternity leave period.

PRIMARY SCHOOL REGISTRATION

As noted earlier, antinatalist measures were incorporated in 1973 in the annual registration of Primary One school children conducted in the middle of the year for them to commence schooling in January the following year. Over the years various changes were introduced in this annual registration exercise, and by 1986 priority was given to children of families with up to three children, except for one category in Phase 2C (see Table 10.1).

With effect from the registration exercise held in mid-1987 for children commencing Primary One education in January 1988, Phase 2C was amended as indicated in Table 10.1. The extension of priority to the three-child family in the second category of Phase 2C removed the remaining penalty imposed on the third child. Priority for a third child has already been accorded in all the other stages in the registration exercise.

TABLE 10.1
Amendment to the Primary School Registration, 1987

Old System	New System
Phase 2C	Phase 2C
Second or third child whose brother/sister is studying in an affiliated school	No change
OR	OR
Child from a one-child or two-child family	Child from a one-child, two-child or three-child family

PERSONAL INCOME TAX

The other method of making the old antinatalist measures less severe has been to make changes to the rules governing personal income tax. Under the old rule implemented in August 1973, the normal child relief was $750 for each of the first two children and $500 for the third child. Under this antinatalist schedule there was no relief for the fourth and subsequent children. A small modification was introduced whereby the relief of the third child was raised to $750 for the 1988 Year of Assessment. Parents submitting their tax returns in 1988 and subsequent years were able to claim this increased amount on their income earned in 1987. This increased relief was applicable to a third child existing at the time of announcement on 4 March 1987 as well as a third child from after this date. The effect of this change was rather negligible since the amount of increase was only $250 for the third child and more importantly, the zero relief for the fourth and subsequent child was retained.

It is therefore not surprising that the Minister for Finance, Mr Richard Hu, announced further liberalization of the above policy in his 1989 Budget Statement delivered in Parliament on 3 March 1989.[15] The normal child relief for personal income tax was doubled from $750 to $1,500 for the first, second and third child. A more notable change was the introduction of a new relief amounting to $1,500 for the fourth child born on or after 1 January 1988. This had the immediate impact of benefiting the parents of some 2,036 children of fourth order born in 1988.

The other modification to the personal income tax rule referred to the numerous changes to the enhanced child relief scheme announced by the Minister for Finance in his budget speech. The scheme, originally introduced in August 1978, served the purpose of inducing mothers with special educational qualifications to remain in, enter or re-enter, the work-force. This scheme gave these women — who had at least five passes at Ordinary Level in the GCE examination and who had opted for separate assessment from their husbands — to claim 5 per cent of their earned income for the first child, 10 per cent for the second child, and 15 per cent for the third child, subject to a maximum of $10,000 per child. This was in addition to their eligibility to claim the normal child relief.

However, the scheme did not give working mothers the right to claim for their fourth and subsequent children. Therefore on 3 March 1989, the Minister announced in Parliament a liberalization of the scheme by extending the enhanced child relief to the fourth child born on or after 1 January 1988, but not backdated to the fourth child born before this date. The working mother was eligible to claim relief for her new-born fourth child 15 per cent of her earned income, subject to the same maximum of $10,000. The other change announced by the Minister refers to the lowering of the educational qualification of the mothers from five passes to three passes at Ordinary Level in the GCE examination. With the change, working mothers possessing any three or four passes could claim enhanced child relief for the first three children born before 1 January 1988 and also for the fourth child born on or after this date. The enhanced child relief was eventually replaced by the working mother's child relief with effect from the 2005 Year of Assessment.

In the longer term, the two modifications to the enhanced child relief scheme will result in a bigger group of working mothers being able to claim this relief for any child up to the fourth one born in 1988 and thereafter. The modifications have the advantage of reinforcing the twofold objective of encouraging working mothers to remain in the work-force as well as to produce more children. These changes constitute a partial liberalization of the antinatalist philosophy underlying the enhanced child relief scheme since it is not applicable to all children irrespective of birth order. Out of a total of 43,664 births born in 1988, some 700 or 0.2 per cent were from the fifth and higher order.

Notes

1. Chua Sian Chin, "Speech by Mr Chua Sian Chin, Minister for Health and Home Affairs, at the World Population Conference, Bucharest, Romania, 19–30 August 1974", *Singapore Public Health Bulletin*, no. 15, January 1975.
2. *Annual Report of the Singapore Family Planning and Population Board* (Singapore: SFPPB, 1977).
3. Saw Swee-Hock, "Too Little Land, Too Many People", in *Singapore Towards the Year 2000*, edited by Saw Swee-Hock and R.S. Bhathal (Singapore: Singapore University Press, 1981).
4. Saw Swee-Hock, *Population Control for Zero Growth in Singapore* (New York: Oxford University Press, 1980).
5. *Sunday Times*, 15 June 1986 and 6 July 1986.
6. *Straits Times*, 4 March 1987.
7. *1987 Budget Statement*, Singapore Government Press Release, Ministry of Communications and Information, 1987.
8. Saw Swee-Hock, "Seventeen Years of Legalized Abortion in Singapore", *Biology and Society* 5, no. 2 (June 1988).

9. *Straits Times*, 4 April 1987.

10. *Straits Times*, 6 March 1987.

11. *Straits Times*, 4 July 1987.

12. *The Employment (Amendment) Act, 1973* (Singapore: Government Printer, 1973).

13. *Straits Times*, 20 August 2000.

14. See "Bonus for Babies and Mothers", *Straits Times*, 1 April 2001. This insert giving details of the Third Child Maternity Scheme was provided by the Ministry of Community Development and Sports.

15. *1989 Budget Statement* (Singapore: Government Press Release, Ministry of Communications and Information, 1989).

11

Introducing Limited Pronatalist Policies

While the previous chapter presents an account of the changes relating to the partial reversal of the old antinatalist policies introduced during the years 1987–2000, this chapter focuses on limited pronatalist measures implemented during the same period. Apart from recommending the loosening of some of the old antinatalist policies, the Inter-Ministerial Population Committee suggested the introduction of some pronatalist measures. But these pronatalist measures, together with those implemented later, were based on the same principle of giving incentives up to at most the fourth child.

The second major group of pronatalist measures were introduced in the new millennium following the traditional address by the Prime Minister, Mr Goh Chok Tong, in the National Day Rally held on 20 August 2000. Among other things, he said, "We must create a total environment conducive to raising a family. Our policy is to have three children or more if you can afford it."[1] It is important to emphasize that the somewhat restricted pronatalist policies are quite different from those completely pronatalist policies adopted in many European countries to raise the level of their below-replacement fertility.

BABY BONUS

By far the most important pronatalist policy promulgated by the Prime Minister in the 2000 National Day Rally was the baby bonus scheme. This scheme was put into effect on 1 April 2000 for parents producing a second or third child on or after this date. The scheme consists of a two-tier payment given annually by the government for a period of six years after the birth of the child. In the first tier, the government gives an outright cash gift, while in the second both the parents and the government contribute to a co-savings account. The scheme has been structured in such a manner as to provide extra funds for the parents to use solely for the benefit of the children. The Family Services Department in the Ministry of Community Development and Sports is responsible for administering the baby bonus scheme.[2]

To be eligible for the baby bonus, the mother must be legally married to the child's father at the time of the child's birth or conception, the child must be a Singapore citizen, and the child must be the second or third child born alive to his mother. This means that step-children or adopted children will not be entitled to the baby bonus, nor can they be counted to determine the birth order of the eligible children. Children born to Singaporeans overseas are entitled to the baby bonus when they take up Singapore citizenship. Multiple births such as twins, triplets and quadruplets are considered as separate births in reckoning the birth order of the children eligible for the baby bonus.[3]

The procedures adopted to administer the scheme are quite established and streamlined. It is not necessary for the parents to apply for the scheme since, based on birth registration records in the Registry of Births and Deaths, an invitation to participate in the scheme is sent automatically by the Ministry of Community Development and Sports. The parents have the option to decline or accept the invitation by returning the completed Declaration Form. Under the first tier, the government pays into the bank account of the parents a cash gift of $500 for the second child and $1,000 for the third child when the baby bonus application is approved. Thereafter, the cash bonus will be paid five times more on the first to the fifth anniversary of the opening of the bank account, bringing the total sum to $3,000 for the second child and $6,000 for the third child. The parents have the discretion to employ the cash gift to defray the costs and incidental expenses of the care and development of the child.

The second tier resembles a co-savings arrangement whereby the government matches dollar-for-dollar the annual amount the parents put into the child's Children Development Account (CDA) opened with the participating bank, DBS Bank. The parents may contribute any amount per year, but the matching payment by the government is subjected to a maximum of $1,000 for the second child and $2,000 for the third child. The matching contribution by the government is made six months after the opening of the CDA, and subsequently every twelve months. The money can be employed to pay for the fees at approved institutions such as kindergartens, childcare centres and other pre-school programmes. Furthermore, the money can be used for all the children in the family and not just for the relevant second or third child. Any funds and interests remaining in the CDA when the child reaches seven years will be transferred to the Edusave account of the child.

A clearer picture of the baby bonus scheme is presented in Table 11.1, showing the numerical examples of the first tier and the second tier. For these two examples, it is assumed that the parents contribute the maximum of $1,000 for the second child and $2,000 for the third. The parents have money to spend for the benefit of the children to the amount of $2,500 per

TABLE 11.1

Baby Bonus Scheme for the Second Child and the Third Child

Year	First Tier	Second Tier		Total ($)
	Government Contribution ($)	Parents' Contribution ($)	Government Contribution ($)	
		Second Child		
First	500	1,000	1,000	2,500
Second	500	1,000	1,000	2,500
Third	500	1,000	1,000	2,500
Fourth	500	1,000	1,000	2,500
Fifth	500	1,000	1,000	2,500
Sixth	500	1,000	1,000	2,500
Total	**3,000**	**6,000**	**6,000**	**15,000**
		Third Child		
First	1,000	2,000	2,000	5,000
Second	1,000	2,000	2,000	5,000
Third	1,000	2,000	2,000	5,000
Fourth	1,000	2,000	2,000	5,000
Fifth	1,000	2,000	2,000	5,000
Sixth	1,000	2,000	2,000	5,000
Total	**6,000**	**12,000**	**12,000**	**30,000**

year from the entitlement of the second child, and $5,000 from the third child. The sum available will of course be less if the contributions from the parent are below the two maximum figures. The baby bonus scheme has been structured in such a manner that financial incentives are not given to parents producing the first child and, more importantly, the fourth and subsequent children. It is a pronatalist policy of a limited kind, and different from those in other countries where restrictions on the utilization of the money are not imposed.

PUBLIC SECTOR LEAVE

The second category of pronatalist measures is related to the leave of employees in the public sector, which is easier to change since government has the authority to alter the working conditions of civil servants. Soon after the National Day Rally speech by the Prime Minister, it was announced on 28 August 2000 by the Chairman of the Working Committee on Marriage and Procreation, Mr Eddie Teo, that a government employee will be permitted to take three days' paid marriage leave when he marries for the first time.[4] This special leave, effective from 1 October 2000, is meant to facilitate civil servants to get married. It was also declared that with effect from the same date, fathers in the civil service will be allowed to take three days' paternity leave to look after their first three children. It was hoped that this pro-family measure would assist husbands to play a bigger role in raising their children.

Earlier on 6 March 1987, the Ministry of Finance had announced the introduction of a pronatalist policy linked to the granting of short unrecorded leave to working mothers in the public sector.[5] With effect from 1 April 1987, working mothers have been entitled to take paid unrecorded leave to attend to their sick children. They can apply for such leave limited to five days for each child under six years of age up to the first three children. Every application must be supported by a medical certificate for the sick child. This special leave is additional to the normal vacation leave and sick leave to which the mother is entitled.

PUBLIC SECTOR FLEXIBLE WORK

Apart from offering special leave, the public sector took the lead in instituting flexible work to permit staff to look after their children and families. With effect from 1 April 1987, a new pronatalist measure was made available to women officers in the civil service with a child under six years of age to convert their full-time job into part-time work up to a maximum of three years.[6] The part-time officer must work 21 hours, equivalent to half of the normal week, and must spread this shortened hours over at least five days a week from Monday to Friday. Her monthly salary will be half that of a full-time officer and she will be entitled to one increment once in two years. The idea behind this policy is to make it easier for some of the married women to have their first child or additional children without having to cease working completely.

Following the National Day Rally held in August 2000, it was announced on 28 August 2000 that government departments would be permitted to adopt flexible working hours for their staff.[7] The working hours of each employee could be adjusted within the framework of 42 hours per week without any loss in productivity and lapse in standard of service. Within these general guidelines, it was possible to come to an arrangement whereby an officer could work five days per week, but working longer hours during the five days to clock a total of 42 hours. The departments must still operate a six-day week. This was replaced by the five-day week in late 2004.

CHILDCARE SUBSIDY

It was recognized that not all working mothers have relatives such as mothers or mothers-in-law or domestic maids to look after their young children at home, and even if they have such persons, they may still need to send their children to childcare centres. A pronatalist financial incentive in the form of a childcare subsidy was therefore offered on 1 April 1987 to parents sending their young children to childcare centres. For the purpose of administering this subsidy, the young children are subdivided into those aged 2 months to below 18 months and those aged 18 months to below 7 years. The government decided to pay a subsidy of $100 per month to working mothers for each of their first three pre-school children under 7 years of age placed in approved full-day childcare centres. If the child remains in the crèche for only half a day, the subsidy is reduced to $50 accordingly. The subsidy was later raised to $150 for full-day childcare and $75 for half-day. At least one of the parents must be a Singapore citizen or permanent resident in order to qualify for the subsidy. By definition the childcare subsidy is applicable to children aged 18 months to less than 7 years old.

A complementary scheme is the infant care subsidy given to working mothers who put their infants aged 2 months to 18 months old in childcare centres. The amount of subsidy is the same, but the fees for these infants are much higher than those for children aged 18 months to below 7 years. Working mothers have to spend very much more in sending their infants to the centres. Another difficulty confronting the mothers is the inadequate number of childcare centres taking care of infants since not all centres provide infant care services. Non-working mothers, ineligible for the two types of subsidies, have been clamouring for some financial assistance. The government finally conceded in January 2002 when a subsidy of $75 per month was given to non-working mothers who enrol their children aged under 18 months or aged 18 months to below 7 years in childcare centres. Regardless of the type of subsidy, the government pays the money to the care centre, and the parents pay the difference between the subsidy they are entitled to and the full fee charged by the centre.

To overcome the shortage of care centres and the reluctance of some mothers to put their children in these centres, the Ministry of Community Development and Sports established the Family Day Care Service scheme for mothers with infant aged 2 to 18 months.[8] Under this scheme the mothers can approach ten childcare centres to matchmake nannies of their choice to take care of their children on a full-day basis in the home of the nannies. In most cases the parents have to take the children to the nanny's home. The nanny is paid about $500 to $625 per month, and the childcare centres are paid up to $30,000 to cover the administration and other expenses incurred in providing the nanny matchmaking services.

PUBLIC HOUSING

In Singapore about 90 per cent of the population live in apartments purchased from or rented from the Housing and Development Board (HDB). Some subsidized apartments are of course governed by a set of rules, including those concerning the sale of existing apartments to purchase bigger apartments. First of all, there was the rule that if the owners had stayed in the apartment for less than five years, they could not sell the apartments in the open market at usually a higher price, but had to sell it back to the HDB. There was another rule requiring the apartments to be sold back to HDB and not in the open market if they were the second or third apartments ever owned. As for the larger apartments that the owners wish to buy, the application would be placed in a queue to be processed on a first-come-first-served basis.

A new pronatalist incentive was implemented by the HDB on 4 April 1987 in respect of the sale of an existing apartment to purchase a bigger one.[9] The rules were altered to make it easier for families with a third child born on or after 1 January 1987 to sell their three-room or larger apartment and buy a bigger one. They can jump the queue by backdating their application by three years, thus enabling them to buy the bigger apartment sooner. Moreover, they can sell their existing apartment on the open market even if they had resided in it for less than the required five years, and even if their apartment is a second or third one. Though this liberalized policy applies to couples with a third child, the HDB will also consider, on its own merit, couples with a fourth child wishing to take advantage of the new policy. This new policy making it easier for HDB dwellers to upgrade to larger apartments was formulated to enable them to accommodate more children.

The HDB has also revised other rules to give some pronatalist incentives to couples staying in its apartments. The first change refers to rules concerning the third child. If the mother's first pregnancy results in twins, the child born in the second pregnancy will be treated as the third child. If the third pregnancy results in twins, the couple can still benefit from the new policy though they have four children. The second change concerns divorcees who remarry. The number of children they are given custody of will be counted in the application of the new policy.

The implementation date of the new policy was backdated to 1 January 1987, and the benefits will be restricted to existing children born during 1 January to 4 March 1987, children due to be born, and children from future pregnancies. HDB couples with existing children born before 1987 cannot benefit from the new policy. Finally, although they are not given any direct financial incentives from the HDB or the government, they can in fact gain financially by selling their existing apartment in the open market rather than being compelled to sell back to the HDB.

SPECIAL TAX REBATES

An important pronatalist measure was announced in the 1987 Budget Statement delivered by the Minister for Finance, Mr Richard Hu, in Parliament in March 1987.[10] This incentive refers to the granting of a special tax rebate from the 1988 Year of Assessment to couples who had their third child on or after 1 January 1987. In the following year, the rebate was extended to couples having their fourth child on or after 1 January 1988 to take effect from the 1989 Year of Assessment as declared by the Minister for Finance in Parliament in early 1988.[11] Finally, the rebate was extended to the second child born on or after 1 January 1990 on condition that the mother was below 31 years of age at the time of delivery.

The amount of tax rebate was fixed at $20,000 for the third or fourth child, but it varied according to the age of the mother in the case of the second child as shown below:

Age of Mother at Delivery Date	Amount of Rebate ($)
Below 28	20,000
Below 29	15,000
Below 30	10,000
Below 31	5,000

The purpose of varying the amount of tax rebate according to age was to help mothers to bear the second child as early as possible.

The special tax rebate for each qualifying child could be utilized within a period of nine years from the Year of Assessment following the year of birth of the qualifying child. The rebates for the second, third and fourth children may be claimed consecutively within a cumulative period of 27 years. The rebate could be utilized to set-off against either the husband's or wife's income tax liabilities, but the rebate in the husband's account could even be transferred to the wife's account, and vice versa. Another feature of the tax rebate scheme was that if the working wife had opted for separate assessment, she was entitled to a further tax rebate equivalent to 15 per cent of her earned income in lieu of maternity leave not made available to mothers giving birth to the third or fourth child.[12] However, this rebate could only be employed to offset the wife's tax liabilities. Her earned income was defined to include income received from trade, business, profession, vocation or employment.

There are of course certain conditions attached to the granting of the special tax rebates. Only legitimate children or stepchildren were eligible for the tax rebate, and adopted children did not qualify the parents for the rebate. All the children must be Singapore citizens at the time of birth or within 12 months after birth to ensure that only families committed to the country could benefit from this pronatalist incentive. If the qualifying child was given up for adoption or the marriage was dissolved by divorce, the tax rebate would cease from the Year of Assessment following the year of divorce. The impact of this pronatalist policy should be more extensive and lasting as almost all parents with two, three or four children were tax payers, and thus stand to gain from this financial incentive every year until the fourth child starts working years later. The special tax rebate was replaced by the parenthood tax relief with effect from the 2005 Year of Assessment.

A different kind of pronatalist incentive linked to personal income tax refers to medical expenses incurred in childbirth. With effect from 1 January 1988, delivery and hospital expenses for a fourth child can be offset against the earned income of the parents, subject to a maximum of $3,000. The tax structure is such that this incentive will benefit mostly parents earning $2,000 or more per month. But the implementation date of 1 January 1988 implies that parents with an existing fourth child or expecting a fourth child before 4 March 1987 cannot benefit from this new policy. The financial incentive is confined not only to future births, but to the fourth child only and not to the third child. The influence of this policy will probably be not so significant as the amount of financial gain is relatively small and receivable on a one-off basis.

CONCLUSION

The limited nature of the pronatalist policies would result in some additional births, but certainly not to the maximum as in the case of those with no restrictions at all. For one thing, the pronatalist benefits are not given to parents producing the fifth and subsequent children. It would appear that there still exists the concern that too many children are being produced by certain segments of the population. It is therefore not surprising that fertility has not been given the maximum possible boost and has continued to proceed well below replacement level.

Notes

1. *Straits Times*, 21 August 2000.
2. Ministry of Community Development and Sports, < www.babybonus.gov.sg >, 17 March 2001.

3. *Baby Bonus*, Ministry of Community Development and Sports, n.d.
4. *Business Times*, 29 August 2000.
5. *Straits Times*, 7 March 1987.
6. The details are given in a Ministry of Finance circular and published in the *Straits Times*, 7 March 1987.
7. *Business Times*, 29 August 2000.
8. *Straits Times*, 17 January 2004.
9. *Straits Times*, 4 April 1987.
10. *1987 Budget Statement*, Government Press Release, Ministry of Communications and Information, 1987.
11. *Straits Times*, 4 April 1987.
12. Inland Revenue Authority of Singapore, < www.iras.gov.sg >, 27 April 2001.

12

Strengthening Old Pronatalist Incentives

NEED FOR FURTHER CHANGE

We have observed that on the basis of the recommendations of the Inter-Ministerial Population Committee, the government implemented a wide range of incentive measures in 1987 aimed at encouraging women to produce more children. This was subsequently followed by a few pronatalist measures announced by the Prime Minister in the National Day Rally held in August 2000. The effectiveness of all the measures has not been very encouraging mainly because they were formulated to loosen some of the old antinatalist measures and to introduce some limited pronatalist measures. Furthermore, the socio-economic factors favouring small family norms have continued to exert a strong influence in prolonging the movement of low fertility below the replacement level.

In an attempt to evaluate the effectiveness of the above measures, one must take into account the influence of the Tiger Year and Dragon Year in the Chinese lunar calendar during the period under consideration. Viewed in terms of producing babies among the Chinese community, the Tiger Year in 1998 was an inauspicious year and the Dragon year in 2000 an auspicious year. This has resulted in some distortions in the annual movement of fertility during the period from 1997 onwards. The total fertility rate (TFR) was recorded as 1.68 in 1997 when the above measures were first implemented, and one would expect an increase to be registered the very next year. Instead, the TFR witnessed a pronounced decline of 8.3 per cent to 1.54 in the Tiger Year 1998, and remained at this level in the following year. The Dragon Year 2000 experienced a break in the fertility down trend when the TFR rose to 1.68. Despite the introduction of some pronatalist measures in 2000, the TFR resumed its downward movement in the next few years, falling to 1.48 in 2001, 1.45 in 2002, and 1.33 in 2003.

The government became extremely concerned about the continuous decline of the low fertility below the replacement level and the attendant fall in the number of births from 46,997 in 2000 to the record low of 37,485 in 2003. In presenting his Budget to Parliament on 22 February 2004, the then Deputy Prime Minister and Finance Minister, Mr Lee Hsien Loong, said:

> Our existing measures are not enough. We must take a more comprehensive approach to solving this problem. We must encourage young people to marry and marry earlier, and make it easier for young couples to start and raise a family... The approach must be both holistic and coherent, addressing parents' concerns from childbirth through the years of bringing up their children.[1]

In March 2004 the government established a Working Committee on Population with Mr Eddie Teo, Permanent Secretary to the Prime Minister's Office, as the chairman. Other members of the committee were the permanent secretaries of several ministries and chiefs of some statutory boards and government departments.[2] The Working Committee was required to submit its findings to a five-member Steering Group on Population chaired by Mr Lim Hng Kiang, Minister in the Prime Minister's Office. The other members of this group consisted of Dr Yacoob Ibrahim, Minister for Community Development and Sports, Dr Ng Eng Hen, Acting Minister for Manpower, and two Members of Parliament, Mrs Lim Hwee Hua and Dr Amy Khor.[3]

In formulating the new package of pronatalist measures, the Steering Group has benefited from extensive feedback from public e-mails, telephone calls, letters to the press, media stories, and tripartite consultation with employee and union representatives. By August 2004, the Steering Group was able to complete its deliberations and submitted its recommendations. The main features of the new package were made known by the new Prime Minister, Mr Lee Hsien Loong, in his National Day Rally held on 22 August 2004 (See Appendix E). More information was provided a few days later in a press conference held by the Steering Group with all five members engaged in a question-and-answer session. The details of the new package were given in a press release and also in the websites of relevant ministries, especially the Ministries of Community Development and Sports, of Manpower and of Health.

The new package of measures seeks to ease the burden, financial or otherwise, of parenthood in promoting marriage, facilitating conception, making childbirth more affordable, increasing childcare options, providing financial support to raising children, and encouraging a conducive work-life situation. Some of the measures constitute a further relaxation of old antinatalist policies as well as a further strengthening of the limited pronatalist policies implemented earlier. The more important point to note is that the new package also contains a wide range of new pronatalist measures, some of which constitute a radical departure from traditional beliefs and practices. A discussion of these new pronatalist measures will be presented in the next chapter, while the strengthening of the old pronatalist measures are examined in this chapter.

USE OF MEDISAVE

We have noted in Chapter 10 that the use of Medisave for medical expenses incurred in childbirth was extended from the first two children to the first three with effect from 1 March 1987. Under the new Medisave maternity package, the use of Medisave for maternity purposes has been extended to women giving birth to their fourth child on or after 1 August 2004. Another concession is that Medisave can be utilized for the pre-delivery and delivery medical expenses incurred by women giving birth to the fifth and subsequent child provided the parents have a combined Medisave balance of at least $15,000 at the time of delivery.[4] This minimum balance is necessary to prevent premature depletion of the Medisave accounts of the parents so that they would have sufficient funds for future hospitalization needs, particularly during their old age.

The Medisave maternity package has also been structured in such a manner as to assist couples with delivery expenses and pre-delivery medical expenses such as consultations and ultrasound. Under the new arrangement, parents are allowed to withdraw up to $450 more from their Medisave to pay for the delivery and pre-delivery medical expenses of the fourth birth born on or after 1 August 2004. This scheme can also be extended to similar expenses of the fifth and subsequent birth if the parent have a combined Medisave balance of $15,000 at the time of delivery. The reason for this minimum sum has been explained earlier.

Another liberalization of the use of Medisave concerns the current practice of allowing it to be used to pay for expenses arising from assisted conception procedures, subject to a withdrawal limit of $4,000 per treatment cycle up to a maximum of three treatment cycles. To increase the ability of couples to undergo this type of treatment, the withdrawal limit has been raised to $6,000, $5,000 and $4,000 for the first, second and third treatment cycles respectively. Couples undergoing treatment on or after 1 August 2004 can benefit from this revised limits since they can use more Medisave and thereby reduce their out-of-pocket payment. However, the use of Medisave for assisted conception procedures is still restricted to a maximum of three treatment cycles as the success rates tend to fall sharply after the third cycle. The restriction is meant to prevent a large increase in the number of claimable cycles from rapidly depleting the Medisave funds meant primarily for future use in old age.

EXTRA PAID MATERNITY LEAVE

One of the antinatalist policies implemented in the early seventies to discourage women from producing too many children was the amendment to the Employment Act to restrict paid maternity leave of eight weeks to the first two children. In April 2001 this maternity leave scheme was relaxed to allow women to take eight-week maternity leave when they give birth to the third child, but their normal salary during this period was paid by the government instead of their employer. The maternity leave scheme was further relaxed in 2004 by extending maternity leave to working women giving birth to their fourth child and, more importantly, by lengthening the leave period from eight weeks to twelve weeks for the first four births.[5] For the first two confinements, the employers would continue to pay for the eight-week maternity leave according to the Employment Act, and the government would pay for the extra four weeks subject to a maximum of $10,000. As for the third and fourth confinements, the government would fund the full twelve weeks with a cap of $30,000. The extra four weeks for the first and second birth and the full twelve weeks for the third and fourth birth are provided by an amendment of the Children Development Co-Savings Act enacted in Parliament on 21 September 2004. The amended Act also gives woman executives, managers, confidential staff, civil servants and statutory board employees the entitlement to the extended paid maternity leave.

In practice, the salary will continue to be paid to the mother by the employer for the duration of the extra maternity leave, and the employer will in turn claim reimbursement from the government. The employer is not required to pay above the capped amounts, though he can choose to do so voluntarily. The additional four weeks can be taken in a flexible manner over a period of six months from the birth of the child with the mutual agreement of the both the employee and employer. Otherwise, the four-week leave has to be consumed as a block immediately after the first eight weeks. The latest relaxation of maternity leave is aimed at encouraging working mothers to have more children by relieving some of their financial burden and by giving them more time to rest and take care of their newborn. Moreover, the option accorded to them to take the additional four weeks flexibly will give them more time to arrange for good infant care and ease back into the work-place.

In order to qualify for the government disimbursement through her employer under the enhanced maternity leave scheme, a female employee must fulfil the following requirements:

(a) Her child is a Singapore citizen at the time of birth, and must be born on or after 1 October 2004.
(b) She has not more than three children at the time of her confinement.
(c) She is lawfully married to the child's father at the time of child's conception or birth.
(d) She has worked for her employer for at least 180 days before the birth of the child.

Self-employed married women are also entitled to the government-paid maternity leave. In addition to satisfying requirements (a), (b) and (c), they must fulfil two other conditions. First, they must have been engaged in a particular business/trade/profession as their vocation for at least 180 days before the birth of the child. Second, they must have lost income as a result of not engaging in their trade, business, profession or vocation during the maternity leave period.

We have observed the ineligibility of adopted children to benefit from the mandatory eight-week paid maternity for the first two births under the Employment Act and from the government-paid third child maternity leave scheme discussed in Chapter 10. Similarly, adopted children do not qualify for the extra maternity leave scheme. As part of its pro-family gesture, the government decided to introduce a special scheme whereby it will fund up to four weeks of maternity leave for a mother who adopts a child on or after 1 August 2004 if the employer agrees to provide the leave on a voluntary basis. The funding is capped at $10,000, including CPF contributions, and the mother must satisfy the following conditions:

(a) She is married, widowed or divorced at the time of the child's adoption or naturalization.
(b) She must have fewer than four children, excluding adopted children and stepchildren.
(c) The adopted child is a Singapore citizen or becomes one at the time of adoption or naturalization.
(d) The adoption and naturalization process, where applicable, must be completed before the child reaches six months old.
(e) The leave is consumed before the child turns six months old.

According to the procedure put in place by the government, the female employee is required to submit a declaration form to her employer at least a week before she commences her maternity leave. She should reach an agreement beforehand with her employer regarding the manner in which she would like to take the extra leave. Her employer will make an initial check to ensure that she qualifies for the benefit and seek reimbursement from the government later. She would continue to receive her salary from her employer throughout her maternity leave as if she had been working without any break. The employer would submit a claim to the government for reimbursement after the employee has completed her extra four weeks of maternity leave for the first or second birth and twelve weeks for the third or fourth birth.

CPF TOP-UP GRANT FOR HDB APARTMENTS

Apart from the further relaxation of the above two earlier antinatalist measures, the government strengthened some of the limited pronatalist measures discussed in the previous chapter. We have noted a minor relaxation of the method of downpayment for the purchase of an apartment for first-time couples with effect from 28 August 2000. The use of subsidized public housing to promote marriage among young Singaporeans was reinforced in August 2004 with the introduction of the CPF housing top-up grant scheme. Under this scheme, a married couple can apply to top up the singles grant to family grant for the present apartment they wish to retain as their matrimonial apartment. As for the purchase of another resale apartment, they receive a top-up grant equivalent to the difference between the current family grant of $30,000 for their existing apartment or $40,000 for a resale apartment and the singles grant they have already received.

Under the singles grant scheme, the grant can be employed to pay the downpayment, and if there is any balance left, it must be employed to reduce the mortgage loan. The singles grant cannot be used to offset the cash payment where the declared resale price exceeds the market valuation. To qualify for the singles grant scheme, the applicant must be a Singapore citizen, at least 35 years old and a single person who is unmarried, divorced or widowed.[6] The gross monthly household income must not exceed $3,000, and the applicant can only purchase up to a five-room apartment.

With the introduction of the CPF top-up grant scheme, an apartment owner who had received the singles grant earlier can apply to top up the singles grant to a family grant for the current flat to be retained as a matrimonial apartment. The top-up grant can be used for lump-sum repayment or full redemption of the mortgage loan, but cannot be employed to pay the monthly instalments. If the top-up grant exceeds the outstanding mortgage loan, the applicant and the spouse can decide on the amount to be deducted from the respective amount each will receive to redeem the loan. If the top-up grant is more than enough to discharge the mortgage loan, the balance will be deposited into the applicant's or the spouse's CPF account. This unused amount of top-up grant can be used to purchase another HDB apartment in the future, or it can remain as part of the CPF money available for withdrawal under the CPF rules when the applicant or the spouse reaches 55 years of age.

The CPF top-up grant can also be employed to purchase another resale apartment with the spouse. The top-up grant derived from the difference between the singles grant and family grant will be deposited into the applicant's CPF account or the spouse's account, or both their accounts according to the approved proportions. The top-up grant can be used to pay the downpayment of the resale flat if the applicant does not have sufficient CPF savings. Any balance left must be utilized to reduce the mortgage loan. The top-up grant must not be used to offset the cash payment where the resale price exceeds the market valuation. If the applicant is purchasing a resale flat with a bank loan, the top-up grant will be treated as part of the applicant's or the spouse's CPF fund, which can be employed to pay for the CPF portion of the downpayment, but not the cash portion, or to reduce the mortgage loan.

EXTENDING BABY BONUS TO FIRST AND FOURTH CHILD

The previous chapter discussed the introduction of a limited pronatalist measure in April 2000 in the form of a baby bonus for the second and third child. To lighten further the financial burden of raising children, the baby bonus scheme was extended to the first and fourth child born on or after 1 August 2004. Under the enhanced baby bonus scheme, the cash gift that parents can receive from the government amounts to $3,000 each for the first and second child, and $6,000 each for the third and fourth child. In addition, the co-savings arrangement will enable the parents to receive a maximum of $6,000 for the second child and a maximum of $12,000 for each of the third and fourth child from the government.[7] The co-savings arrangement does not apply to the first child. On the whole, the parents can expect to receive from the government a maximum sum of $3,000 for the first child, $9,000 for the second child, and $18,000 each for the third and fourth child.

In the 2000 baby bonus scheme, the cash gift from the government was paid to the parents in six annual instalments over a period of six years. As of 2004, the cash gift is now given out earlier in five equal instalments over a shorter period of eighteen months from the birth of the child so that the parents can choose to use the cash for more immediate expenses consequent on the newborn. The cash gift for each entitled child is given within three weeks after the mother joins the scheme, and the subsequent cash contributions are provided when the child reaches six, twelve and eighteen months of age (see Table 12.1). The cash gift is deposited directly into the nominated bank account of the parents.

TABLE 12.1
Cash Gift Schedule

Age of Child	Birth Order	
	First & Second	Third & Fourth
Within 3 weeks after joining the scheme	$750	$1,500
6 months	$750	$1,500
12 months	$750	$1,500
18 months	$750	$1,500
Total	$3,000	$6,000

The co-savings to be contributed by both the parents and the government are deposited in a special savings account opened for the child at any Post Office Savings Bank (POSB) branch. This account, also known as the Children Development Account, recognizes that the primary responsibility for providing for the child rests with the parents. The government will match dollar-for-dollar the amount of savings the parents contribute to their child's account. There are six co-savings periods, with the first period beginning with the opening of the account and ending on the last day the month before the child's first birthday. Subsequent co-savings periods are of one year each and start from the child's month of birth. For each co-savings period, the parent's savings would be matched in the child's month of birth up to a maximum of $1,000 for the second child, and $2,000 for the third and fourth child (see Table 12.2). As mentioned earlier, there is no co-savings arrangement for the first child. The funds in the account may be employed to pay the fees of approved childcare centres, kindergartens and special schools. The funds can be used by all their children attending the approved institutions.

For a child to qualify for the baby bonus scheme, the following conditions must be fulfilled:

(a) born on or after 1 August 2004;
(b) is a Singapore citizen or becomes a Singapore citizen;
(c) is the first to fourth child born alive to the mother;
(d) the mother is lawfully married to the child's father at the time of the child's birth or conception.

TABLE 12.2
Government Matching in Co-Savings Schedule

Age of Child (in years)	Birth Order	
	Second	Third & Fourth
1	Up to $1,000	Up to $2,000
2	Up to $1,000	Up to $2,000
3	Up to $1,000	Up to $2,000
4	Up to $1,000	Up to $2,000
5	Up to $1,000	Up to $2,000
6	Up to $1,000	Up to $2,000
Total	Up to $6,000	Up to $12,000

An adopted child is also eligible for the baby bonus scheme if the adoption occurred on or after 1 August 2004. Furthermore, the adopted child must be less than six years old on or after 1 August 2004, a Singaporean citizen, and the first and fourth child of the adoptive mother, divorcee or widower. Regardless of whether the child is adopted or the natural child of the mother, stepchildren and children who are not Singapore citizens are not considered in the counting of birth order.

INCREASED INFANT CARE SUBSIDY

It may be recalled that the government has been providing a subsidy of $150 through childcare centres to working mothers who put an infant aged two months to below eighteen months or a child aged eighteen months to less than seven years in a care centre. But the fee charged by the centre is very much higher for the infant than for the child. As part of the overall package of pronatalist incentives, the government increased with effect from 1 August 2004 the monthly subsidy for infant care from $150 to $400. This subsidy is available to an infant aged two months to below eighteen months who is a Singapore citizen and belonging to the birth order from first to fourth.[8] This increased subsidy makes it more affordable and easier for working mothers to take care of their children by enrolling their infant in infant care programmes in licensed care centres.

TABLE 12.3
Infant Care Monthly Subsidy Rates

Programme (Daily Care)	Working Mother	Non-working Mother
Full-day Care	$400	$75
Half-day Care	$200	$75
Flexible Programme Number of Hours Per Week	**Working Mother**	**Non-working Mother**
12 hours to 24 hours	$100	$25
Above 24 hours to 36 hours	$200	$50
Above 36 hours to 48 hours	$300	$75
Above 48 hours	$400	$75

The increased infant care subsidy is also available on a pro-rated basis for infants receiving less than a full-day care as shown in Table 12.3. It is to be noted that the subsidy has remained at $75 per full-day or half-day for non-working mothers. Single fathers who are divorced or widowed are also entitled to the infant care subsidy. The monthly subsidy according to the schedule shown in Table 12.3 is paid by the government to the care centre which will collect from the parent the subsidized fee equivalent to the difference between the full-fee and the government subsidy.

PARENTHOOD TAX RELIEF

One of the limited pronatalist measures discussed in the previous chapter refers to the special tax rebate which amounted to $20,000 for the third or the fourth child, and $5,000 to $20,000 for the second child of the mother depending on the age of the mother. This special tax rebate had been replaced by a more liberal parenthood tax rebate with effect from the 2005 Year of Assessment.[9] As compared to the special tax rebate, the parenthood tax rebate has been liberalized in the following manner:

1. It does not have an age requirement for the mother to claim rebate for the second child as in the special tax rebate.
2. It has no time limit of nine years for claiming the rebate as in the special tax rebate. It can be claimed any time until the rebate is fully utilized.
3. It does not require the child's elder siblings to be Singapore citizens as in the special tax rebate.

The new tax rebate system will provide parents with greater financial support for raising their children.

To qualify for the parenthood tax rebate, the mother must be legally married to the child's father, and the child must be a Singapore citizen at the time of birth or become one within twelve months thereafter. An adopted child is also entitled to the rebate, but must be legally adopted, a Singapore citizen at the time of adoption or become one within twelve months thereafter. However, the rebate is made available to a legitimate second, third or fourth child born to the family on or after 1 January 2004 or to a second child or fourth child legally adopted on or after 1 January 2004 while the claimant is married, divorced or widowed. The birth order of the children is based on the date of birth or the date of legal adoption in the case of adopted children. This means that an adopted child will be considered as the second child in the family even though the first child born to the family is younger.

The amount of rebates for the second, third and fourth child under the parenthood tax rebate as compared to that provided under the old special tax rebate is presented in Table 12.4. The amount of rebate can be used by either parents or shared between parents in their filing of the income tax returns. Any unutilized rebate balance can be carried forward to future assessments until such time as the rebate is fully utilized. It is important to note that the parenthood tax rebate is only available to parents producing their second, third and fourth child. There is therefore no financial support under this scheme provided by the government to couples producing the first or fifth child and subsequent child. In this sense, the liberalized parenthood tax rebate is still considered as a limited type of pronatalist policy.

TABLE 12.4
Comparison of Rebates Under the Old and New Schemes

Birth Order	Parenthood Tax Rebate	Special Tax Rebate	
			Mother's Age
Second	$10,000	$20,000	Below 28
		$20,000	Below 29
		$20,000	Below 30
		$20,000	Below 31
Third	$20,000	$20,000	
Fourth	$20,000	$20,000	

WORKING MOTHER'S CHILD RELIEF

The previous chapter observed the numerous changes made to the enhanced child relief and the special tax rebate which were designed to provide some financial assistance for working women with children to support. These two schemes were replaced by the working mother's child relief with effect from the 2005 Year of Assessment.[10] This new relief scheme still retains the original twofold aim of providing some financial support to working women to produce more children and to rejoin or continue to be part of the work-force after childbirth.

The quantum of tax relief given to working mothers varies according to the birth order of the child as shown below:

Birth Order	Percentage of Mother's Earned Income
First Child	5 per cent
Second Child	15 per cent
Third Child	20 per cent
Fourth Child	25 per cent

The total amount of relief for each child is capped at $25,000. Working women who are married women, divorcees or widows with children qualify for the relief. Unlike the parenthood tax relief, the working mother's child relief cannot be shared by the husband since it is specifically meant for working women.

A married, divorced or widowed working woman can claim the relief if the child is:

1. unmarried;
2. a Singapore citizen as at the end of the year preceding the Year of Assessment of claim;
3. the claimant's legitimate child, stepchild or legally adopted child;
4. below the age of sixteen or receiving full-time education at any educational institution or is handicapped; and
5. is not receiving an annual income of more than $2,000 in that year.

Working women producing or adopting a fifth and subsequent child are not eligible for the working mother's child relief which is therefore only a limited type of pronatalist measure.

Notes

1. Lee Hsien Loong, *Budget Statement 2004* (Singapore Government Press Release, Ministry of Finance, 2004).
2. *Straits Times*, 18 March 2004.
3. Ibid.
4. Ministry of Health, <www.moh.gov.sg> 5 October 2004.
5. Ministry of Manpower, <www.mom.gov.sg> 5 October 2004.
6. *Streats*, 1 September 2004.

7. Ministry of Community Development, Youth and Sport, <www.babybonus.gov.sg> 5 October 2004.

8. Ministry of Community Development, Youth and Sport, <www.childcarelink.gov.sg> 6 October 2004.

9. Inland Revenue Authority of Singapore, <www.iras.gov.sg> 10 October 2004.

10. Ibid.

13

Introducing New Pronatalist Incentives

The package of pronatalist incentives implemented soon after the National Day Rally held in August 2004 can be separated into two broad groups. As noted in the previous chapter, the first group consists of incentives designed to implement some changes to the measures introduced in the past so as to make them stronger and more effective. The second group contains entirely new measures that were quite essential for preventing any further deterioration of the exceedingly low level of fertility prevailing at the time. The formulation of the overall package in terms of financial and non-financial incentives was in fact viewed by the government as a "holistic and coherent approach" towards creating a more congenial environment for couples to produce and raise children in Singapore.

TWO-DAY CHILDCARE LEAVE

One of the new pronatalist incentives introduced in 2004 is the two days of statutory childcare leave granted to each working parent provided by an amendment to the Employment Act passed in Parliament on 21 September 2004.[1] With effect from 1 October 2004, parents are entitled to take two days per year of this statutory employer-paid leave if they have at least a child under seven years of age. The leave is granted on the basis of per parent and not per child, i.e. each parent can only take two days in a year even if there are more than one child under seven years old in the family. However, parents have full flexibility to use this leave to spend time with their children for whatever purpose since it is not predicated on other conditions such as illness of the child. As part of the overall package of measures to support parenthood, the childcare leave somewhat allows working parents to take time off to care for their children without any loss of income and to achieve a more harmonious work-life environment.

The childcare leave is also made available to working parents with any stepchildren or legally adopted child below age seven.[2] The parents can be single, divorced or widowed, and they can be regular employees, fixed-term contract workers, or temporary or part-time employees. The important condition is that they must have worked for a period of no less than three months. Foreign workers are eligible for the childcare leave as long as they are covered under the Employment Act and meet the above requirements. In fact, foreign employees can take the childcare leave together with their annual leave to go back to their home countries to spend time with their children. Employees are required to submit an application to their employer and it can be refused if the employer believes that the leave will be used for purposes other than taking care of their children.

LOWER MAID LEVY

Faced with the non-availability of Singaporeans to work as domestic maids in private homes, families have to employ foreign maids from neighbouring countries. To control the total number of foreign maids working in Singapore, the government requires families to pay a monthly maid levy of $345 per foreign maid in addition to the salary that has to be paid to the maid. As part of the package of new pronatalist measures, the government reduced the monthly foreign domestic maid levy to $250 for families with children aged less than twelve years of age, or with elderly person aged sixty-five and above.[3] This maid levy concession will make the employment of foreign maids more affordable for families who need help in providing full-time domestic care for young children or elderly persons at home.

With effect from 1 August 2004, an employer is eligible for a lower levy rate per month for each foreign domestic worker if any one of the following conditions is fulfilled:

(a) the employer or spouse has a child below the age of twelve years who is a Singapore citizen staying in the same household as the employer; or

(b) the employer or co-residing spouse is a Singapore citizen aged sixty-five years or above; or

(c) the employer has a parent, parent-in-law, grandparent or grandparent-in-law aged sixty-five years or above who is a Singapore citizen staying in the same household as the employer.

The employer is eligible for levy concession for up to a maximum of two foreign domestic maids at any one time subject to the conditions being met. It should be mentioned that employers need not be working in order to qualify for the lower maid levy, but the need for maids would be greater in families with both parents working.

GRANDPARENT CARE-GIVER RELIEF

It is not unusual for grandparents to help in taking care of grandchildren, especially when both parents are working. A new pronatalist measure was announced in August 2004 to recognize the important role played by grandparents in childcare by implementing a grandparent caregiver relief of $3,000 for working mothers to claim this relief from the 2005 Year of Assessment if their parents or parents-in-law look after their children aged not more than twelve years. A working mother, whether married, divorced or widowed, can claim the relief if she satisfies the following conditions:[4]

1. Her parent or parent-in-law taking care of children must not be working as an employee or self-employed person receiving income during the Year of Assessment claim.
2. The parent or parent-in-law must be staying in Singapore.
3. The child must be a Singapore citizen aged twelve years or younger.
4. The child must be a legitimate child, stepchild or legally adopted child.
5. The claimant is the only person claiming the relief in respect of one particular parent or parent-in-law.

Once the claimant applies for the relief on the basis that her mother is taking care of her children, her siblings cannot submit another claim even though her mother has been taking care of her nephews and nieces. If her mother takes care of her children and her father takes care of her sister's children, both she and her sister are entitled to submit a claim each. Her husband is not allowed to share the relief in his income tax submission since it is meant for working mothers. She can claim the grandparent care-giver relief in respect of her mother in addition to the parent relief because they are for different objectives. Furthermore, if she has a domestic maid in addition to her mother to care for her children, she can claim both the lower foreign maid levy as well as the grandparent care-giver relief.

FIVE-DAY WORKING WEEK

One of the major issues confronting working parents with young children is the difficulty of having more time to spend with their children during the weekend when they are required to work more than five days a week. The clamour for a five-day working week in the civil service was frequent, but the government had always refused to accede to this request. In the meantime, a few government departments and statutory boards implemented their own alternate-week system where employees took an alternate Saturday off, with business as usual on Saturdays manned by about half the staff strength. For the private sector there is a wider variety of working week practices adopted in the different sectors of the economy as determined by the nature of the business of each company. A clear picture of private sector practice can be gleamed from the results of a survey on conditions of employment conducted by the Ministry of Manpower in June 2002.[5]

A summary of the survey results presented in Table 13.1 reveals some 37.5 per cent of the employees in the private sector observed the five-day working week as compared to 17.1 per cent with a six-day working week and 15.7 per cent with 5½-day week. The five-day working week was extremely prevalent in the financial serviced industry with close to two-thirds (64 per cent) of the employees working a five-day week. This shorter working week was also observed by most of the employees in business and real-estate services (48.3 per cent), manufacturing (46.9 per cent) and wholesale and retail trade (46.3 per cent). Another type of shorter working week practised by some companies refers to employees working 5½ days in certain weeks and five days in other weeks so that these companies can still remain open for business on Saturdays. This was quite noticeable in the community and personal services (23.1 per cent), transport and communications (20.3 per cent), and financial services (18.2 per cent).

In June 2003, the Remaking Singapore Committee recommended, among other things, the adoption of a five-day working week in the civil service.[6] This recommendation was promptly rejected by the government,

TABLE 13.1

Percentage Distribution of Full-Time Employees by Type of Work, Week Pattern and Industry, 2002

Industry	5-Day	5½-Day	6-Day	5½-Day with some Saturday Off	6-Day with some Saturday Off	Others
Manufacturing	46.9	17.3	6.8	4.8	1.8	22.4
Construction	6.7	24.5	56.2	7.0	3.6	2.0
Services	40.1	12.2	12.9	15.6	1.5	17.7
Wholesale & Retail Trade	46.3	13.6	11.1	11.8	2.3	14.9
Hotels & Restaurants	6.0	6.7	37.3	5.7	1.6	42.6
Transport & Communications	33.0	15.7	5.3	20.3	0.4	25.3
Financial Services	64.4	1.0	0.3	18.2	0.9	15.3
Business and Real-Estate Services	48.3	13.5	17.1	12.7	0.9	7.5
Community and Personal Services	21.8	17.1	18.3	23.1	2.7	17.1
Total	37.5	15.7	17.1	10.8	1.9	17.0

but was subsequently handed over to the Steering Group on Population for further consideration. In a surprise move, a shift from a 5½-day working week to a five-day week in the civil service was presented as one of the new pronatalist incentive in August 2004 to arrest the declining low fertility. This break from an ancient practice was reported in the press as the slaughter of a sacred cow.[7] Clearly, the government has come to the inescapable conclusion that a shorter working week is badly needed to give parents a longer weekend to spend more time with their children.

Under the new five-day working week system, the total number of hours clocked in by an employee during the shortened week has still remained at forty-two hours. What it means is that the hours previously observed on Saturdays are now redistributed and collapsed into the five-day week with longer hours from Monday to Friday. An important requirement of the system is the continued opening of public counters and essential services on Saturdays by certain departments or sections within a department. It is not necessary to adhere to a common pattern of working hours during the five-day week, and government departments and statutory boards are presented with a choice of five patterns of working hours to select in accordance with their own needs, but benefiting most of their employees (see Table 13.2).[8]

TABLE 13.2
Pattern of Working Hours for Five-Day Week

1.	Monday to Thursday	7.30 am to 5.00 pm
	Friday	7.30 am to 4.30 pm
2.	Monday to Thursday	8.00 am to 5.30 pm
	Friday	8.00 am to 5.00 pm
3.	Monday to Thursday	8.30 am to 6.00 pm
	Friday	8.30 am to 5.30 pm
4.	Monday to Thursday	9.00 am to 6.30 pm
	Friday	9.00 am to 6.00 pm
5.	Monday to Thursday	9.30 am to 7.00 pm
	Friday	9.30 am to 6.30 pm

EQUAL MEDICAL BENEFITS

One of the archaic terms of employment in the public sector has been the unequal medical benefits for the two sexes. A female civil servant was not entitled to claim medical benefits for her husband and children, regardless of whether her husband was employed as a civil servant. There were constant calls to abolish this unequal treatment, but the government had refused to change this policy. More recently, this issue was revived in the Remaking Singapore Committee and its recommendation for providing equal medical benefits in the civil service was submitted to the Steering Group on Population for consideration.[9]

Recognizing the importance of adopting a comprehensive approach to the problem of solving the current baby shortage, the government finally decided to slaughter another sacred cow by giving equal medical benefits to female civil servants as part of the total package of pronatalist incentives offered in August 2004. With this change, female employees are allowed to claim medical benefits for their husbands and unmarried children under the age of eighteen with effect from 1 January 2005.[10] It is hoped that this change will facilitate greater sharing of care-giving responsibilities between married couples and keep pace with the increasing tendency for women to play a greater role in supporting their families. This is in line with the new policy of promoting a more pro-family work environment and a better work-life balance in the public sector.

WORK-LIFE WORKS! FUND

We have observed in the early years that an increase in the female labour force participation rate has been a significant factor in influencing the rapid decline in fertility. The difficulty faced by married workers in trying to maintain a satisfactory balance between work and family life will continue to assert a strong influence on fertility even when it falls below the replacement level. A conducive work-life environment will also benefit businesses since workers in a better position to care for their families tend to be more committed and engaged at the work-place, thus enhancing the performance of companies. A good work-life strategy will enable companies to attract and sustain talented staff. In order to assist companies develop an effective work-life strategy at the workplace, the Ministry of Manpower established a $10 million WOW! (Work-Life Works!) Fund in September 2004.[11]

All private sector organizations, including non-profit organizations, can apply for grants from the fund to defray the cost of introducing measures that can help employees to better achieve work-life harmony. The government will co-fund up to 70 per cent of the costs incurred for approved projects, subject to a cap of $30,000 per project per organization. The subsidy will help to mitigate the upfront costs of introducing a work-life strategy at the work-place, and hence spread the long-run benefits to more organizations. Prior approval must be obtained by the organizations before starting the work-life project which must be completed within a year. The grant will be disbursed in two instalments, the first 30 per cent for approved items after the approval of the project and the remaining 70 per cent after the completion of the project.

The WOW! Fund can be utilized for the following purposes:

1. Training of human resource (HR) managers and line supervisors on work-life implementation, including training to develop good HR management systems.
2. On a case-by-case basis, one-time infrastructural costs in implementing flexible work arrangements and selected employee support schemes that contribute towards care of dependants.
3. Engaging a qualified work-life consultant.
4. Employing or deploying staff dedicated to drive work-life implementation within the organization.

In evaluating proposals from organizations, greater priority will be given to projects aimed at introducing flexible work arrangements which are deemed to have long-term benefits in facilitating work-life harmony. This pro-family stance constitutes an integral part of the package of pronatalist measures meant to create a better environment for working women to produce and raise children.

OVERVIEW OF 2004 MEASURES

The 2004 package of pronatalist measures is by far the most comprehensive, offering a wide range of financial as well as non-financial incentives. It seeks to address, among others, three key issues that were raised through public debates and tripartite feedback from workers and their employers. Firstly, the new measures have sought to meet the concerns of parents in having larger families. The measures will give parents an opportunity to spend more time with their children, pursue a range of childcare options, and strike a better balance between work and family life. Secondly, as compared with previous ones, the new measures contain fewer conditions with the removal of mother's age and education as qualifying criteria for any of the measures. Thirdly, the new measures have provided parents greater flexibility in supporting the variety of choices that they make because of their differing circumstances, i.e. a wider range of childcare arrangements. A rough estimate of the cost of the new package to the government stood at about $300 million per year, bringing the total annual expenditure on pro-family measures to about $800 million.[12]

The general public has shown keen interest in the new package, seeking clarification on many issues and voicing their views in letters to the media, the Steering Group on Population and the Prime Minister. There were also numerous calls to the Parenthood hotline and e-mails to the Parenthood website. Public feedback on the new package has been positive, with many Singaporeans expressing satisfaction and strong support.[13] Responding to concerns that some families may become worse off with the new package, the Steering Group pointed out that the government has put in place some transitional arrangements to ensure that no Singaporean will be worse off under the new package. On whether some parents, such as stay-at-home mothers and employees not covered by the Employment Act, might not benefit at all, the Steering Group gave an assurance that the package will benefit most families. Responding to calls that the 1 August 2004 implementation date of some schemes be pushed back to encompass more families, the Steering Group emphasized that even parents with children from before this date will receive some benefits from the new schemes, such as childcare leave, infant care subsidy, lower foreign maid levy, and revised tax breaks.

It was mentioned that the pronatalist measures implemented in 2004 would benefit a larger group of families with the removal of age of mother, education of mother and income of parents as criteria qualifying for the measures. However, there is still scope for more babies to be produced if we allow these measures to be made available to all children and not only those up to the fourth order as in the extra paid maternity leave, baby bonus, parenthood tax relief and working mother's child relief. In this respect, the recently-introduced incentives may still be regarded as a limited kind of pronatalist policies, unlike those adopted in many European countries confronted with the same problem of below-replacement fertility.

TABLE 13.3

Distribution of Births by Birth Order, 2000–03

Birth Order	Number				Percentage			
	2000	2001	2002	2003	2000	2001	2002	2003
1st	19,930	17,595	17,524	16,434	42.4	42.4	43.0	43.7
2nd	16,948	14,501	14,873	13,548	36.1	35.0	36.5	36.0
3rd	7,164	6,651	6,009	5,515	15.2	16.0	14.7	14.7
4th	2,134	1,909	1,674	1,505	4.5	4.6	4.1	4.0
5th	557	524	446	421	1.2	1.3	1.1	1.1
6th & above	260	266	230	207	0.6	0.6	0.6	0.6
Total	46,997	41,451	40,760	37,633	100.0	100.0	100.0	100.0

The distribution of births according to birth order is presented in Table 13.3.[14] The number of births pertaining to the fifth and subsequent order amounted to 817 (1.8 per cent) in 2000, 790 (1.9 per cent) in 2001, 676 (1.7 percent) in 2002, and 628 (1.7 per cent) in 2003. It would make more sense to widen the eligibility of the incentives to all children since the proportion belonging to births for the fifth and subsequent order is very small. There would be savings in money and manpower in the administration of the measures if they are made available to all children regardless of birth order. Moreover, children who are of the fifth and subsequent order would not feel discriminated against and unwanted. The important consideration is that they do contribute to the national population number.

In the late eighties the Inter-Ministerial Population Committee was disbanded once it had completed its task and submitted its recommendations to the government. After the implementation of the latest package of pro-family measures in 2004, both the Working Committee on Population and the Steering Group on Population remain in existence, with some minor changes in the membership. Mr Eddie Teo continues to be the chairman of the former committee, while Mr Wong Kan Seng, Minister for Home Affairs and Deputy Prime Minister, has taken over the chairmanship of the latter from Mr Lim Hng Kiang. The government has also appointed Mr Wong to be in overall charge of population matters. He said that his role as minister-in-charge of population issues is to "review the government's population and demographic objectives, and chart new directions for a comprehensive approach to these population challenges".[15] This is an improvement over the position in the late nineties when no Minister or committee was designated to look after national population affairs.

Notes

1. *Straits Times*, 22 September 2004.
2. Ministry of Manpower, <www.mom.gov.sg>, 5 October 2004.
3. Ibid.
4. Inland Revenue Authority of Singapore, <www.iras.gov.sg>, 25 August 2004.
5. Ministry of Manpower, *Conditions of Employment 2002*, Occasional Paper, 10 January 2003.
6. *Straits Times*, 23 August 2004.
7. *The Newpaper*, 24 August 2004.
8. Public Service Division, Prime Minister's Office, PMO (PSD) Circular No. 15/2004, 25 August 2004.
9. *Straits Times*, 23 August 2004.
10. Public Service Division, Prime Minister's Office, Press Release on "Civil Service Moves Ahead with Changes to Promote a Pro-Family Environment and Better Work-Life Balance for Civil Servants", 25 August 2004.
11. Ministry of Manpower, "When You Need to Balance Work and Family", *Sunday Times*, 5 September 2004.
12. *Business Times*, 26 August 2004.
13. Press Release on "Strong Support for Baby Package". <http://fed.citizen. gov.sg>, 7 September 2004.
14. *Yearbook of Statistics Singapore 2004* (Singapore: Department of Statistics, June 2004).
15. *Business Times*, 4–5 September 2004.

14

Prolonged Below-Replacement Fertility

INTRODUCTION

This chapter examines the salient features of fertility movement below the level of replacement during a span of some thirty years since 1975. In studying this long-term trend we should bear in mind three broad groups of factors that can affect the level of fertility in Singapore. Firstly, there are the important social and economic factors that will always continue to assert a strong influence on the level of fertility. Secondly, there are the government policies and programmes that were introduced to change the course of fertility. Thirdly, there is the special influence of the Tiger Year and the Dragon Year in the twelve-animal zodiac signs in the Chinese lunar calendar.[1] Needless to say, the 2004 package of pronatalist measures will only have an impact on the level of fertility from late 2005 onwards.

The analysis of fertility trend will be carried out in terms of the total fertility rate (TFR), the computation of which requires some explanation. The base female population used in the computation is derived from the distribution of the female resident population rather than the total female population, classified by five-year age groups from age 15 to 49. This is because figures for the intercensal and postcensal years are only available for the resident population. Furthermore, the figures for the female resident population for the years 1991–99 are obtained from the revised estimates prepared after the 1990 Census.[2] Another point to note is that the distribution of births by five-year age group of mothers from age 15 to 49 refers to births borne by the total female population and not by the female resident population. Birth statistics for the latter only are not available.[3]

FERTILITY TRENDS BELOW REPLACEMENT LEVEL

After the unprecedented decline during the years up to 1975, the overall fertility in Singapore has continued to proceed downwards below the replacement level.[4] The figures reveal that from the slightly below-replacement level of 2.08 in 1975, the total fertility rate edged up to 2.11 in the very next year but after that it moved down continuously to touch the low of 1.42 in 1986. Thereafter, the rate fluctuated somewhat but — on account of the influence of the Tiger and Dragon Years in the Chinese calendar and the effect of the population policy changes — was still below the replacement level.

The sharp drop of 12.3 per cent in the total fertility rate in 1986 coincided with the inauspicious Tiger Year for Chinese couples with respect to producing babies. Bearing in mind this unique influence in 1986, it is not surprising that the recovery was immediate in the following year when the rate moved up by 15.5 per cent to the level of 1.64. The great upsurge of 20.7 per cent, which brought the rate to the high of 1.98 in 1988, was caused by the relaxation of some old antinatalist measures and the introduction of some limited pro-natalist measures in early 1987. However, the upsurge was also partly due to 1988 coinciding with the auspicious Dragon Year for Chinese births. As the rush to take advantage of the new incentives, financial or otherwise, diminished and the influence of the Dragon Year ran its course, the total fertility rate fell again by about 9.6 per cent to 1.79 in 1989.

The next two years witnessed less violent fluctuations in the total fertility rate because other animals in the Chinese zodiac calendar have no influence on the Chinese in terms of producing babies.[5] In 1990, the rate was raised by 5.0 per cent to 1.88, but the rise may be attributed partly to the utilization of the female resident population, instead of the female total population, to calculate the total fertility rate for 1990 and the years that followed. In the following year, the rate was lowered by 5.3 per cent to 1.78 and remained at about this level until 1997 when it fell again to the low of 1.68 in 1997. The important point is that the 1987 policy changes arrested the downward trend in fertility for a few years only but as of 2003 had not succeeded in pushing it back to the replacement level of 2.15 (see Table 14.1).

The Tiger Year in 1998 witnessed a steep drop of 8.3 per cent in the total fertility rate to the low of 1.54, notwithstanding the introduction of some pronatalist incentives in the previous year. As the postponed births began to be born and as the incentives commenced to exert some

TABLE 14.1

Annual Births and Total Fetility Rate, 1975–2003

Year	Number of Births	Total Fertility Rate	Annual Changes (%)	
			Birth	TFR
1975	39,948	2.08	—	—
1976	42,783	2.11	+7.1	+1.4
1977	38,369	1.82	−10.3	−13.7
1978	39,441	1.80	+2.8	−1.1
1979	40,778	1.79	+3.4	−0.6
1980	41,219	1.74	+1.1	−2.8
1981	42,250	1.72	+2.5	−1.1
1982	42,654	1.71	+1.0	−0.6
1983	40,585	1.59	−4.9	−7.0
1984	41,556	1.61	+2.4	+1.3
1985	42,484	1.62	+2.2	+0.6
1986	38,379	1.42	−9.7	−12.3
1987	43,616	1.64	+13.6	+15.5
1988	52,957	1.98	+21.4	+20.7
1989	47,669	1.79	−10.0	−9.6
1990	51,142	1.88	+7.3	+5.0
1991	49,114	1.78	−4.0	−5.3
1992	49,402	1.77	+0.6	−0.6
1993	50,225	1.79	+1.7	+1.1
1994	49,554	1.76	−1.3	−1.7
1995	48,635	1.73	−1.9	−1.7
1996	48,577	1.73	−0.1	0.0
1997	47,333	1.68	−2.1	−2.9
1998	43,669	1.54	−7.8	−8.3
1999	46,336	1.55	−0.8	+0.6
2000	46,997	1.68	+7.8	+9.1
2001	41,451	1.48	−11.8	−11.9
2002	40,760	1.45	−1.7	−0.2
2003	37,485	1.33	−7.9	−8.3

FIGURE 14.1
Annual Births and Total Fertility Rate, 1970–2003

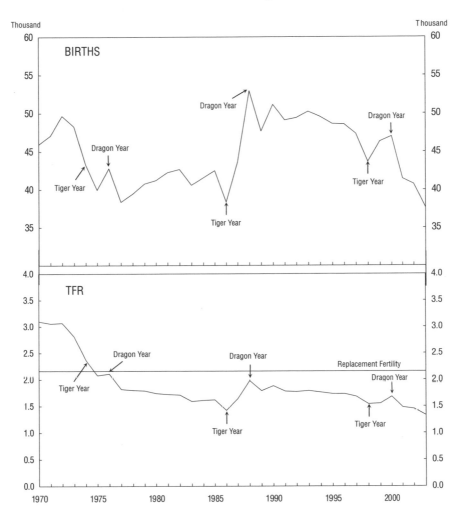

influence, fertility immediately stopped falling and edged up slightly to 1.55 in 1999. In the previous Tiger Year 1986, there was also a perceptible dip in fertility along the trend line, falling by 12.3 per cent in that inauspicious year.

The year 2000 is quite unique viewed in terms of favourable factors influencing the reproductive behaviour of the population. Among the more important factors are the desire for Dragon babies among some Chinese couples, the thrill of having new millennium babies, and the continuous influence of the 1987 pronatalist incentives. The increase in births was not as spectacular as one would expect since fertility was pushed up by only 9.1 per cent in 2000 as against the corresponding result of 20.7 per cent in the previous Dragon Year 1988. This is perhaps a manifestation of the dominant influence of social and economic factors as Singapore continues to move up the rank of developed countries. Indeed, the few pronatalist incentives implemented in 2000 did not make much difference as fertility continued its relentless downward path to touch the all-time low of 1.33 in 2003.

A diagram of the long-term movements in the total number of births and the total fertility rate is depicted in Figure 14.1.

FERTILITY TREND OF THREE MAIN RACES

It may be recalled that the three main races of Singapore's population, viz. Chinese, Indians and Malays, managed to reach replacement fertility at the same time in 1975, and it would be interesting to see what happened to their fertility trends after this remarkable achievement. Table 14.2 gives the figures for the total fertility rates of the three main races. The Chinese fertility edged up to the target of replacement level equivalent to 2.15 in 1976, after falling slightly below this level in the previous year. But this was only a flash in the pan as it resumed its downward trend immediately, to reach the low of 1.45 in 1983. Thereafter, a minor rise was recorded when the Chinese fertility moved up to 1.46 in 1984 and 1.50 in 1985. But this gentle uptrend was abruptly broken by the Tiger Year which caused the Chinese fertility to shrink by 16.0 per cent and to reach the lower point of 1.26 in 1986. It recovered by 17.5 per cent to 1.48 in the following year and then shot up by 27.0 per cent to reach 1.88 in the Dragon Year of 1988. It took an immediate downtown to 1.60 in the following year.

TABLE 14.2

Total Fertility Rates for Three Main Races, 1975–2003

Year	Chinese	Malays	Indians	Annual Change (%)		
				C	M	I
1975	2.07	2.14	1.96	—	—	—
1976	2.15	1.91	1.85	+3.9	−10.7	−5.6
1977	1.81	1.88	1.69	−15.8	−1.6	−8.6
1978	1.78	1.84	1.80	−1.7	−2.1	+6.5
1979	1.77	1.85	1.88	−0.6	+0.5	+4.4
1980	1.66	2.04	1.93	−6.2	+10.3	+2.7
1981	1.62	2.09	1.94	−2.4	+2.5	+0.5
1982	1.60	2.11	1.96	−1.2	+1.0	+1.0
1983	1.45	2.06	1.91	−9.4	−2.4	−2.6
1984	1.46	2.10	1.95	+0.7	+1.9	+2.1
1985	1.50	2.11	1.94	+2.7	+0.5	−0.5
1986	1.26	2.05	1.89	−16.0	−2.8	−2.6
1987	1.48	2.16	1.95	+17.5	+5.4	+3.2
1988	1.88	2.31	2.11	+27.0	+6.9	+8.2
1989	1.60	2.40	2.18	−14.9	+3.9	+3.3
1990	1.67	2.70	1.93	+4.4	+12.5	−11.5
1991	1.56	2.65	1.86	−6.6	−1.9	−3.6
1992	1.55	2.62	1.94	−0.6	−1.1	+4.3
1993	1.57	2.57	1.97	+1.3	−1.9	+1.5
1994	1.53	2.56	1.85	−2.5	−0.4	−6.1
1995	1.53	2.53	1.75	0.0	−1.2	−5.4
1996	1.51	2.53	1.79	−1.3	0.0	+2.3
1997	1.46	2.50	1.77	−3.3	−1.2	−1.1
1998	1.29	2.44	1.75	−11.6	−2.4	−1.1
1999	1.30	2.44	1.62	+0.7	0.0	−7.4
2000	1.45	2.45	1.62	+11.5	+0.4	0.0
2001	1.22	2.48	1.61	−15.9	+1.2	−0.6
2002	1.20	2.33	1.61	−1.6	−6.0	0.0
2003	0.98	2.17	1.45	−21.6	−7.3	−11.0

FIGURE 14.2
Annual Fertility Rates for Three Main Races, 1975–2003

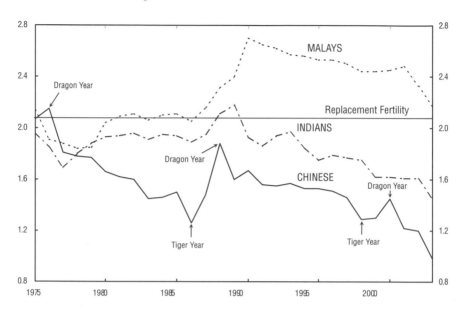

Since the Tiger and Dragon Years have such an important impact on not only the fertility level but also the marriage incidence, a more detailed analysis of the phenomenon is presented below:

Year	Chinese Marriages	Annual Changes in Chinese Gross Total Fertility Rate (%)			
		1st Order	2nd Order	3rd Order	4th Order
1984	18,255	−2.7	+6.5	−0.7	−7.6
1985	16,747	+3.9	−0.9	−5.5	−11.3
1986	13,824	−8.1	−20.3	−16.2	−25.6
1987	16,904	−2.8	+29.3	+35.2	+29.7
1988	17,861	+24.7	+23.5	+48.4	+28.9

The 16 per cent decline in Chinese fertility during 1986, the Tiger Year, was related to the corresponding pronounced drop in the gross total fertility rates for the first to the fourth order. One would expect the

Chinese fertility in the following year to recover to above the level prevailing prior to 1986 because of the postponed births occurring in 1987, but this did not happen as the total fertility rate went up to only 1.48, which was still below the 1985 figure of 1.50. This is because the upturn took place at the second order (29.3 per cent), third order (35.2 per cent) and fourth order (29.7 per cent), but failed to do so in the first order with only a small rise of 2.8 per cent. This failure to bounce back may be attributed directly to the dip in Chinese marriages in the Tiger Year, resulting in a smaller number of first order births than usual in the following year. The Dragon Year in 1988 saw the Chinese fertility go up by the all-time high of 27.0 per cent to reach 1.88, and this was caused by the sharp rise in the first to the fourth order births (see Figure 14.2).

It is not surprising that after the pronounced rise in the Dragon Year, there should be a substantial fall of 14.9 per cent in the Chinese fertility in the following year 1989 since some couples have already brought forward their births to the Dragon Year. After this decline, it moved up by 4.9 per cent to 1.67 in 1990, but this may be partly attributed to the use of the resident female population instead of the total female population to compute the TFR. Thereafter, the Chinese fertility experienced a fairly steady downward trend until 1997 to reach 1.46.

The late nineties was exposed once more to the distortions engendered by the Tiger Year and the Dragon Year. The Chinese fertility fell by 11.6 per cent in the Tiger Year 1998, remained nearly stationary in the following year, rose by 11.5 per cent in the Dragon Year 2000, and fell again by 15.9 per cent in 2001. It continued to fall slightly by 1.6 per cent to reach 1.20 in 2002. In the following year 2003, the Chinese fertility recorded an enormous fall of 21.6 per cent, bringing the TFR to the all-time low of 0.98. The decrease of 21.6 per cent represents the largest fertility decline ever experienced in Singapore and the TFR of 0.98 is the lowest ever recorded by any ethnic group.

The path taken by the Malay fertility was by comparison more simple and constant. After attaining the replacement level in 1975, the Malay fertility continued to proceed downwards to the lowest level of 1.84 in 1978, after which it crept up steadily back to the replacement level of 2.16 in 1987.[6] In response to the introduction of pro-baby incentives at the beginning of 1987, the Malay fertility went up more decisively above the replacement level to touch 2.70 in 1990. It then moved down very slowly to 2.50 in 1997, after which it dropped to 2.44

in 1998 and remained at about this level until 2001. The last two years recorded a sharper decline to touch 2.33 in 2002 and 2.17 in 2003. Unlike the Chinese fertility, the Malay fertility stayed slightly below the replacement level for about a decade after 1975 and remained above this level until today. The population policy shifts appear to have exerted a more positive and lasting impact on the fertility level of the Malay community.

The Indian fertility seemed to stay somewhere in between the Chinese and Malay fertility in most years. However, once it fell below the replacement level, it did not recover as in the case of the Malay fertility, and continued to move downwards between this level. After 1975, it remained somewhat stable just below the replacement level until the late eighties. In the nineties, there was a slow and steady movement in the Indian fertility downwards from 1.93 in 1990 to 1.62 in 1999. There was no change to this level for the first three years in the new millennium, but in the latest year 2003 the Indian fertility also experienced a pronounced fall of 11.0 per cent to touch the low of 1.45.

BIRTH SHORTFALL BELOW REPLACEMENT LEVEL

To what extent did the annual number of births produced by women in 1975 and thereafter fail to ensure that the population would be able to replace itself in the future? An overview of this birth shortfall is presented in Table 14.3. The estimated annual number of births shown in the third column has been calculated on the assumption that the age-specific fertility rates corresponding to a total fertility rate (TFR) of 2.13 and a net reproduction of 1.00 would prevail. This is done to scale up the age-specific fertility rates for each year so that the resultant TFR would be equal to 2.13 and to apply these adjusted rates to the mid-year resident female population in the various reproductive age groups to give us the estimated births.[7]

The figures reveal that a TFR of 2.37 in 1974 yielded 43,268 births, giving an excess of 4,194 over the 39,074 births produced at the replacement fertility level of 2.13. In 1975 the TFR of 2.08 yielded 39,948 births, about 755 or 1.9 per cent shortfall of the number required to ensure that the population would be replacing itself in the future. The existence of this birth shortfall not only persisted, but also became more significant over the years as fertility moved on a steep downward trend.

TABLE 14.3

Annual Births According to Actual Fertility and Replacement Fertility, 1974–2003

Year	Actual Fertility		TFR = 2.13	Birth Shortfall	
	TFR (1)	Births (2)	Births (3)	Number (4)	Percentage (5)
1974	2.37	43,268	39,074	+4,194	+10.7
1975	2.08	39,948	40,703	755	1.9
1976	2.11	42,783	43,035	252	0.6
1977	1.82	38,369	44,788	6,424	14.3
1978	1.80	39,441	46,521	7,080	15.2
1979	1.79	40,778	48,887	8,108	16.6
1980	1.74	41,219	50,235	9,018	18.0
1981	1.72	42,250	52,176	9,926	19.0
1982	1.71	42,654	53,576	10,924	20.4
1983	1.59	40,585	54,316	13,731	25.3
1984	1.61	41,556	54,174	12,618	22.3
1985	1.62	42,484	55,900	13,416	24.0
1986	1.42	38,379	55,532	17,153	30.9
1987	1.64	43,616	56,661	13,045	23.0
1988	1.98	52,957	56,739	3,782	6.7
1989	1.79	47,669	57,252	9,583	16.7
1990	1.88	51,142	57,944	6,802	11.7
1991	1.78	49,114	60,087	10,973	18.3
1992	1.77	49,402	59,448	10,046	16.9
1993	1.79	50,225	59,765	9,540	16.0
1994	1.76	49,554	59,968	10,414	17.4
1995	1.73	48,635	59,874	11,239	18.8
1996	1.73	48,577	59,808	11,231	18.8
1997	1.68	47,333	60,011	12,678	21.1
1998	1.54	43,669	60,392	16,728	27.7
1999	1.55	46,336	59,537	16,207	27.7
2000	1.68	46,997	59,579	12,582	21.1
2001	1.48	41,451	59,152	17,701	29.9
2002	1.45	40,760	60,035	19,275	32.1
2003	1.33	37,485	60,269	22,784	37.8

FIGURE 14.3

Annual Births According to Actual Fertility and Replacement Fertility, 1974–2003

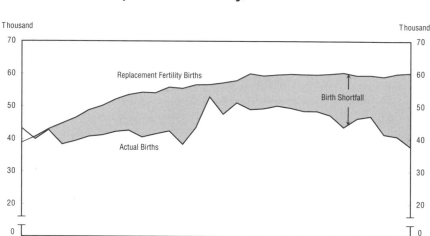

From the first year of 1.9 per cent in 1975, the birth shortfall rose consistently to reach the high of 25.3 per cent in 1983. It fell to 22.2 per cent in the following year, but immediately worsened to 24.0 per cent in 1985 and 30.9 per cent in the Tiger Year. Not surprisingly, the birth shortfall improved to 23.0 per cent in the following year and to only 6.7 per cent in the Dragon Year 1988, by far the smallest shortfall during the whole thirty-year period of below-replacement fertility. This remarkable improvement may be partly attributed to the emerging influence of the pronatalist incentives introduced in 1987.

The percentage of the birth shortfall immediately went up to 16.7 per cent in 1989 and remained generally below the 19-level until 1996. In the late nineties the birth shortfall took a turn for the worse, with the percentage reaching 27.7 per cent in the Tiger Year 1998 and remaining at the same level in the following year. There was an improvement in the Dragon Year 2000, but the 21.1 per cent was not that satisfactory. Even more discouraging events occurred in the next three years, when the birth shortfall was pushed up to 29.9 per cent in 2001, 32.1 per cent in 2002, and finally 37.8 per cent in 2003. The continuous presence of the birth shortfall is the result of the limited effectiveness of government pronatalist measures in lifting fertility back to the replacement level once it had remained well below this level for so many years. The important task of eliminating the birth shortfall has led the government to acknowledge that immigration can be a major source of replenishing our population.[8]

FUTURE FERTILITY TRENDS

A general view of the possible direction of fertility in Singapore in the years ahead may be examined in terms of the experience of other countries that have been recording fertility below the replacement level. To this end, we have laid out in Table 14.4 the figures for the total fertility rate for some typical countries for the last three decades or so.[9] It is to be noted that, without any exception, fertility has remained consistently below the replacement level in these countries, and has failed to rise above this level irrespective of whether pronatalist incentives have been provided by the government.[10] The same situation has persisted in Singapore even with government intervention, and fertility cannot be possibly pushed back to the replacement level.

The government has therefore not repeated the demographic objective of the seventies in maintaining fertility at exactly the replacement level in order to achieve zero population growth to stabilize the population at a certain size in the future. Instead, the government is realistic enough

TABLE 14.4

Total Fertility Rate of Selected Countries, 1970–2002

Country	1970	1975	1980	1985	1990	1995	2000	2001	2002
Singapore	3.0	2.1	1.7	1.6	1.9	1.7	1.7	1.5	1.5
Hong Kong	3.3	2.8	2.1	1.5	1.2	1.2	1.0	0.9	1.0
Japan	2.1	1.9	1.7	1.7	1.5	1.4	1.4	1.4	1.3
France	2.5	2.0	2.0	1.8	1.8	1.7	1.9	1.9	1.9
Italy	2.4	2.2	1.6	1.5	1.4	1.2	1.2	1.2	1.3
Switzerland	2.1	1.6	1.6	1.5	1.6	1.5	1.5	1.4	1.5
United States	2.4	1.8	1.8	1.8	2.0	2.0	2.0	2.1	2.1
Canada	2.3	1.8	1.7	1.7	1.8	1.6	1.5	1.5	1.5
Austalia	2.9	2.2	1.9	1.9	1.9	1.8	1.8	1.8	1.8

to recognize that the objective of the new package of pronatalist incentives is to raise the extremely low fertility prevailing nowadays to as near the replacement level as possible.[11] The extent to which this objective will be achieved can of course be known only from late 2005 onwards. The inevitable birth shortfall will have to be replenished by fresh immigration which is an integral part of the portfolio of the Ministry of Home Affairs under Mr Wong Kan Seng, the minister-in-charge of population matters. The government will have to pay more attention to the question of attracting new immigrants to work and settle in Singapore. This will require a review of the rules governing the admission of foreigners, the offer of permanent resident status, and finally, the granting of Singapore citizenship.

Notes

1. The twelve animals of the zodiac in order of appearance are rat, ox, tiger, rabbit, dragon, snake, horse, goat, monkey, cock, dog, pig.
2. *Trends in Singapore Resident Population 1990–2000* (Singapore: Department of Statistics, 2001).
3. *Report on Registration of Births and Deaths* for various years (Singapore: Department of Statistics, 2001).
4. Saw Swee-Hock, "A Decade of Fertility Below Replacement Level in Singapore", *Journal of Biosocial Science* 18, no. 4 (October 1986).
5. Neil Somerville, *Your Chinese Horoscope for 1988* (Weillingborough: The Aquarian Press, 1987).
6. Saw Swee-Hock, "Muslim Fertility Transition: The Case of the Singapore Malays", *Asia-Pacific Population Journal* 4, no. 3 (September 1989).
7. Saw Swee-Hock, *The Population of Singapore* (Singapore: Institute of Southeast Asian Studies, 1999).
8. *Straits Times*, 30 August 2004.
9. *Demographic Yearbook* for various years (New York: Department of Economic and Social Affairs, Statistical Office, United Nations), *World Fertility Report 2003* (New York: Department of Economic and Social Affairs, Population Division, United Nations), *World Development Indicators* for various years (Washington, D.C.: Development Data Centre, The World Bank).
10. Kingsley Davis, Mikhall S. Bernstam and Rita Ricado-Cambell, eds, *Below Replacement Fertility in Industrial Societies: Causes, Consequences, Policies, Population and Development Review*, A Supplement to Vol. 12, 1986.
11. *Business Times*, 4–5 September 2004.

15

Future Population Trends

INTRODUCTION

An examination of the most plausible course of population trends in the future and the social and economic consequences of such trends are presented in this chapter. To do this, population projections need to be prepared on the basis of certain assumptions concerning the future course of migration, mortality and fertility, the three factors determining the rate of increase or decline in any population. In Singapore the future path of mortality movement is not difficult to decide, while the movement of fertility in the future is somewhat more problematic to resolve. It is of course quite impossible to reckon the flow of migration in the future, which depends primarily on the need for foreigners in the various sectors of the economy that is greatly dependent on external factors outside the control of Singapore.

Three sets of population projections based on three different assumptions in regard to the future course of fertility have been computed to provide us with a better insight into the possibilities of the growth and structure of the population in the years ahead. In addition, we have constructed another population projection on the assumption that the total fertility rate will move up to the replacement level of 2.13 and remain at this level indefinitely. The results of this projection based on a somewhat unrealistic fertility assumption are only meant to illustrate the previously-mentioned concepts such as zero population growth, population replacement, and stationary population.

METHODOLOGY

The population projections were prepared by the component method which involves the separate projection of the number of males and females in each age group of the population.[1] Since the base resident population in 2005 has been divided into quinary age group, the projections are computed for five-year intervals of time so that at the end of the five-year period all the survivors of one age group would have moved into the next older age group. Each cohort of the sex-age group is diminished to account for the impact of mortality over time. This step requires a set of five-year survival ratios (P_x) which are deemed to represent mortality in each cohort during specific-periods of time subsequent to 2005. A multiplication of the original number in each sex-age group by the relevant survival ratio will give us the estimated number of persons five years older at a date five years later. A repetition of this procedure will yield the estimated population aged ten years older than those at the base date and at a date ten years later.

The second step involves the essential task of estimating the future number of children born in each five-year time interval subsequent to the base date in 2005 in order to fill in the vacuum in the first age group 0–4 at periods of time five years later. To begin with, it is necessary to fix the most plausible assumption concerning the future course of fertility in terms of the total fertility rate with its equivalent age-specific fertility rates from age 15 to 49. These rates are then employed in conjunction with the female population in the reproductive age groups to derive the estimated number of births to the various five-year periods. The total births are split into male births and female births by applying the sex ratio at birth for the three-year period 2001–03. The number of births for each sex surviving at the end of a given five-year period is estimated by multiplying the number of births during the period with the survival ratio (P_b).

The three population projections were prepared on the assumption that the resident population is a closed one not subject to immigration and emigration. Mortality as measured by the life expectancy at birth is assumed to improve from 76.9 in 2005 to 77.7 in 2010 and to remain constant thereafter for the males, with the corresponding figure for the females improving from 80.9 in 2005 to 81.7 in 2010 and remaining constant thereafter for the females. In the case of fertility, three different assumptions are adopted to prepare the following projections.

Low Projection: Fertility is assumed to increase from 1.33 in 2003 to 1.43 in 2005 and to remain constant thereafter.

Medium Projection: Fertility is assumed to increase from 1.33 in
2003 to 1.43 in 2005 and 1.63 in 2010 and to
remain constant thereafter.

High Projection: Fertility is assumed to increase from 1.33 in
2003 to 1.63 in 2005 and 1.83 in 2010 and to
remain constant thereafter.

The results of the population projections mentioned above will
provide a fairly good idea of the possibilities of the growth and structure
of the resident population in the years ahead. As mentioned earlier, a
fourth projection was prepared on the assumption that fertility will
move up from 1.33 in 2003 to 1.63 in 2005 and 2.13 in 2010, and remain
at this replacement fertility level thereafter. The results of this
Replacement Projection will allow us to illustrate the various aspects of
a stationary population.

The postcensal estimates for the resident population classified by sex
and quinary age group from age 0 to 80 and over are available for the
year 2004 but not yet for 2005.[2] The figures for 2005 are calculated by
means of linear interpolating the 2003 and 2004 estimates for the various
age groups, and applying the same increase or decrease to the respective
age groups in 2004 to give us the required 2005 base population.

STATIONARY POPULATION

If a population is closed against migration and is subject to a net
reproduction rate of $R_0 = 1$ and a constant mortality indefinitely, the
population will eventually reach a stage where it will experience a rate
of population growth of r equivalent to zero.[3] At this point of time and
thereafter, the population is said to be a stationary population possessing
certain inherent properties. The size of the population will remain
constant, the annual number of births and deaths will remain not only
constant but equal, the age composition will be invariable, and the crude
death rate equal to the inverse of the expectation of life at birth. A less
restrictive population model is the stable population where the population
need not be stationary. It may be constructed from independent schedules
of mortality and fertility, permitting some annual increase or decrease in
r as determined by the level of the net reproduction rate R_0 above or
below unity. In a stable population the total size of the population varies
by a constant rate r, the crude birth rate and the crude death rate are

constant but the annual numbers of births and deaths vary at a constant rate r, and the age composition of the population is fixed. It should be noted that a stationary population is in fact a special case of the more general family of the stable populations in which $r = 0$. The rate of population growth in a stable state is known as the intrinsic rate of natural increase or the Lotka rate. Lotka established the approximate functional relationship as $(1 + r)^x = R_o$, where $r = 0$ if $R_o = 1$.

In life table terminology the annual number of persons reaching each year of age in a stationary population is indicated by the l_x column. The annual number of deaths at each age is given in the d_x column. The mid-year population at age x is shown by the L_x column, and the sum of the numbers in this column provides the total size of the stationary population which is equivalent to the value of T_o shown as the first entry of the T_x column. The crude death rate is naturally the total annual number of deaths divided by this total population. The number of births occurring each year is equivalent to the value of l_o, ordinarily fixed at a constant number 10,000. The crude birth rate is therefore $\dfrac{l_o}{T_o} \times k$. Since the number of births and the number of deaths each year must be equal, the crude death rate is also equal to $\dfrac{l_o}{T_o} \times k$. Since the expectations of life at birth is $\dfrac{l_o}{T_o}$, the crude death rate and the crude birth rate are both equal to the inverse of the expectation of life at birth, that is, $\dfrac{l_o}{e_o} \times k$.

The results of the Replacement Projection based on constant mortality from 2010 onwards and also constant fertility at the replacement level of TFR = 2.13 from 2010 onwards are presented in Table 15.1. As mentioned earlier, the possibility of fertility returning to this level in Singapore is quite remote. The figures given in the table are of very little practical use and can only serve to illustrate the kind of resident population that would emerge if we could in theory achieve the demographic goal, propounded in the seventies, of attaining a stationary population with zero growth in the future.

The data laid out in Table 15.1 demonstrate that the resident population is expected to grow from the initial size of 3,538,500 in 2005 to the peak of 4,016,343 in 2030. After that it will fluctuate somewhat, decrease to 3,939,309 in 2035, increase to 3,944,708 in 2040, decrease to 3,899,200 in 2045, and then increase again to 3,902,451 in 2050. Thereafter

TABLE 15.1
Future Resident Population According to
Replacement Projection, 2005–50

Year	Resident Population	Increase		
		Number	Percentage	
			5-Year	Annual
2005	3,538,500	—		
2010	3,670,125	131,625	3.7	0.7
2015	3,793,315	123,190	3.4	0.7
2020	3,884,754	100,439	2.6	0.5
2025	3,977,395	92,600	2.4	0.5
2030	4,016,343	38,948	1.0	0.2
2035	3,939,309	−77,034	−1.9	−0.3
2040	3,944,708	5,399	0.1	0.0
2045	3,899,200	−45,508	−1.1	−0.2
2050	3,902,451	3,251	0.1	0.0

the resident population of Singapore is expected to remain stationary at about 3.9 million forever. The implied annual growth rate will be lowered from 0.7 per cent during 2005–10 to 0.2 per cent in 2025–30, and after that it will oscillate slightly around zero growth. The small fluctuations in the annual growth rate after 2030 may be attributed to the initial disturbances in the age structure of the resident population which has engendered the unstable number of annual births in the first place. The base resident population in 2005 has an abnormal age pyramid with a bulge at the working ages contributed by permanent residents, most of whom were of working ages.[4] If the initial age structure had the normal shape of a pyramid, the annual growth rate would remain about constant at zero after 2030 when the resident population would be in a stationary state.

FUTURE POPULATION GROWTH

The availability of two separate figures for the population of Singapore in recent years requires some explanation before examining the results of the population projections. Resident population, the focus of attention in this chapter, has been defined to include Singapore citizens and permanent residents. Total population, however, refers to the overall population which includes these two groups of persons as well as the transient group of foreigners collectively known as non-resident population. The latter comprise primarily of foreign workers on employment pass or work permit, foreign students on student visa, and foreigners on short-term social visit pass. According to the 2000 Population Census, the total population of 4,017,733 composed of 3,263,209 resident population and 754,524 non-resident population. Among the resident population, there were 3,060,248 (93.8 per cent) Singapore citizens and 202,961 (6.2 per cent) permanent residents.[5] In 2004 the total population was estimated to number 4,240,300, split into 3,486,900 resident population and 753,400 non-resident population; separate figures for citizens and permanent residents are not available in postcensal estimates.[6] As mentioned earlier, the resident population employed in the base year 2005 as the starting point of our projection was estimated to number 3,538,500. It is customary nowadays to use the figure for the resident population, without the temporary and volatile foreign component, to represent the population of Singapore.

The results of the three projections based on three different assumptions concerning the possible course of fertility in the future are summarized in Table 15.2 and Figure 15.1, while the detailed figures by sex and age group are presented in Tables 15.4–15.12 for the benefit of prospective users. If fertility remains constant indefinitely at the low level of TFR = 1.43 as assumed in the Low Projection, the resident population is expected to grow from the original size of 3,538,500 in 2005 to the peak of 3,659,068 in 2020, an increase of 120,568 or 3.4 per cent. After that, it will commence to shrink steadily to reach 3,458,773 in 2035, smaller than the size prevailing at the beginning in 2005. The contraction of the resident population consequent on negative growth rate will continue to proceed up to the end of the projection period in 2050 when it will number 2,986,824. Though we do not have the projected figures to show, the resident population, according to stationary population theory, will continue to shrink beyond 2050 if the TFR is held constant at 1.43 indefinitely.

The above results of the population projections is based on the rather pessimistic view that fertility will continue to be very low in the future. However, there is a possibility that the 2004 package of pronatalist incentives might be somewhat more effective as to move fertility up to the moderate level of 1.63. As can be observed from the results of the

TABLE 15.2

Resident Population According to
Three Different Projections, 2005–50

Year	Resident Population	Increase		
		Number	Percentage	
			5-Year	Annual
Low Projection (TFR = 1.43)				
2005	3,538,500	—	—	
2010	3,612,364	73,864	2.1	0.4
2015	3,649,738	37,374	1.0	0.2
2020	3,659,068	9,330	0.3	0.1
2025	3,639,805	−19,263	−0.5	−0.1
2030	3,576,382	−63,423	−1.7	−0.3
2035	3,458,773	−117,609	−3.3	−0.7
2040	3,353,808	−104,965	−3.0	−0.6
2045	3,173,969	−179,839	−5.4	−1.0
2050	2,986,824	−187,145	−5.9	−1.3
Medium Projection (TFR = 1.63)				
2005	3,538,500	—	—	
2010	3,628,899	90,399	2.6	0.5
2015	3,690,522	61,623	1.7	0.3
2020	3,723,322	32,800	0.9	0.2
2025	3,727,420	4,098	0.1	0.0
2030	3,697,029	−30,391	−0.8	0.1
2035	3,593,766	−103,263	−2.8	−0.6
2040	3,517,123	−76,643	−2.1	−0.4
2045	3,373,352	−143,771	−4.1	−0.8
2050	3,222,738	−150,614	−4.5	−0.9
High Projection (TFR = 1.83)				
2005	3,538,500	—	—	
2010	3,651,530	113,030	3.2	0.6
2015	3,737,408	85,878	2.4	0.5
2020	3,797,161	59,753	2.0	0.3
2025	3,825,277	28,116	1.0	0.2
2030	3,807,478	−17,799	−0.5	−0.1
2035	3,740,501	−66,977	−1.8	−0.3
2040	3,693,252	−47,249	−1.3	−0.2
2045	3,591,647	−101,605	−2.1	−0.4
2050	3,483,520	−108,127	−3.0	−0.6

FIGURE 15.1

Actual and Projected Resident Population, 1990–2050

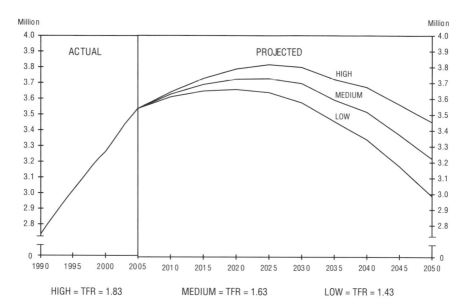

HIGH = TFR = 1.83   MEDIUM = TFR = 1.63   LOW = TFR = 1.43

Medium Projection, the resident population can now be expected to grow more rapidly from 3,538,500 in 2005 to the higher peak of 3,727,420 five years later in 2025. Thereafter, the negative growth will trigger the shrinking of the resident population, but at a slower pace to reach the higher figure of 3,222,738 in 2050. During the uptrend, the amount of increase for every five-year period will become progressively smaller, being reduced from 90,399 during 2005–10 to only 4,098 during 2020–25. The implied annual growth rate will slacken from 0.5 per cent to zero per cent. A completely different picture will emerge during the downturn when the amount of decrease will worsen from 30,391 during 2025–30 to 150,614 during 2045–50. The negative annual growth rate will fluctuate somewhat, moving up from 0.1 per cent during 2025–30 to 0.6 per cent during the next period, down during 2035–40, and up again to 0.9 per cent during 2045–50. This scenario will probably be the nearest the resident population will resemble in the future, and the detailed figures by sex and age group according to

FIGURE 15.2
Actual and Projected Annual Births, 1990–2050

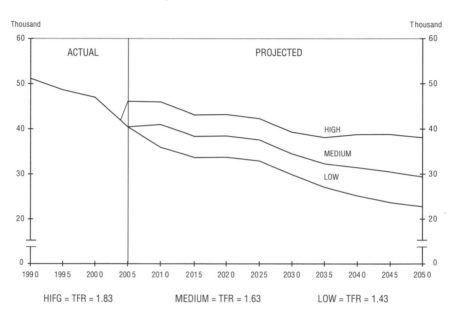

HIFG = TFR = 1.83   MEDIUM = TFR = 1.63   LOW = TFR = 1.43

the Medium Projection presented at the end of this chapter should therefore be preferred by prospective users.

If the upturn in fertility towards the replacement level happens to be more robust as reflected in the High Projection with TFR = 1.83, the resident population is expected to expand faster to reach a higher peak and thereafter shrink more slowly until the end of the projection period (see Figure 15.1). As the figures in Table 15.2 show, the resident population will grow more quickly for twenty-five years from 3,538,500 in 2005 to the high of 3,825,277 in 2025, after which it will reverse course to dwindle more slowly to reach the larger size of 3,483,520 in 2050. In all likelihood, this outcome of the future resident population will not be easy to realize since the fertility assumption of TFR rising from 1.33 in 2003 to remain constant at 1.83 from 2010 onwards will be almost impossible to achieve, notwithstanding the comprehensive package of pronatalist incentives introduced in 2004.

A common feature displayed by the results of the three projections is the inevitable shrinkage of the resident population after 2020, or the latest 2025. It may be recalled that the stationary population theory tells us that a population will not be able to replace itself in the future as long as fertility continues to remain below the replacement level. In other words, the excess of births over deaths will occur up to a point only, and beyond this point there will be a deficit of births over deaths as the former will be reduced progressively in the future. The decline in the annual number of births in all the three projections is depicted in Figure 15.2.

FUTURE AGE STRUCTURE

Another aspect of the future resident population that we can examine is the changing character of the age structure presented in Table 15.3. This table includes only the figures derived from the Medium Projection, the most likely outcome of the future resident population. For a more convenient and meaningful analysis, the figures have been summarized in terms of four functional age groups. A well-defined shift in the age composition will be experienced in the first half of the present millennium when the first three age groups will record a contraction and the older age group an expansion. The number of young children aged 0–4, after rising during the first five years from 194,600 to 207,016 in 2010, will fall consistently during the rest of the period to reach the low of 149,387 in 2050. The corresponding proportion to the total resident population will be raised from 5.5 per cent to 5.7 per cent during the first five years, followed by a steady reduction until the end of the period when it is expected to stand at 4.6 per cent.

A more clear-cut pattern is revealed by the figures for the schooling age group 5–15. The whole projection period will witness a continuous decrease in this age group from 496,800 in 2005 to 312,930 in 2050. This is accompanied by a downtrend in the proportion in this age group during the same period, falling consistently from 14.0 per cent to 9.7 per cent. Clearly, this tendency may not augur well for the supply of local labour in the future, but may offer excellent opportunities for improving the educational system. The lessening pressure for school places will provide a good chance for achieving enhanced quality education by eliminating double sessions, reducing class size, having better facilities, and maximizing the utilization of financial resources.

Except for a minor rise in the first decade, the working age group 15–64 will encounter a noticeable contraction from 2,674,767 in 2015 to

TABLE 15.3
Future Resident Population by Four Broad Age Groups
According to Medium Projection, 2005–50

Year	0–4	5–15	15–64	65 & over	Total
			Number		
2005	194,600	496,800	2,552,500	294,600	3,538,500
2010	207,016	429,512	2,659,920	332,451	3,628,899
2015	197,862	401,005	2,674,767	416,888	3,690,522
2020	191,657	404,254	2,591,760	535,651	3,723,322
2025	186,675	388,922	2,479,358	672,465	3,727,420
2030	179,741	380,749	2,339,585	786,954	3,687,029
2035	166,581	368,848	2,221,268	837,069	3,593,766
2040	158,970	345,813	2,111,455	900,885	3,517,123
2045	154,441	325,050	2,041,040	852,821	3,373,352
2050	149,387	312,930	1,990,769	769,652	3,222,738
			Percentage		
2005	5.5	14.0	72.2	8.3	100
2010	5.7	11.8	73.3	9.2	100
2015	5.4	10.9	72.4	11.3	100
2020	5.1	10.9	69.6	14.4	100
2025	5.1	10.4	66.5	18.0	100
2030	4.9	10.3	63.5	21.3	100
2035	4.6	10.3	61.8	23.3	100
2040	4.5	9.8	60.1	25.6	100
2045	4.6	9.6	60.5	25.3	100
2050	4.6	9.7	61.8	23.9	100

the low of 1,990,769 in 2050. The proportion in this age group is expected to record a small rise from 72.2 to 73.3 per cent in 2010, and thereafter a steady diminution to 61.8 per cent in 2050. The deterioration in the supply of working age persons, already obvious since the late eighties, will offer no respite in the future and will surely perpetuate the current dependency on foreign labour. The other challenge concerns the nature of the dependency burden that will have to be borne by the working persons. The shrinking proportion of working persons will be obliged not only to shoulder a heavier dependency burden, but also to divert much of their personal effort and resources towards the care of the elderly rather than the young.

TABLE 15.4
Total Resident Population by Age Group According to High Projection, 2005–50

Age Group	2005	2010	2015	2020	2025	2030	2035	2040	2045	2050
0 – 4	194,600	229,647	222,143	218,654	213,770	203,463	193,074	191,787	193,621	191,905
5 – 9	235,300	194,366	229,371	221,875	218,390	213,512	203,219	192,842	191,556	193,388
10 – 14	261,500	235,146	194,239	229,221	221,730	218,247	213,373	203,087	192,716	191,431
15 – 19	243,900	261,183	234,860	194,004	228,943	221,461	217,984	213,115	202,840	192,482
20 – 24	218,500	243,295	260,534	234,275	193,523	227,378	220,910	217,345	213,011	202,336
25 – 29	248,300	217,785	242,493	259,673	233,508	192,885	226,626	220,181	216,634	212,846
30 – 34	303,500	247,437	217,007	241,621	258,738	231,668	192,192	225,809	219,388	215,861
35 – 39	305,600	302,237	246,409	216,084	240,582	257,623	230,666	191,366	224,805	218,444
40 – 44	333,600	303,732	300,401	244,915	214,751	239,092	256,026	229,233	190,182	223,410
45 – 49	315,000	332,324	300,775	297,498	242,552	212,642	236,734	253,499	226,964	188,306
50 – 54	261,100	310,166	327,218	296,222	293,039	240,926	204,492	233,086	249,586	223,450
55 – 59	196,000	253,993	301,758	318,339	288,283	285,250	234,554	199,002	226,747	242,787
60 – 64	127,000	187,768	243,312	289,129	305,003	276,377	273,582	225,015	190,767	217,222
65 – 69	105,300	117,967	174,406	225,973	268,633	283,357	257,059	268,655	209,544	177,406
70 – 74	79,000	91,751	102,810	151,992	196,913	234,175	246,991	254,699	234,179	183,069
75 – 79	56,900	63,514	73,749	82,666	122,203	158,298	188,363	198,647	206,242	188,346
80 & above	53,400	59,219	65,923	75,020	84,716	111,124	144,656	178,884	202,865	220,831
TOTAL	3,538,500	3,651,530	3,737,408	3,797,161	3,825,277	3,807,478	3,740,501	3,696,252	3,591,647	3,483,520

TABLE 15.5

Male Resident Population by Age Group According to High Projection, 2005–50

Age Group	2005	2010	2015	2020	2025	2030	2035	2040	2045	2050
0 – 4	100,100	118,439	114,569	110,979	110,517	104,935	99,577	98,939	99,860	98,974
5 – 9	121,800	99,970	118,285	114,420	110,834	110,373	104,799	99,448	98,810	99,730
10 – 14	135,000	121,714	99,900	118,202	114,340	110,756	110,296	104,726	99,378	98,741
15 – 19	125,300	134,784	121,519	99,740	118,013	114,157	110,579	110,120	104,558	99,219
20 – 24	110,700	124,861	134,312	121,093	99,391	117,600	113,757	110,192	109,735	104,192
25 – 29	118,300	110,157	124,249	133,653	120,499	98,904	117,024	113,200	109,652	109,735
30 – 34	145,300	117,684	109,584	123,602	132,958	119,872	98,390	116,415	112,611	109,082
35 – 39	149,600	144,385	116,942	108,893	122,823	132,120	119,116	97,770	115,652	111,902
40 – 44	167,900	148,418	143,244	116,018	108,032	121,852	131,076	118,174	96,998	114,738
45 – 49	158,600	167,751	146,518	141,410	114,532	106,649	120,292	129,398	116,661	95,756
50 – 54	132,200	155,158	164,110	143,338	138,341	112,046	99,443	117,681	126,590	114,129
55 – 59	98,000	127,375	149,494	158,119	138,106	133,291	107,956	95,813	113,385	121,969
60 – 64	62,300	92,238	119,885	140,703	148,821	129,985	125,453	101,608	90,179	106,717
65 – 69	50,300	55,939	82,821	107,644	126,337	133,626	116,713	126,644	91,234	80,972
70 – 74	36,300	42,383	47,134	69,785	90,701	106,451	112,593	98,342	106,710	76,874
75 – 79	25,300	27,642	32,275	35,893	53,141	69,069	81,062	85,740	74,887	81,260
80 & above	20,400	22,772	25,121	28,600	32,137	42,494	55,592	68,095	76,656	75,514
TOTAL	1,757,400	1,811,670	1,849,962	1,872,092	1,879,523	1,864,180	1,823,718	1,792,305	1,743,556	1,699,504

TABLE 15.6
Female Resident Population by Age Group According to High Projection, 2005–50

Age Group	2005	2010	2015	2020	2025	2030	2035	2040	2045	2050
0 – 4	94,500	111,208	107,574	107,675	103,253	98,528	93,497	92,848	93,761	92,931
5 – 9	113,500	94,396	111,086	107,455	107,556	103,139	98,420	93,394	92,746	93,658
10 – 14	126,500	113,432	94,339	111,019	107,390	107,491	103,077	98,361	93,338	92,690
15 – 19	118,600	126,399	113,341	94,264	110,930	107,304	107,405	102,995	98,282	93,263
20 – 24	107,800	118,434	126,222	113,182	94,132	109,778	107,153	107,153	103,276	98,144
25 – 29	130,000	107,628	118,244	126,020	113,009	93,981	109,602	106,981	106,982	103,111
30 – 34	158,200	129,753	107,423	118,019	125,780	111,796	93,802	109,394	106,777	106,779
35 – 39	156,000	157,852	129,467	107,191	117,759	125,503	111,550	93,596	109,153	106,542
40 – 44	165,700	155,314	157,157	128,897	106,719	117,240	124,950	111,059	93,184	108,672
45 – 49	156,400	164,573	154,257	156,088	128,020	105,993	116,442	124,101	110,303	92,550
50 – 54	128,900	155,008	163,108	152,884	154,698	128,880	105,049	115,405	122,996	109,321
55 – 59	98,000	126,618	152,264	160,220	150,177	151,959	126,598	103,189	113,362	120,818
60 – 64	64,700	95,530	123,427	148,426	156,182	146,392	148,129	123,407	100,588	110,505
65 – 69	55,000	62,028	91,585	118,329	142,296	149,731	140,346	142,011	118,310	96,434
70 – 74	42,700	49,368	55,676	82,207	106,212	127,724	134,398	156,357	127,469	106,195
75 – 79	31,600	35,872	41,474	46,773	69,062	89,229	107,301	112,907	131,355	107,086
80 & above	33,000	36,447	40,802	46,420	52,579	68,630	89,064	110,789	126,209	145,317
TOTAL	1,781,100	1,839,860	1,887,446	1,925,069	1,945,754	1,943,298	1,916,783	1,903,947	1,848,091	1,784,016

TABLE 15.7
Total Resident Population by Age Group According to Medium Projection, 2005–50

Age Group	2005	2010	2015	2020	2025	2030	2035	2040	2045	2050
0 – 4	194,600	207,016	197,862	191,657	189,675	179,741	166,581	158,970	154,441	149,387
5 – 9	235,300	194,366	206,766	197,624	191,427	189,447	179,524	166,380	158,778	154,255
10 – 14	261,500	235,146	194,239	206,630	197,495	191,302	189,324	179,433	166,272	158,675
15 – 19	243,900	261,183	234,360	194,004	206,379	197,255	191,070	189,095	179,215	166,071
20 – 24	218,500	243,295	260,534	234,275	193,523	205,867	196,765	190,595	188,626	178,770
25 – 29	248,300	217,785	242,493	259,673	233,508	192,885	205,187	196,115	189,966	188,004
30 – 34	303,500	247,437	217,007	241,621	258,738	231,668	192,192	204,449	195,410	189,283
35 – 39	305,600	302,237	246,409	216,084	240,582	257,623	230,666	191,366	203,568	194,569
40 – 44	333,600	303,732	300,401	244,915	214,751	239,092	256,026	229,233	190,182	202,307
45 – 49	315,000	332,324	300,775	297,498	242,552	212,642	236,734	253,499	226,964	188,306
50 – 54	261,100	310,166	327,218	296,222	293,039	240,926	204,492	233,086	249,586	223,450
55 – 59	196,000	253,993	301,758	318,339	288,283	285,250	234,554	199,002	226,747	242,787
60 – 64	127,000	187,768	243,312	289,129	305,003	276,377	273,582	225,015	190,767	217,222
65 – 69	105,300	117,967	174,406	225,973	268,633	283,357	257,059	268,655	209,544	177,406
70 – 74	79,000	91,751	102,810	151,992	196,913	234,175	246,991	254,699	234,179	183,069
75 – 79	56,900	63,514	73,749	82,666	122,203	158,298	188,363	198,647	206,242	188,346
80 & above	53,400	59,219	65,923	75,020	84,716	111,124	144,656	178,884	202,865	220,831
TOTAL	3,538,500	3,628,899	3,690,522	3,723,322	3,727,420	3,687,029	3,593,766	3,517,123	3,373,352	3,222,738

TABLE 15.8
Male Resident Population by Age Group According to Medium Projection, 2005–50

Age Group	2005	2010	2015	2020	2025	2030	2035	2040	2045	2050
0 – 4	100,100	106,768	102,046	98,846	97,824	92,701	85,914	81,988	79,652	77,046
5 – 9	121,800	99,970	106,629	101,913	98,718	97,697	92,580	85,802	81,881	79,548
10 – 14	135,000	121,714	99,900	106,554	101,841	98,649	97,629	92,515	85,742	81,824
15 – 19	125,300	134,784	121,519	99,740	106,383	101,678	98,491	97,473	92,367	85,605
20 – 24	110,700	124,861	134,312	121,093	99,391	106,011	101,322	98,146	97,132	92,044
25 – 29	118,300	110,157	124,249	133,653	120,499	98,904	105,491	100,825	97,665	96,656
30 – 34	145,300	117,684	109,584	123,602	132,958	119,872	98,390	104,942	100,301	97,157
35 – 39	149,600	144,385	116,942	108,893	122,823	132,120	119,116	97,770	104,280	99,669
40 – 44	167,900	148,418	143,244	116,018	108,032	121,852	131,076	118,174	96,998	103,456
45 – 49	158,600	167,751	146,518	141,410	114,532	106,649	120,292	129,398	116,661	95,756
50 – 54	132,200	155,158	164,110	143,338	138,341	112,046	99,443	117,681	126,590	114,129
55 – 59	98,000	127,375	149,494	158,119	138,106	133,291	107,956	95,813	113,385	121,969
60 – 64	62,300	92,238	119,885	140,703	148,821	129,985	125,453	101,608	90,179	106,717
65 – 69	50,300	55,939	82,821	107,644	126,337	133,626	116,713	126,644	91,234	80,972
70 – 74	36,300	42,383	47,134	69,785	90,701	106,451	112,593	98,342	106,710	76,874
75 – 79	25,300	27,642	32,275	35,893	53,141	69,069	81,062	85,740	74,887	81,260
80 & above	20,400	22,772	25,121	28,600	32,137	42,494	55,592	68,095	76,656	75,514
TOTAL	1,757,400	1,799,999	1,825,783	1,835,804	1,830,585	1,803,095	1,749,113	1,700,956	1,632,320	1,566,196

TABLE 15.9

Female Resident Population by Age Group According to Medium Projection, 2005–50

Age Group	2005	2010	2015	2020	2025	2030	2035	2040	2045	2050
0 – 4	94,500	100,248	95,816	92,811	91,851	87,040	80,667	76,982	74,789	72,341
5 – 9	113,500	94,396	100,137	95,711	92,709	91,750	86,944	80,578	76,897	74,707
10 – 14	126,500	113,432	94,339	100,076	95,654	92,653	91,695	86,918	80,530	76,851
15 – 19	118,600	126,399	113,341	94,264	99,996	95,577	92,579	91,622	86,848	80,466
20 – 24	107,800	118,434	126,222	113,182	94,132	99,856	95,443	92,449	91,494	86,726
25 – 29	130,000	107,628	118,244	126,020	113,009	93,981	99,696	95,290	92,301	91,348
30 – 34	158,200	129,753	107,423	118,019	125,780	111,796	93,802	99,507	95,109	92,126
35 – 39	156,000	157,852	129,467	107,191	117,759	125,503	111,550	93,596	99,288	94,900
40 – 44	165,700	155,314	157,157	128,897	106,719	117,240	124,950	111,059	93,184	98,851
45 – 49	156,400	164,573	154,257	156,088	128,020	105,993	116,442	124,101	110,303	92,550
50 – 54	128,900	155,008	163,108	152,884	154,698	128,880	105,049	115,405	122,996	109,321
55 – 59	98,000	126,618	152,264	160,220	150,177	151,959	126,598	103,189	113,362	120,818
60 – 64	64,700	95,530	123,427	148,426	156,182	146,392	148,129	123,407	100,588	110,505
65 – 69	55,000	62,028	91,585	118,329	142,296	149,731	140,346	142,011	118,310	96,434
70 – 74	42,700	49,368	55,676	82,207	106,212	127,724	134,398	156,357	127,469	106,195
75 – 79	31,600	35,872	41,474	46,773	69,062	89,229	107,301	112,907	131,355	107,086
80 & above	33,000	36,447	40,802	46,420	52,579	68,630	89,064	110,789	126,209	145,317
TOTAL	1,781,100	1,828,900	1,864,739	1,887,518	1,896,835	1,883,934	1,844,653	1,816,167	1,741,032	1,656,542

TABLE 15.10

Total Resident Population by Age Group According to Low Projection, 2005–50

Age Group	2005	2010	2015	2020	2025	2030	2035	2040	2045	2050
0 – 4	194,600	190,481	173,592	168,145	166,251	156,596	142,048	130,402	118,000	112,159
5 – 9	235,300	194,366	190,252	173,384	167,942	166,051	156,406	141,877	130,246	117,858
10 – 14	261,500	235,146	194,239	190,128	173,271	167,832	165,943	156,305	141,785	130,161
15 – 19	243,900	261,183	234,860	194,004	189,897	173,061	167,629	165,742	156,115	141,613
20 – 24	218,500	243,295	260,534	234,275	193,523	189,425	172,632	167,213	165,331	155,727
25 – 29	248,300	217,785	242,493	259,673	233,508	192,885	188,800	172,062	166,661	164,786
30 – 34	303,500	247,437	217,007	241,621	258,738	231,668	192,192	188,121	171,443	166,061
35 – 39	305,600	302,237	246,409	216,084	240,582	257,623	230,666	191,366	187,312	170,890
40 – 44	333,600	303,732	300,401	244,915	214,751	239,092	256,026	229,233	190,182	186,152
45 – 49	315,000	332,324	300,775	297,498	242,552	212,642	236,734	253,499	226,964	188,306
50 – 54	261,100	310,166	327,218	296,222	293,039	240,926	204,492	233,086	249,586	223,450
55 – 59	196,000	253,993	301,758	318,339	288,283	285,250	234,554	199,002	226,747	242,787
60 – 64	127,000	187,768	243,312	289,129	305,003	276,377	273,582	225,015	190,767	217,222
65 – 69	105,300	117,967	174,406	225,973	268,633	283,357	257,059	268,655	209,544	177,406
70 – 74	79,000	91,751	102,810	151,992	196,913	234,175	246,991	254,699	234,179	183,069
75 – 79	56,900	63,514	73,749	82,666	122,203	158,298	188,363	198,647	206,242	188,346
80 & above	53,400	59,219	65,923	75,020	84,716	111,124	144,656	178,884	202,865	220,831
TOTAL	3,538,500	3,612,364	3,649,738	3,659,068	3,639,805	3,576,382	3,458,773	3,353,808	3,173,969	2,986,824

TABLE 15.11

Male Resident Population by Age Group According to Low Projection, 2005–50

Age Group	2005	2010	2015	2020	2025	2030	2035	2040	2045	2050
0 – 4	100,100	98,240	89,529	86,720	85,743	80,764	73,237	67,254	58,982	56,063
5 – 9	121,800	99,970	98,112	89,413	86,607	85,632	80,657	73,142	67,167	58,905
10 – 14	135,000	121,714	99,900	98,043	89,350	86,546	85,572	80,601	73,091	67,120
15 – 19	125,300	134,784	121,519	99,740	97,886	89,207	86,408	85,435	80,472	72,974
20 – 24	110,700	124,861	134,312	121,093	99,391	97,543	88,895	86,106	85,136	80,190
25 – 29	118,300	110,157	124,249	133,653	120,499	98,904	97,065	88,459	85,684	84,719
30 – 34	145,300	117,684	109,584	123,602	132,958	119,872	98,390	96,560	87,999	85,238
35 – 39	149,600	144,385	116,942	108,893	122,823	132,120	119,116	97,770	95,952	87,445
40 – 44	167,900	148,418	143,244	116,018	108,032	121,852	131,076	118,174	96,998	95,194
45 – 49	158,600	167,751	146,518	141,410	114,532	106,649	120,292	129,398	116,661	95,756
50 – 54	132,200	155,158	164,110	143,338	138,341	112,046	99,443	117,681	126,590	114,129
55 – 59	98,000	127,375	149,494	158,119	138,106	133,291	107,956	95,813	113,385	121,969
60 – 64	62,300	92,238	119,885	140,703	148,821	129,985	125,453	101,608	90,179	106,717
65 – 69	50,300	55,939	82,821	107,644	126,337	133,626	116,713	126,644	91,234	80,972
70 – 74	36,300	42,383	47,134	69,785	90,701	106,451	112,593	98,342	106,710	76,874
75 – 79	25,300	27,642	32,275	35,893	53,141	69,069	81,062	85,740	74,887	81,260
80 & above	20,400	22,772	25,121	28,600	32,137	42,494	55,592	68,095	76,656	75,514
TOTAL	1,757,400	1,791,471	1,804,749	1,802,667	1,785,405	1,746,051	1,679,520	1,616,822	1,527,783	1,441,039

TABLE 15.12

Female Resident Population by Age Group According to Low Projection, 2005–50

Age Group	2005	2010	2015	2020	2025	2030	2035	2040	2045	2050
0 – 4	94,500	92,241	84,063	81,425	80,508	75,832	68,811	63,148	59,018	56,096
5 – 9	113,500	94,396	92,140	83,971	81,335	80,419	75,749	68,735	63,079	58,953
10 – 14	126,500	113,432	94,339	92,085	83,921	81,286	80,371	75,704	68,694	63,041
15 – 19	118,600	126,399	113,341	94,264	92,011	83,854	81,221	80,307	75,643	68,639
20 – 24	107,800	118,434	126,222	113,182	94,132	91,882	83,737	81,107	80,195	75,537
25 – 29	130,000	107,628	118,244	126,020	113,009	93,981	91,735	83,603	80,977	80,067
30 – 34	158,200	129,753	107,423	118,019	125,780	111,796	93,802	91,561	83,444	80,823
35 – 39	156,000	157,852	129,467	107,191	117,759	125,503	111,550	93,596	91,360	83,445
40 – 44	165,700	155,314	157,157	128,897	106,719	117,240	124,950	111,059	93,184	90,958
45 – 49	156,400	164,573	154,257	128,088	128,020	105,993	116,442	124,101	110,303	92,550
50 – 54	128,900	155,008	163,108	156,088	154,698	128,880	105,049	115,405	122,996	109,321
55 – 59	98,000	126,618	152,264	152,884	150,177	151,959	126,598	103,189	113,362	120,818
60 – 64	64,700	95,530	123,427	160,220	156,182	146,392	148,129	123,407	100,588	110,505
65 – 69	55,000	62,028	91,585	148,426	142,296	149,731	140,346	142,011	118,310	96,434
70 – 74	42,700	49,368	55,676	118,329	106,212	127,724	134,398	156,357	127,469	106,195
75 – 79	31,600	35,872	41,474	82,207	69,062	89,229	107,301	112,907	131,355	107,086
80 & above	33,000	36,447	40,802	46,773	52,579	68,630	89,064	110,789	126,209	145,317
TOTAL	1,781,100	1,820,893	1,844,989	1,856,401	1,854,400	1,830,331	1,779,253	1,736,986	1,646,186	1,545,785

Another transformation of no less significance may be seen to occur in the last age group 65 and over. Since the statutory retirement age has been raised to 62 and some workers have had their retirement extended to 65, we have decided to adopt the cut-off period for the old age group as 65 rather than 60. The number of persons in this old age group can be expected to balloon from the initial size of 294,600 to 769,652 at the end of the period, an enormous expansion of some 493,854 or 168 per cent. It is important to bear in mind that this continuation of the present rapid ageing process was mainly engendered by the sharp decline in fertility prior to 1975 and the subsequent below-replacement fertility rather than by a rise in life expectancy.

IMPLICATIONS OF FUTURE TRENDS

One of the vital issues confronting the people of Singapore pertains to the sluggish growth of the resident population up to 2025 and the inevitable shrinking of the population thereafter. The extremely low fertility in the past and the future has resulted in the inability of the resident population to produce enough babies to replace itself. Since 1987 the government has attempted to address this population problem by taking various pronatalist initiatives to encourage married couples to produce more babies. This intervention on the part of the government has culminated in the most recent package of pronatalist measures introduced in 2004, but this package is by no means exhaustive and final. It is still possible to strengthen this pronatalist package by fine-tuning some of the existing policies and adding new ones.

Listed below are some of the improvements that can be considered in the future:

1. The eligibility of pronatalist incentives currently restricted to births up to the fourth order can be extended to the fifth and subsequent births, amounting to less than 2 per cent of the annual births. Apart from the small additional cost involved, this will remove the discrimination, and stigma, against fifth and subsequent children and simplify the administration of these incentives, where applicable.

2. The quantum of money provided under certain existing measures linked to financial rewards can be increased to make them more attractive and effective. The government can afford to allocate more financial resources to the present population problem involving the very survival of the nation-state.

3. The different incentive measures contained in the present package are certainly not all that can be adopted by a country to induce its people to produce more babies. The possibility of introducing other measures such as paid paternity leave can be carefully considered.
4. The Voluntary Sterilization Act, legislated in the early seventies to control population growth, can be reviewed and amended to render it more difficult for men and women to undergo sterilization, having served its original purpose.
5. The Abortion Act, also legislated in the early seventies for the same purpose, can certainly be re-examined and amended to make it less easy for women to seek abortion. Instead, pregnant married women can see through their pregnancy, and the pronatalist package will provide financial and other assistance. For unmarried women, they can keep their babies or give away to deserving couples for adoption.

The anticipated shortage of births will require the relentless promotion of immigration to augment the resident population in Singapore. In this respect, we must bear in mind that the process of permanent residents taking up citizenship does not constitute an addition to the resident population. It merely represents a shift from the permanent resident component to the citizen component within the resident population. Addition to the resident population through immigration can only take place through the granting of permanent residence to foreigners already in the non-resident population as well as new foreigners entering Singapore. The possibility of enlarging the pool of permanent residents from the non-resident population is rather limited. Most of the non-residents, such as domestic maids and construction workers on work permit, are not eligible for permanent resident status. Those on employment pass are reluctant to become permanent residents as their primary purpose in coming to Singapore is to work for a few years rather than to settle down permanently.

There is a need to review the present rules governing the granting of permanent residence to make them as simple and generous as possible. The importance of attracting more immigrants has now been recognized by the government as mentioned by Mr Wong Kan Seng, Deputy Prime Minister in charge of national population affairs.[7] In fact, a new scheme was announced by the Monetary Authority of Singapore (MAS) whereby foreigners worth at least $20 million will be granted permanent resident status if they place $5 million in financial institutions. "We hope this will boost total assets under management and attract high net-worth individuals and their families to take up residency here," said Senior Minister Goh Chok Tong, Chairman of MAS.[8] This is additional to the existing Global Investor Programme administered by the Economic Development Board (EDB) which gives permanent resident status to foreigners investing at least $1 million in business or $1.5 million in venture capital, foundations and trusts.

The slackening rate of population growth, followed by a reduction in the proportion of persons in the working ages, will tend to reinforce the current dependency on foreign workers in certain sectors of the economy. What it implies is that the policy of allowing selected foreigners to work in Singapore on employment pass or work permit basis has to be preserved. Needless to say, the inflow of foreign workers would depend on the demand for such workers as determined by the health of the economy, and have to be supervised closely to minimize the number of over-stayers and illegal immigrants. As explained earlier, the admission of foreigners to work in Singapore is intertwined with the question of promoting immigration. Special consideration, or even incentives, can be offered to such foreigners to take up permanent resident status, thus enlarging the resident population.

The ageing of the resident population is expected to gather momentum in the future as evidenced by the enormous expansion of old persons aged 65 and over. This rapid ageing process was triggered by the sharp decline in fertility since the early-sixties and the continued below-replacement level since the mid-seventies.[9] Among the more serious consequences of population ageing is the availability of social support system for the fast rising number of elderly persons. The family will have to continue to be the primary source of support for the elderly, viewed in terms of shelter and care, not forgetting the greater role to be played by institutional homes. In the course of time, senior citizen villages or condominiums run on a private basis might be able to provide additional shelter for the elderly.

Another implication of the ageing population is related to the modification of the healthcare system to meet the medical needs of the elderly population. Obviously, a higher proportion of the nation's resources, such as medical personnel, physical facilities and finance, will have to be devoted to the needs of the elderly sick. The expected rise in the number of chronic sick and disabled among the old population will require more old age nursing homes. The other issue that is of greater concern to the old people directly is in the area of personal finance. For most of them, the perennial anxiety is related to the adequacy of their CPF savings to enable them to maintain a reasonable standard of living during their old age. Extending the mandatory age for employees to retire, and even allowing some to work beyond this age under mutually-agreed terms, will help to ease the financial burden of the elderly and mitigate the tight labour market accompanying the sluggish growth of the resident population.

Notes

1. United Nations, *Manual III: Methods of Population Projections by Sex and Age*, Population Studies No. 25 (New York: Department of Economics and Social Affairs, 1956).
2. *Monthly Digest of Statistics* (Singapore: Department of Statistics, November 2004).
3. For a discussion of the theory of stationary and stable populations, see Louis Dublin and Alfred J. Lotka, "On the True Rate of Natural Increase", *Journal of the American Statistical Association* 20, no. 150 (September 1925) and Alvaro Lopez, *Problems in Stable Population Theory* (Princeton: Office of Population Research, 1961).
4. Saw Swee-Hock, *The Population of Singapore* (Singapore: Institute of Southeast Asian Studies, 1999).
5. Leow Bee Geok, *Census of Population 2000: Advanced Data Release* (Singapore: Department of Statistics, 2001).
6. *Yearbook of Statistics 2004* (Singapore: Department of Statistics).
7. *Straits Times*, 4 September 2004.
8. *Straits Times*, 1 December 2004.
9. Saw Swee-Hock, "Dynamics of Ageing in Singapore's Population", *Annals of Academy of Medicine*, October 1985, no. 4.

APPENDIX A

TALENT FOR THE FUTURE

by
Lee Kuan Yew

(Prepared text delivered at the National Day Rally
on 14 August 1983)

Our performance for the first half of 1983 has been more than fair with $5\frac{1}{2}$ per cent growth. If the American recovery continues, we may achieve real growth for 1983 of 6 to 7 per cent.

However, several sectors have suffered: Manufacturing down 8 per cent; external trade down 2 per cent; cargo handled down 1 per cent; tourism down 2 per cent.

We made up by boosting construction up 31 per cent, and banking and financial services up 18 per cent. So on our 18th National Day we have cause for relief and congratulations.

How has this been achieved? It is the cumulative result, since 1959, of nearly 24 year of hard work, savings for investments, and consistent policies of rewards based on merit and performance, since 1959.

For the first four to six years, we settled urgent basic problems of unrest and insecurity caused by communist subversion, demonstrations, labour strikes, walkouts, sit-ins, go-slows, riots and general political agitation.

Then in 1965, when we had about established confidence that we could get on top of the communist problems, we suffered a blow to our prospects for long-term economic viability by separation from Malaysia. Then came the withdrawal of the British bases announced in 1968.

It took another five years, to 1970, for us to establish our viability. We established it by restoring discipline and efficiency in society.

Strikes went down, social and work discipline prevailed, and the Employment Act changed the rules governing relations between management and workers. Then investments and trade grew steadily.

We maximized our assets. We had to keep morale up. In November 1964, in the depression after our communal riots, we had campaigns against beggars, stray dogs, and cattle. We had become a scruffy town.

In October 1968, we had our first Keep Singapore Clean campaign. In October 1969, we had a campaign to Keep Singapore Mosquito-Free. Our first tree-planting campaign was in June 1963. It stalled. There were too many political crises. We resumed it in 1971.

We added on the anti-litter campaign to make Singapore clean and green. By the middle 1970s, we moved on to courtesy campaigns. The first Productivity Campaign was in 1975. We were not ready for it.

Five years later, in the 1980s, we relaunched a movement for increased productivity. We were better prepared for it to respond to better education, better training, better work attitudes and good human relations.

The results of better education and the drive for higher productivity are going to take 10 to 20 years before their full benefits are felt. Those campaigns which can give simple, quick returns have all been done.

The swiftest gains were when we established confidence in our stability, discipline, efficiency and security. Now comes the more difficult, long haul to do better: better education, better performance, zero defects, better productivity.

Eventually, we shall reach our maximum potential. And that maximum is determined by our inherent capabilities, the kind of people we are, as individuals, and as a society.

From our 1982 school examinations, we can improve on our present talent pyramid and project that our population will consist of the very able, about 0.1 per cent of each year's school intake who become scholars; the able: 7 per cent tertiary educated, up from 2 per cent in 1980; the above-average: 9 per cent upper secondary, up from 5 per cent; the average: 52 per cent secondary, up from 13 per cent; the below-average: 20 per cent primary, down from 37 per cent; the slow learners: 12 per cent, down from 44 per cent.

Each is capable of learning to achieve her respective potential and must be helped to do so.

From the 1980 Census, we know that the better educated the people are, the less children they have. They can see the advantages of a small family. They know the burden of bringing up a large family.

And when a well-educated wife with high income is not working, the disruption to the wife's career and loss in joint family income is serious. This is having serious consequences, but more on it later.

A person's performance depends on nature and nurture. There is increasing evidence that nature, or what is inherited, is the greater determinant of a person's performance than nurture (or education and environment).

Researches on identical twins who were given away at birth to different families of different social, economic classes show that their performance is very close although their environments are different.

One such research, for over a decade, is by Prof Thomas Bouchard of the University of Minnesota, which has located identical twins wherever they can be found at whatever age — 20 plus, 30 plus, 40 plus.

They test their vocabulary, their habits, their likes and dislikes, of colours, food, friends. The conclusion the researchers draw is that 80 per cent is nature, or inherited, and 20 per cent the differences from different environment and upbringing.

Even though only 20 per cent of the performance of a human being is due to nurture, much more than 20 per cent of the performance of human beings as a group depends on training and organisation.

Compare the East Germans and the West Germans. Their genetic make-up is the same but the performance is vastly different. So with the North and South Koreans. These differences arise from differences in the social, administrative and economic system.

So it is crucial to help every Singaporean, whatever his inherited characteristics, to achieve his best through improved training and education.

The 1980 Census disclosed that whilst we have brought down the birth rate, we have reduced it most unequally. The better educated the woman is, the less children she has.

Ironically, she has the greater resources to provide her children with a better environment, nurturing and care. A woman below age 40 with no educational qualifications, on average, produces about three children although she has limited income and few resources to give her children the extra attention, help and stimulation required.

With primary education, she produces about two on average; with secondary education, $1\frac{1}{4}$; with upper secondary education, $1\frac{1}{3}$; with tertiary education, $1\frac{1}{4}$.

I was so disturbed by these figures that I refused to use them as the basis for the future. They show how many children for each ever-married women aged 10 to 39. I asked for figures of the older women aged 35 to 39. They have slightly more children.

Adjusted for those women in the group who remain unmarried, the mean figures are:

No education — 3.5
Primary — 2.7
Secondary — 1.9
Upper Secondary — 2.0
Tertiary — 1.65

If the younger women, aged 10 to 34, turn out to have the same pattern as the older, aged 35 to 39, the position is not so disastrous, though still bad. Those without education still have more than double the children of those with tertiary or secondary education who have not reproduced themselves.

I shall base my arguments tonight on these less disturbing figures. I suspect the actual results will be that the younger women will have slightly more children than at present, but less than the older women.

Before 1960, most girls had no education. The law permitted and people practised polygamy.

We have altered our pattern of procreation producing the next generation, first by educating everyone, second by giving women equal employment opportunities, and third by establishing monogamy since 1960.

We gave universal education to the first generation in the early 1960s. In the 1960s and 70s, we reaped a big crop of able boys and girls. They came from bright parents, many of whom were never educated.

In their parents' generation, the able and not-so-able both had large families. This is a once-ever bumper crop which is not likely to be repeated. For once this generation of children from uneducated parents have received their education in the late 1960s and 70s, and the bright ones make it to the top, to tertiary levels, they will have less than two children per ever-married woman. They will not have large families like their parents.

The results are going to be felt in Singapore, not in one to two hundred years as in Europe, but in one generation, in 25 years.

Unlike Europe, we do not have a large rural community, where most farmers were uneducated, and so the uneducated but able parents had as many children as their less able but equally uneducated neighbours.

If we continue to reproduce ourselves in this lop-sided way, we will be unable to maintain our present standards. Levels of competence will decline.

Our economy will falter, the administration will suffer, and the society will decline. For how can we avoid lowering performance when for every two graduates (with some exaggeration to make the point), in 25 years' time there will be one graduate, and for every two uneducated workers, there will be three? Worse, the coming society of computers and robotics needs more, not less, well-educated workers.

In all societies, the trend is for the better-educated people to have less children than the less-educated. But no other society has ever compressed this process into just over one generation, from the 1950s to the 1970s, and we have the first statistical evidence in the 1980 Census.

A minority of women, about 14 per cent of all ever-married women age 10 to 39, have four to seven children, and a smaller minority, about 0.4 per cent of all ever-married women age 10 to 39, have eight and more children.

Nearly all of them (97 per cent) have no secondary education. In future, such women will be better educated and will be urged to stop at two. Singapore does not have the space or the resources for such an explosive family expansion.

The government has concentrated on better health, education and housing to improve performance through better environment. Parents must be made to do their part in family nurturing which is only possible in small families.

From data collected by the Ministry of Education on the educational qualifications of the parents of Primary 1 students for 1981–83, we discover that women marry their educational equals or their educational superiors.

In other words, the Singaporean male marries his educational equal or his inferior. Seldom does he marry his educational superior.

The result is a considerable loss in well-educated women remaining unmarried at 40 plus and not represented in the next generation: $13\frac{1}{2}$ per cent of all tertiary-educated women, $8\frac{1}{2}$ per cent of all upper secondary-educated women, and $10\frac{1}{2}$ per cent of all secondary-educated women.

It could be male ignorance and prejudice which lead to his preference of a wife less educated than himself. Or it may be that an educated woman shies away from a husband with less educated ways. Whatever it is, this is a new problem.

In the old days, matchmakers settled these matters. Now we are caught betwixt and between. We have gone for Western-style individual free choice. At the same time, the Singapore male is chauvinist enough not to like marrying women better educated than himself.

Most men hope that their children will be as bright as themselves. After all, they carry their father's surname. Many men are ignorant of the fact that biologically and genetically, every mother and father contributes equally to the child's physical and mental attributes.

Meantime, to make up for this loss of replacement at the top of the educational pyramid, we must increase recruitment of top talent from outside. It is slow and difficult.

Our projected losses through graduates not reproducing themselves under present patterns will be over 20 per cent (based on the mean of 1.65 children born alive per ever-married woman aged 35 to 39) of about 2,000 graduates per year or about 400 graduates.

Our recruitment at present is less than 80 graduates per annum, and unlikely ever to exceed 200 however much we try.

Our most valuable asset is in the ability of our people. Yet we are frittering away this asset through the unintended consequences of changes in our education policy and equal career opportunities for women. This has affected their traditional role as mothers.

It is too late for us to reverse our policies and have our women go back to their primary role as mothers, the creators and protectors of the next generation. Our women will not stand for it. And anyway, they have already become too important a factor in the economy.

Therefore, we must further amend our policies, and try to reshape our demographic configuration so that our better-educated women will have more children to be adequately represented in the next generation.

I am sanguine that we can succeed in getting the few with families of four to 10 or more down to two, as the majority have done. I am not sure we can persuade those with families of one to have two. They need incentives, not disincentives.

Incentives for more children have not worked in Europe. Anyway, it is no offence not to marry and to have any children at all. All the same, we must think deep and long on the profound changes we have unwittingly set off.

In some way or other, we must ensure that the next generation will not be too depleted of the talented. Government policies have improved the part of nurture in performance. Government policies cannot improve the part nature makes to performance.

This only our young men and women can decide upon. All the government can do is to help them and lighten their responsibilities in various ways.

COMPARATIVE EDUCATION LEVELS OF SPOUSES

Education level	Men		Women	
	% whose wives have LOWER education	% whose wives have HIGHER education	% whose husbands have LOWER education	% whose husbands have HIGHER education
No schooling	0%	47.9%	0%	88.4%
Primary	20.6%	16.7%	2.5%	41.6%
Secondary	44.3%	3.3%	18.0%	19.5%
Upper secondary	75.0%	1.7%	31.4%	24.3%
Tertiary	69.1%	0%	16.2%	0%
Total	37.6%	9.5%	9.5%	37.6%

Note: Definitions of categories used in chart

No Qualification: Never attended school or did not pass PSLE.

Primary: Passed PSLE.

Secondary: Passed at least one 'O' level or equivalent.

Upper Secondary: Passed at least one 'A' level or equivalent examination in Poly or Ngee Ann.

Tertiary: Passed university or equivalent qualification.

• *These definitions are in accordance with those used in the 1980 Census.*

APPENDIX A.1
NUMBER OF CHILDREN OF WOMEN (AGED BELOW 40) BY EDUCATION

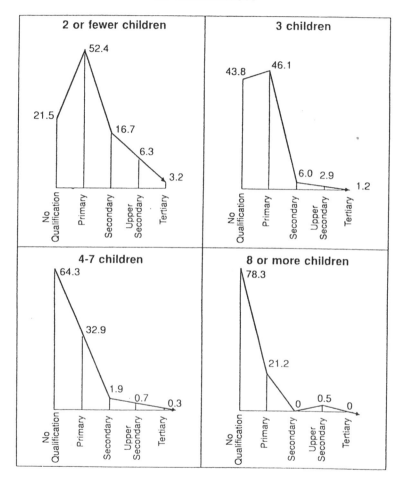

Note: Definitions of categories used in charts

No Qualification: Never attended school or did not pass PSLE.
Primary: Passed PSLE.
Secondary: Passed at least one 'O' level or equivalent.
Upper Secondary: Passed at least one 'A' level or equivalent examination in Poly or Ngee Ann.
Tertiary: Passed university or equivalent qualification.

• *These definitions are in accordance with those used in the 1980 Census.*

APPENDIX B

WHEN COUPLES HAVE FEWER THAN TWO

by
Saw Swee-Hock

(Article published in *Sunday Times* on 15 June 1986)

Our long-term demographic goal is to stabilize the population at a certain number sometime in the first half of the 21st century. To attain this goal, two conditions must be fulfilled.

The first is that we must reduce our fertility to the replacement level, or the two-child family level; the other is to maintain it at this level indefinitely.

The first condition was accomplished in 1975 when our fertility was reduced to the two-child family level. But we were not able to realize the second condition in that fertility continued to fall below this level to reach the low point of 1.5-child family level in 1985.

The continuous decline of our fertility below that two-child family level can be attributed to our comprehensive population control programme as well as to many economic, social and cultural factors favouring a small family size among our general population.

To elaborate on the above points, I have prepared three alternative population projections based on three different fertility assumptions.

In the first projection, it is assumed that our fertility will move back from the 1.5-child family level in 1985 to the replacement level of the two-child family in the year 2000, and will continue to be at this level indefinitely.

In the second projection, fertility is assumed to remain constant indefinitely at the 1.5-child family level.

In the third, it is assumed that fertility will continue to decline slightly from the 1.5-child family level in 1985 to the 1.3-child level in the year 2000.

If we succeed in moving fertility back to the two-child family level in the year 2000, the total population of Singapore will reach the peak of about 3.39 million in the year 2030 and will remain just slightly below this figure indefinitely. This means that zero population growth will be experienced from the year 2030 onwards, with births equalling deaths each year.

If our fertility is not pushed back to the two-child family level and is allowed to continue indefinitely at the 1.5-child level, our population will peak at about 3.02 million in the year 2015. After that, it will decline continuously until it reaches 2.46 million in the year 2050. During this period, deaths will progressively exceed births each year.

The position would be worse if we were to allow our fertility to drop further from the 1985 level to the 1.3-child family level in the year 2000. In this case, the population will reach the maximum of 2.9 million in the year 2010 and, after that, it will decline more rapidly to reach only 2.13 million in the year 2050 as negative growth sets in.

We will now examine the impact of the three paths of population trends on manpower supply and the ageing of the population.

With a two-child family level, the number of children under 15 years of age will rise from 624,000 in 1985 to 682,000 in the year 2000, and then remain slightly below this level during the rest of the period.

But the number will shrink continuously if fertility were not moved back to the two-child family level. With a 1.5-child family level, the number will be reduced from 624,000 in 1985 to 355,000 in the year 2050. The shrinkage is even more severe when the level is a 1.3-child family, the number will then go down to 252,000 in the year 2050.

With the exceptionally rapid decline in our fertility from the high level of about six-child family in the late 1950s to the two-child family level in 1975, ageing in our population has begun.

As for the process of ageing, according to the first projection, the proportion of our population aged 60 and over will increase from 7.8 per cent in 1985 to the peak of 24.5 per cent in the 2030, and fall slightly towards the end of the period in 2050.

According to the second projection, the proportion will increase from 7.8 per cent in 1985 to very near 29.3 in the year 2050.

The third projection sees the proportion increasing from 7.8 per cent in 1985 to 33.7 per cent in the year 2050.

The movement back to the two-child family in the year 2000 is, therefore, necessary not only to prevent our population from declining in the early 21st century, but also to avoid a worsening of our problems associated with our manpower shortage and aged population.

An accelerated ageing process of our population, accompanied by a severe shrinkage in manpower supply, will have dire consequences viewed in terms of many aspects of our society.

Taking into consideration the above scenario, it is advisable for us to make some changes to our population policies in order that our national demographic goal of stabilizing our population in the future can be successfully attained.

The aim of stabilizing our population at about 3.4 million in the future makes sense in view of our small country with limited land space and natural resources.

An ultimate population size of 3.4 million is what Singapore can afford. But with the current pattern of reproduction, the population will fall short of the ultimate size.

To prevent this from happening, we must raise our fertility to at least replacement level. Families which can afford to have at least two children should do so.

HOW POPULATION WILL GROW
(in thousands)

Year	2-child family	1.5-child family	1.3-child family
1985	2,558	2,558	2,558
1990	2,703	2,691	2,686
1995	2,850	2,809	2,789
2000	2,987	2,900	2,858
2005	3,102	2,961	2,896
2010	3,191	3,000	2,911
2015	3,266	3,018	2,905
2020	3,328	3,014	2,873
2025	3,372	2,979	2,807
2030	3,391	2,912	2,708
2035	3,382	2,814	2,577
2040	3,358	2,698	2,429
2045	3,332	2,577	2,275
2050	3,317	2,460	2,125

NUMBER OF CHILDREN UNDER 15

(in thousands)

Year	2-child family	1.5-child family	1.3-child family
1985	624	624	624
1990	621	609	604
1995	659	618	598
2000	682	595	553
2005	681	552	492
2010	660	509	440
2015	642	481	410
2020	643	468	393
2025	660	457	374
2030	671	438	346
2035	669	412	315
2040	659	387	288
2045	651	368	268
2050	654	355	252

PERCENTAGE OF OLD PEOPLE OVER 59

Year	2-child family	1.5-child family	1.3-child family
1985	7.8	7.8	7.8
1990	8.5	8.6	8.6
1995	9.3	9.5	9.5
2000	10.5	10.8	11.0
2005	11.5	12.0	12.3
2010	14.2	15.1	15.5
2015	17.4	18.8	19.6
2020	21.1	23.3	24.4
2025	23.8	26.9	28.5
2030	24.5	28.5	30.6
2035	24.4	29.3	32.0
2040	23.2	28.9	32.1
2045	22.4	28.9	32.7
2050	22.0	29.3	33.7

APPENDIX C

WHO IS HAVING TOO FEW BABIES?

by
Saw Swee-Hock

(Article published in *Sunday Times* on 6 July 1986)

In an earlier article ("When couples have fewer than two", The *Sunday Times*, June 15) I discussed the impact of fertility trends in Singapore on the future size of our population.

Singapore women, as a whole, have been having too few babies to keep our population from declining in the future. But there are differences in birth patterns among women from the different ethnic and educational groups.

For instance, while Malay and Indian women have been having children at a rate of about two per family (the population replacement rate), Chinese women, on average, have been having fewer and fewer.

I will consider the implications of this trend later in the article. First, in order to understand better the population problem that faces Singapore, we need to look at some fertility figures.

Those who watch population trends find a number called the GRR (gross reproduction rate) to be a particularly useful measure of fertility.

It is the average number of daughters a woman will produce during her child-bearing years — provided that she lives through the entire period.

Of course, not all women live until the end of their child-bearing period. So the actual average number of daughters born to women in the population can be calculated from the GRR by taking into account the death rate of women in this age group.

The resulting figure is the net reproduction rate (NRR).

If the NRR is exactly 1 (commonly referred to as the two-child family level, since each woman has one son and one daughter on the average), we can expect the population to replace itself in the future.

If it is less than 1, too few daughters are being born for the population to replace itself.

If it is more than 1, the size of the population will grow, since there will be more daughters than mothers.

When the NRR is exactly 1 in Singapore, the GRR will be about 1.025. This is the replacement fertility level.

Women in Singapore have been having fewer and fewer children since 1958. This decline continued into the early 1970s. In 1970, the average woman had 1.505 daughters over her lifetime.

In 1975, when the fertility rate first dropped below the replacement level of 1.025, the average woman had 1.006 daughters.

Now, if Singapore is to attain the goal of stabilizing its population in the future, two conditions have to be met.

The first is that fertility must drop to replacement level. This it did in 1975.

But the second condition for a stationary population is that fertility needs to remain close to replacement level indefinitely.

This condition has not been met, as fertility has continued to decline after 1975. It fell from 1.006 in 1975 to the low of 0.766 in 1983, after which it went up slightly to 0.779 in 1985.

We can certainly expect fertility to remain below replacement level in 1986 and over the next few years.

Since 1975, our women have been producing fewer children than necessary to keep the population from declining in the future.

For each year since 1975, we can calculate the number of additional births that would have been required to ensure a complete renewal of our population.

First we estimate the number of births that would have occurred each year if replacement fertility (one daughter per woman) had prevailed.

Then, we compare the estimate with the actual number of births for each year.

The difference between the figures for any particular year gives an idea of the extent to which our women have not been producing enough children to ensure that the population will replace itself.

In 1974, there were 43,268 births as compared with the 39,074 births required for replacement. This gives a surplus of 4,194 births. Before 1974, the surpluses were even greater.

In 1975, when fertility dropped below replacement level, the actual number of births was 39,948, a shortfall of 755 below the 40,703 births required for replacement.

In that year, we were therefore 1.9 per cent short of the number of births needed to ensure the future replacement of our population.

As fertility continued to decline after 1975, the birth shortfall became more serious. It increased to 9,018 or 18 per cent in 1980 and to 13,416 or 24 per cent in 1985.

For the whole period 1975–1985, the shortfall was no less than 92,252 births.

We will obviously continue to experience a birth shortfall as long as our fertility remains below replacement level.

It is therefore necessary to take action now to reduce, and eventually to eliminate, the shortfall by making changes to our population control programme so that fertility can move back to replacement level.

Let us now look at the differences in fertility among the three main ethnic groups.

When overall fertility in Singapore first fell to slightly below replacement level in 1975, the fertility of every one of the three ethnic groups fell to near replacement level (1.000 for the Chinese, 1.032 for the Malays and 0.956 for the Indians).

All the three ethnic groups have responded well to our population control programme in the past, and have contributed to the attainment of replacement fertility at the national level.

The fertility of all three groups has remained below replacement level in practically all of the past 11 years.

But the three ethnic groups have differed in the amount by which their fertility has fallen below replacement level.

During the period 1975–1985, while the fertility of Malays and Indians has shown relatively small deviations from replacement level, the fertility of the Chinese has fallen progressively below this level.

In 1985, Malay fertility was 1.034, about 0.9 per cent above replacement level. Indian fertility was 0.939, about 6.1 per cent below replacement level. In contrast, Chinese fertility, at 0.702, was about 31.5 per cent below replacement level.

What was the impact of these differences in fertility on the distribution of births among the ethnic groups? The actual distribution in 1985 was 69.1 per cent Chinese, 19.1 Malays and 7.7 per cent Indians.

Now, if the Chinese women had produced babies in 1985 at a rate required to satisfy replacement fertility, there would have been about 43,125 births to Chinese women instead of the actual 29,355 births.

Assuming that the birth patterns of Malay and Indian women had remained the same, the percentages would then have been 76.7 per cent Chinese births, 14.4 per cent Malay births and 5.8 per cent Indian births.

These percentages are quite close to the population distribution by ethnic group in 1985, which was 76.4 per cent Chinese, 14.9 per cent Malays and 6.4 per cent Indians.

If there had been 43,125 Chinese births, the total number of births in 1985 would have been 56,254. This figure is very near the estimate of 55,900 births required to match replacement fertility in 1985.

Nowadays, the Malays and the Indians are producing children at a rate very close to the two-child family level, while the Chinese are producing well below this point.

The possibility of achieving our demographic goal of stabilizing our population in the future lies with the Chinese population in Singapore.

We will next look at fertility differences among various educational groups, although this analysis is handicapped by inadequate data. Birth statistics classified by educational qualification of mothers have only been compiled recently, since mid-1983.

Also, since we lack good data classified by educational qualification for the female population in non-census years, figures for those years have had to be indirectly estimated from the annual labour force survey.

Our calculations confirm the existence of differences in fertility among educational groups. The 1985 fertility for the three educational groups was as follows:

Educational qualification	GRR
PSLE certificate and below	0.93
O Level certificate	0.58
A Level certificate and above	0.66

We must caution that these rates are crude estimates. This is because the definition of "educational qualification" differs between the birth statistics (where figures are given for those who have successfully obtained their certificates at the three educational stages) and the labour force survey data (where figures refer to those who have merely attended the various stages and need not have obtained the relevant certificates).

A third kind of fertility difference exists among the various income groups. In general, women in the lower income group tend to produce more children than those in the higher income group.

However, it is not possible to compute the variation of GRR with income because birth statistics classified by income of mothers or fathers have never been collected in the birth registration system.

AVERAGE NUMBER OF DAUGHTERS BORN TO WOMEN OVER THE YEARS

Year	No.
1970	1.505
1971	1.478
1972	1.486
1973	1.356
1974	1.135
1975	1.006
1976	1.019
1977	0.878
1978	0.869
1979	0.855
1980	0.841
1981	0.830
1982	0.816
1983	0.766
1984	0.772
1985	0.779

Figures represent gross reproduction rate

HOW BIRTH PATTERNS DIFFER FROM THE
POPULATION DISTRIBUTION

Race	Actual births in 1985		Present racial composition	Birth required for a similar balance
Chinese	29,355	69.1%	76.4%	43,125
Malays	8,104	19.1%	14.9%	8,104
Indians	3,280	7.7%	6.4%	3,280
Others	1,745	4.1%	2.3%	1,745
Total	42,484	100.0%	100.0%	56,254

APPENDIX C.1

HOW FAR OFF TARGET OUR BABY OUTPUT HAS BEEN

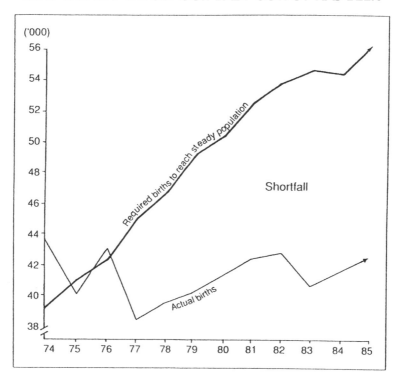

Years	Actual births	Required births	The birth gap	
1974	43,268	39,074	+4,194	+10.7%
1975	39,948	40,703	-755	-1.9%
1976	42,948	42,035	-252	-0.6%
1977	38,364	44,788	-6,424	-14.3%
1978	39,441	46,521	-7,080	-15.2%
1979	40,779	48,887	-8,108	-16.6%
1980	41,217	50,235	-9,018	-18.0%
1981	42,250	52,176	-9,926	-19.0%
1982	42,654	53,578	-10,924	-20.4%
1983	40,585	54,316	-13,731	-25.3%
1984	41,556	54,174	-12,618	-23.3%
1985	42,484	55,900	-13,416	-24.0%

APPENDIX C.2
FERTILITY AMONG THE THREE ETHNIC GROUPS

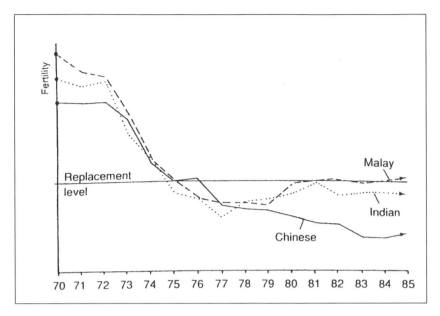

Year	Daughters per woman		
	Chinese	Malay	Indian
1970	1.463	1.720	1.590
1971	1.460	1.627	1.549
1972	1.462	1.599	1.575
1973	1.357	1.390	1.284
1974	1.121	1.195	1.145
1975	1.000	1.032	0.956
1976	1.042	0.912	0.905
1977	0.871	0.897	0.814
1978	0.859	0.896	0.899
1979	0.846	0.886	0.902
1980	0.801	0.983	0.948
1981	0.779	1.008	0.984
1982	0.762	1.023	0.930
1983	0.698	0.989	0.948
1984	0.694	1.016	0.944
1985	0.702	1.034	0.939

Figures represent the gross reproduction rate.

APPENDIX D

THE SECOND LONG MARCH

by
Goh Chok Tong

(Speech delivered at the Nanyang Technological Institute on
4 August 1986)

The title of my talk today is The Second Long March. It is inspired by the Long March of the Chinese communists in 1935.

The Long March began in October 1934 at the south-eastern corner of China, and ended one year later, in another corner in the north-west, a distance of about 10,000 kilometres.

The communists, led by Mao Zedong, trekked over endless expanses of very harsh terrain — raging rivers, snow capped mountains and treacherous marshes. At one point, when there was no water they survived by drinking their own urine.

Of the 90,000 men and women who set out, only 7,000 survived the March. Most of them died of sickness and exhaustion. Only a few were actually killed in battle.

For those who survived, it was a real triumph of human endurance and spirit.

One may disagree with the political ideology of Mao Zedong and his comrades. Yet one cannot help but marvel at the triumph of their spirit over impossible odds.

I feel that the problems we are facing are so complex and immense that they will require strong qualities such as these exhibited by the Long Marchers.

Those are physical and moral courage, perseverance, discipline, dedication, resolution and teamwork.

But when I tested the title on some of my colleagues, they were not the least enthusiastic.

They thought the Long March metaphor suggested that I was an admirer of the Chinese communists.

They also pointed out that the Long March was not an all-conquering march, but was, in fact, a hasty retreat of the Red Army.

I looked for alternative titles, such as The Tasks Ahead and Certainties and Uncertainties.

In the end I felt The Second Long March was still the most apt. It captures the spirit of determination and toughness of purpose most vividly.

Singapore's First Long March

My Long March metaphor may be inspired by the Chinese communists but the numerical order is not.

I use the word "second" not after the Long March in China but after a Long March in Singapore.

For, in my view, the struggle for survival of Singapore as an independent nation is also a triumph of the human spirit, a victory of conviction and determination, over impossible odds.

The PAP Old Guard fought the communists, and defeated them.

Our Prime Minister has no doubt that, had the communists won, they would have pulled out his fingernails.

Singapore's survival as an independent nation was also a hard struggle. To begin with, Singapore's birth was not a normal one. It was a painful Caesarian operation done without anaesthesia. Older Singaporeans were convinced that the newborn Singapore was not meant to survive. But, like a Spartan baby left overnight under a cold open sky, it did.

It is now, of course, history how the Prime Minister and the PAP Old Guard rallied the people, struggled and kept newborn Singapore warm and alive. In retrospect, it looks easy. But at that point of time, nothing was certain.

I remember how the Government flattened the hills and filled up the swamps in Jurong, to turn it into an instant Industrial estate. I was working in the Economic Planning Unit then. Success was far from certain. For years, Jurong sprouted only a few factories and Jurong

Industrial Estate became known as "Goh's folly" (not this Goh, but Dr Goh).

The Second Long March

We have grown up. We will be 21 years old in a few days' time.

It is an opportune time for us to re-assess and reaffirm certain basic facts and premises before we plunge into adulthood. Where are we heading? What is the landscape like before us?

Singapore is unique as a nation — small, no natural resources, a city-state, a country without a country-side, a nation of many different races and religions.

Given these basic facts, Singapore will always be vulnerable to internal and external forces. Take, for example, the vulnerability of our economic prosperity.

I was made vividly aware of this when I first started work in 1964. Trade with Indonesia came to a sudden standstill because of Sukarno's Confrontation against Malaysia. Jobs were suddenly lost. The bumboats were all tied up along the Singapore River. The large number of unemployed youths was described as "the army of the unemployed".

When Confrontation ended, and with Independence, Singapore grew. It grew rapidly until 1985, when we suddenly plunged into recession. Our economy shrank.

Workers became unemployed again. A new army of the unemployed? Of mainly officer grades? We have to worry about creating jobs all over again.

Creating jobs and economic growth is, therefore, like climbing mountains. The mountains are always there.

Mountain Ranges

Looking ahead, I can see several other peaks we have to scale. You may say that once you have successfully conquered a mountain peak, there is nothing to climbing the next one.

But these mountains are permanently covered with snow, and scaling them is always dangerous, even for the most experienced mountaineer.

At this point of time, we may not be able to plan in detail how to climb since we do not have full information on the topography. But at least we are better equipped than Mao Zedong.

What I aim to do in my speech is not to tell you how to climb the mountains, but to outline the obstacles we are likely to encounter. Then I would like to hear your views, after my speech, on how to climb them.

After all, the group of Singaporeans who have to participate most actively in The Second Long March will be the young men and women like you.

Physical Constraints of Growth

Our immediate problem is to pull ourselves out of the current economic recession. Our longer-term problem is how to overcome the many constraints on our growth.

For example, our land, water and manpower resources are finite, and we are almost reaching their limits. I have spoken on these issues at a similar forum in NUS last year.

The Acting Minister for Trade and Industry has also spoken to you on Recession and Economic Recovery. I shall, therefore, not elaborate on this point tonight.

But I want to reiterate that we should go easy on wage increases for another year at least, and to advise you to learn to live with slower economic growth, which means lowering your income expectations.

Human Problems

The constraint of physical resources is not as difficult to overcome as the human resource problem. This type of problem requires us to change attitudes and tread on sensitivities. It concerns people directly.

When we deal with people, we are basically dealing with emotions, their hopes and fears, their pride and prejudices, their joys and sorrows.

The human resource problem cannot, therefore, be tackled in the same efficient, computerized manner as we can the non-human ones. Unless they are properly handled, any attempt to solve them can itself cause further problems. People are what make Singapore. They are our most valuable resource.

I think the most serious challenge we are going to face is how to cope with the changing demographic profile — its size, composition and age distribution.

I know this is a longer-term problem, but if we do not address it now, it can only become more serious.

Our population now stands at 2.6 million. It will grow to three million in the year 2020, and then decline.

Our population will decline because the number of babies born each year in the last 10 years has fallen short of the number required.

Professor Saw Swee Hock, professor of statistics at the National University of Singapore, has calculated that for our population to replace itself, that is, one person for one person, we required 56,000 babies for 1985.

But only 42,000 babies were born last year. There was, therefore, a shortfall of 14,000 babies.

You may think producing babies is the most natural thing to do. But apparently the facts seem to indicate otherwise. It seems that the more we educate our girls, the more reluctant they are to have babies. I do not know whether the reluctance is theirs alone, or whether the boys must also share the blame. This not a joke. It is a fact.

The girls who have only a Primary School Leaving Examination education have no problems. They are reproducing themselves, one for one.

For a population to replace itself, on average, each girl must produce another girl. The girls with an O level certificate and above are not doing that. They are under-producing by as much as 40 per cent. So, here we have the nub of the problem.

Prosperity

We have to pay close attention to the trend and pattern of births because of their consequences on our prosperity and security — in fact, on our survival as a nation.

You may be puzzled why having fewer babies can result in a less prosperous nation. Let me explain.

Economic growth comes from two sources — growth in the size of the work force and growth in its productivity. Productivity itself depends on the ability of the population. If the work force does not increase, then productivity must increase to generate economic growth.

But there is a limit to productivity growth as the economy becomes more developed.

The Japanese are a highly productive people. Yet in the last 20 years, their growth in productivity has not exceeded 4 per cent per annum.

The Japanese are good. Do you think we can do better? I doubt it. It would be extremely difficult to do better than the Japanese people.

Not Enough Young Workers

Economic growth will slacken for another related reason. With fewer babies each year, the proportion of younger people in the population will become smaller. Put in another way, our work force will become increasingly older.

Today, the average or median age of our work force is 27, that is, half the work force is above this age, and half below it. It will go up to 35 years by the year 2000, and then 43 years by the year 2030.

Will our work force be vigorous and dynamic? Will investors be attracted to a country which does not have enough young workers? Even now, you can see that many companies prefer to employ younger workers. Not only are they cheaper to employ, but they are also more nimble with their hands, and are more up-to-date in their skills and training.

Ageing Population

Our changing demographic profile will throw up another grave problem — how to cope with a fast ageing population.

At present, there are about 200,000 people aged 60 and above. The number will quickly increase to over 300,000 in 15 years' time. It will balloon to 800,000 30 years later.

You will be among those 800,000 people. How are you going to support yourselves when you are no longer working?

You may say that your children can support you, but bear in mind, at the rate we are going, many Singaporeans will have only one or even not a single child in their lifetime.

The older population that is without a steady income will need medical care, housing and to move around. These services will have to be paid for, not by the Government, but by those who are working.

Singapore has no natural wealth. The only way for the Government to raise the required revenue to take care of the older population is to levy more taxes on those who are working. And they will squeal.

The tax burden can be extremely heavy if it has to support some 30 per cent of the population who are over 60 years old. How do we reconcile the interest of the young and the needs of the old? How do we solve the dilemma? I hope you will tell me later.

Security

I now move on to explain the effect of fewer and fewer births on security. Put simply, there will not be enough young men to defend the country.

We have already extended reserve service to 13 years. Do we extend it to 20? Does it really solve our problems even if we do? Do we enlist girls for national service?

Security is a perennial problem. It is another one of those perennially snow-capped mountains.

You cannot assume that once you are born a Singaporean, you will always remain a Singaporean. Let me illustrate this point by giving you a bit of my personal history. I have changed nationality many times.

I was born a British subject. Before I could even walk, the Japanese dropped their bombs on Singapore. Soon Singapore fell, and I became, I suppose, a Japanese subject. The Japanese lost the war in 1945. Singapore was returned to the British, and I became a British subject again. In 1959, when I was still in school, I became a Singapore citizen. In 1963, when I was in the university, I became a Malaysian when Singapore became part of Malaysia. Two years later, soon after I started work, I reverted to Singapore citizenship.

So, all in all, I have changed nationality five times! I hope there will not be a sixth time.

What I am talking about is our ability to defend ourselves in the future. You may not realize it, but it takes 20 years to produce a soldier — 18 years to grow him and two years to train him.

What Can Be Done?

What can be done? What should be done? Does the solution lie simply in exhorting our people to produce more babies? Who should do the producing?

How do we get those who can afford and should have at least two children to have at least two children? Do we change our family planning policy of 'Two is Enough" to "Three is Better"?

This matter has to be carefully considered, because by trying to check and anticipated population decline, we may overshoot the target. Then we will have the reverse problem of having too many people on too small a piece of land.

National Harmony

The problems I have raised today are not really new. But like the mountain ranges in front of Mao, we have to cross them, again and again.

Each crossing is always difficult, always tricky, always perilous. It requires unity of mind and singleness of purpose. It requires us to work in harmony. National harmony is absolutely crucial for us to conquer our problems.

A country at peace with itself can achieve many things. A country at odds with itself will lose everything.

I can think of no better example to illustrate this point than Sri Lanka. I have been to Sri Lanka several times. I have some friends there. It is, therefore, with some concern that I see what is taking place there.

Some years ago, when I was in Colombo, they showed me their proposed economic zone. They were going to model it after Jurong Industrial Estate. As recently as a year ago, Air Lanka advertised in our press and on SBC: Come to Sri Lanka for "A Taste of Paradise". Today, investors are not going. Neither are the tourists. The violent disharmony between Tamils and Sinhalese is keeping them away.

The Sri Lankans are not an unintelligent people. Our Senior Minister came from Sri Lanka. Their Minister of National Security (Mr Lallith Athulathmudali) taught law in Singapore. He has also taught my wife.

They have a high rate of literacy. They also practise democracy. It is not that they do not know that national harmony is important. Everybody knows that national harmony is crucial to progress. But it does not follow that just because you know that it is important that there will be national harmony. It depends ultimately on the politics of the country, its government, and its ability to get the people to work together.

Our Mission

The time has come for our generation to work together, to face the future together, to shoulder the responsibilities of state, and to keep Singapore going.

We have already begun our Long March. We will face our share of adversaries and our own mountains. We have to call on our own skill, resolve and courage to overcome them.

The problems are great because, besides the basic internal problems I have discussed, there will be external pressures and uncertainties. For one, the world is becoming more protectionist and more competitive. Making a living is going to be tougher. For another, the whole South-east Asian region is undergoing a political change. And change invariably means uncertainty.

The older generation of Singaporeans has marched together to overcome its problems. Our generation must likewise march together to overcome ours. Only then can we cross our mountains successfully.

I have discussed only some of the problems today, such as physical resource limitations, declining number of births, particularly by the better-educated girls, and ageing population. There are many more. Besides mountains, there are ravines, gorges, landslides, flash floods, and swamps we have to contend with. Singapore's problems are unique.

We can look at other countries which are facing similar problems and get some idea on how we can approach or tackle ours.

But, finally, because of our unique circumstances, we will still have to find our own unique solution to our own set of problems. You will notice I did not attempt to offer any solution.

EDUCATION AND FERTILITY

Educational qualification	Gross reproduction rate*
PSLE certificate and below	0.93
'O' level certificate	0.58
'A' level certificate and above	0.68

*GRR (gross reproduction rate) is a measure of fertility. It refers to the average number of daughters a woman will produce during her child-bearing years, provided that she lives during the entire period. However, since not all women live until the end of their child-bearing period, the actual average number of daughters born to women in the population is lower than the GRR. The GRR minus the death rate of women in this age group gives the net reproduction rate (NRR).

If the NRR is exactly 1 (commonly referred to as the two-child family level, since each woman has one son and one daughter on the average), we can expect the population to replace itself in the future.

If it is less than 1, too few daughters are being born for the population to replace itself.

If it is more than 1, the size of the population will grow, since there will be more daughters than mothers.

When the NRR is exactly 1 in Singapore, the GRR will be about 1.025. This is the replacement fertility level.

The reason for my not doing so is simple. When you go mountaineering, every climber must play his part. You know it is a risky venture. You have to take precautions, such as linking the climbers with a rope tied round their waists, for mutual support in case one slips.

If one slips or stumbles, he will be saved by the others. The climbers work as a team. They place their trust in one another.

We are going to climb the mountains together, and I want to know how you think we can conquer them.

POPULATION BY AGE
in thousands

	1985	2000	2030
Under 15	624	586	399
15–59	1735	1989	1681
60 & over	199	327	841
Total	2558	2902	2921

OLD DEPENDENCY RATIO
(%)

1985	11%
2000	16%
2030	50%

APPENDIX D.1

EDUCATIONAL PROFILE OF OLDER SINGLES

Percentage of those in 40-44 years age group

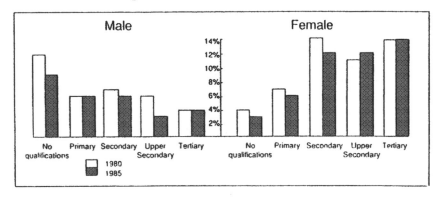

APPENDIX D.2

WHO WILL REMAIN UNMARRIED EACH YEAR IN FUTURE

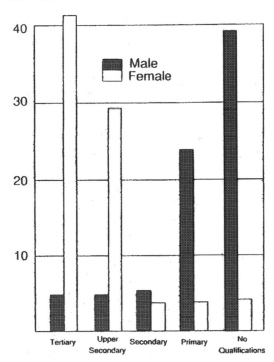

APPENDIX D.3

DISTRIBUTION OF POPULATION BY AGE AND SEX

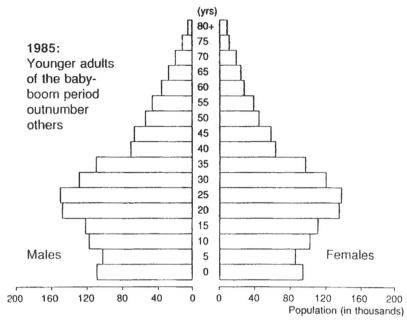

1985:
Younger adults
of the baby-
boom period
outnumber
others

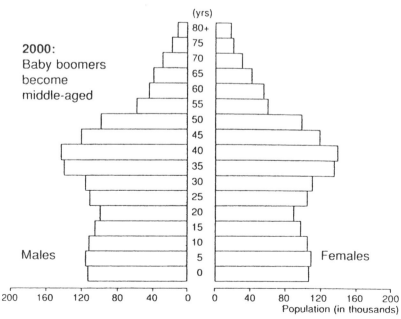

2000:
Baby boomers
become
middle-aged

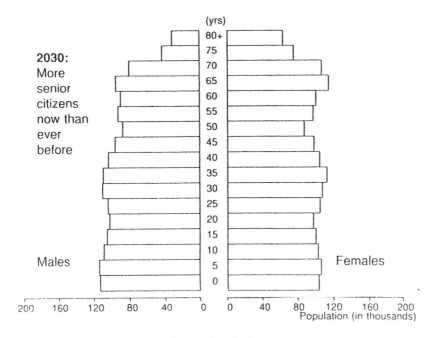

(yrs)

2030:
More
senior
citizens
now than
ever
before

Males

Females

Population (in thousands)

APPENDIX D.4
THE AGEING LABOUR FORCE

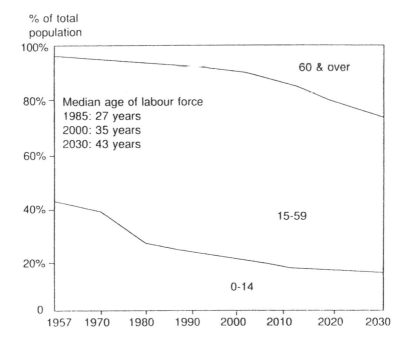

% of total
population

60 & over

Median age of labour force
1985: 27 years
2000: 35 years
2030: 43 years

15-59

0-14

APPENDIX E

BABIES

by
Lee Hsien Loong

(Part of Speech Delivered at the National Day Rally
Held on 22 August 2004)

I have one last subject. It's very late, but I think I will talk about it all the same and this is babies. It's a very serious problem for us and for all the developed countries. Japan, Korea, Hong Kong, Europe. Even the Catholic countries in Europe, Italy has a very low fertility rate, Spain too. The only exception is America where immigration is very high and somehow, the culture is completely different. It's a national problem for us, but it's also an intensely personal business. I asked when did previous Prime Ministers raise such delicate matters? My people tell me, Mr Lee raised it in his 18th National Day Rally. What about Goh Chok Tong? He waited for his tenth National Day Rally. This is my first one. So, new baby, please be understanding.

Our approach is, let's put it like this — this is a matter of values, not of incentives. It's values and priorities, not the financial grants and subsidies, which count. We want people to have babies because you want them and you love them. It's part of a happy family life. It's fulfilling to bring up a child. You can have the most successful career, you can be the richest man on Earth or the most powerful man or woman on Earth, but if you don't have a family and don't have children, I think you're missing something. It starts off with missing changing nappies when you have a child, but then you miss watching a child learning to walk, learning to talk, going to school, getting sick, depending on you, walking with you, playing with you. You are teaching him, doing homework with him or her. Then you'll find that he's got his own temperament, character, personality, he's different from you. He's got his own ideas and after a while, one day, you are helping him or her do homework and he says, "No, no, you do it like this" and I look puzzled and I don't quite know what he is talking about, but he does and you know he's taken a step forward and he's on his own. And then they grow up a bit more and you have to, come a time when they ring up and say, "Can you pick me up at the cineplex?" Then you will worry whether they have found girlfriends or boyfriends. Then you will worry if they have not found girlfriends or boyfriends and you will think by the time they are 20 years old, they would have grown up, but actually, even when they are 50 years old, if I'm still around, I will still be fussing. "Drink your *pao shen*" (ginseng), take care of yourself, don't overstrain because my parents do that and I think if I'm still *compos mentis*, I will do that too.

So, these are not things you can translate into dollars and cents, or careers and promotions. It's fulfilling. It's sad if you don't have it. We wish every Singaporean do and have a couple of children, three, if you can. It's difficult, yes, people say quality time, but actually, some of my friends who have three children say "economies of scale" because with three of them, they form an ecosystem. They learn from each other, they take care of each other, the older ones look after the small ones, which means they learn. The small ones learn to share with the big ones, which means they also learn and if you only have one and you spend quality time with him and he goes to school and the teacher cannot spend quality time with him, and his friend borrows his eraser, he may punch his friend on the nose. So, have two, three. I won't say have half-a-dozen but have a couple. We are not going to micromanage your lives. I mean, we won't say, have the first one by 25 years old, the second one by 30 years old. It's up to you. What we can do is we'll make it easier for families to marry and to have children. You make the decisions.

But I think what we have to do is to change attitudes. We've got to change attitudes of the singles, of the couples and also of employers. It's probably easiest with the employers, you just have to persuade them that they have to be fair to their staff — parents, mothers who have children, give them time off, give them some flexibility. Women who are pregnant, be fair to them and don't sack them because they are about to have a baby. And if you look at the more successful companies, IBM, Hewlett Packard, the American companies, they are very good employers in this respect. They look after their staff. It's not just the Government. We try to be good employers, but they are doing it for commercial reasons and it makes sense for them because they know if they take care of their staff properly, their staff will be loyal to the company and will perform.

Harder to change is the attitudes of singles. They need to have realistic expectations. Don't look for the impossible. If you go for MCS soap opera standard, then no hope. What do I mean by being realistic? I give you a couple of examples. First one is from a very experienced grassroots leader friend of mine who said he counselled his niece many years ago. She was single in her late 20s. He says, "You must get a husband". She said, "But I must find a man who will tell jokes to me, entertain me, pick me up if I am down, look after me in the evenings". So, he told her, "You don't need a husband, you need a TV set". So, she took his advice to heart, got married and is now happily married with children. I should bring him into SDU (Social Development Unit) council some day.

But I asked SDU, do you have problems of high expectations? They said, "Yes". So, I said, "Give me some examples. Don't give me statistics, just give me some examples". So, they gave me a couple. One person said he wants a girl, tall, long hair, intelligent, fair, no spectacles, I don't know what other particulars he specified. So, SDU worked very hard, went through the files, produced the girl — tall, long hair, everything, but wore specs. He went out with the girl, came back, says, "Change". So, the SDU matchmaker says, "Why? She's a perfectly fine lady, why don't you want her? She's wearing specs. Okay, change, she can wear contact lenses". He said, "No. If she wears specs, bad genes. Children will wear specs". So, I asked, what about him? He also wore specs. So, he's still single. Another one says, "I want a girl, this, that, the other, preferably stay in Bukit Timah". So, matchmaker found him somebody nice, suitable social background, so on. Problem? She stayed in Bukit Merah. Wrong Bukit.

So, I think it's not the matchmaker's fault, right? I think we've got to change our mindsets and be realistic and accommodating. I think couples, too, have to change their mindset because we have to share the responsibility more equally and more fairly. In the old days, the man worked, the woman looked after the family. Man brought home the bacon, the woman brought up the kids, and for a lot of homes, they are still like that. If you have done Meet-the-People sessions, you will know. We've seen a lot of women who've been deserted by their husbands,

husbands left, not paid maintenance, trying to go to court, come to look for us. But we very seldom see a husband come, deserted by a woman who's not paid him maintenance and needs our help. That's the reality of our society. It's patriarchal, but that's the way it has worked.

So, because of that, we've always said, for government medical benefits, for the man, your wife and children can get. For the woman, husband and children cannot get because husband is supposed to take care of you, not you of your husband. But a lot of women have felt very angry about this. I know Irene feels strongly. I think Indranee, Penny, they are all watching me carefully and the reality is changing. The reality is changing, our society is changing. The women are working, they are going out. Ten years ago, I don't think you could have imagined a women's team wanting to go and climb Mount Everest, but today, there is and I think that if we're going to talk about shared responsibility, if we are going to shift and try and get couples to split more evenly the duties of bearing and bringing up children, I think we should move. So, after many years, after thinking this over many times and picking up the stone and putting it back again and again, we will now decide to equalise medical benefits for men and women under the new medical schemes. The older schemes which are moribund, we will extend it to their children because I think for the older schemes, there are Civil Service complexities, but for the new schemes, let's treat it as equal. So, philosophically, I accept. The private sector is doing it, I am doing it, but make sure your husband looks after you.

I've got a lot of feedback from the public since March when we had the Budget and I said we're studying this and Hng Kiang is chairing a committee and some of these are very sensible feedback on what we should do as our package for procreation. I'd like to read you just one letter which came in the email. I've got the permission from the person. So, let me tell you what she asked for. She said, "Dear Sir, I am married with a four-year-old son and currently five months-plus pregnant with a pair of twins. We planned to employ a foreign maid to take care of the babies. However, we realised that the maid levy is so much and the maid's salary is so much, excluding her meals". Then she added up — full-day childcare and she already has a son, newborn expenses and so on. "I am writing sincerely to seek your kind assistance. One, maid levy — we hope to pay a lesser amount of maid levy monthly, if possible. Two, Medisave for hospital bill — this time round, I plan to have a Caesarean delivery, thus the hospital bill may be slightly higher. I am worried that I may have to fork out a lot of cash on hospital bills. So, I sincerely hope that we can utilise more Medisave so that we do not have to fork out so much cash. Three, maternity leave (feedback only) — like any other mothers, we feel that eight weeks of maternity leave is quite short. If possible, an additional of four or eight weeks will really be beneficial and valuable to both the mother and the baby. My estimated due date is around beginning of September. I thank you for your precious time in reading my mail, sincerely hope that you can understand my situation. Your kind assistance will be very much appreciated".

I thought this was a very sensible letter because the things she asked for are, in fact, the things which mothers need — maid, delivery expenses, leave. So, I checked up whether her baby is born. She says, "Not yet, two weeks more". So, I will deliver my package before she delivers her baby. I will just sketch out the rough outlines and Lim Hng Kiang will tell you all about it in a few days' time. Childcare — it's a key concern of mothers, both the caring and looking after of their kid when he's young, also the bonding, to form that special tie between mother and baby when the child is growing up. What do you need that will evolve as the infant grows? First few weeks, you need the maternity leave, then you have infant care, then you have childcare, then a little bit older, you still need help around the family. So, for maternity leave, having gone through employers, employees, unions and so on, what we will do is we will extend the leave from eight weeks to 12 weeks — four more weeks. We will go from three children to four children and the Government will reimburse the extra expenses because if we just put it on the employer, I think it's not fair and the employer will say, "I prefer not to have a woman".

Infant care — this is a gap in our system. Now, we have childcare subsidies but we don't have infant care subsidies which are commensurate because infant care is a lot more expensive than childcare. You need almost one caregiver for two babies. So, we will introduce a Centre-based Infant Care subsidy similar to the childcare subsidy but higher. I think it's S$400 per month.

Then we'll have childcare leave — this is a new thing, so let me explain what it is. We could have had, say, five weeks more of maternity leave at the beginning when the baby is born, but we decided, let's have four weeks more and keep this extra one week and let's spread it out over, say, the first seven years of the child's life, two days a year. So, that's actually two weeks more, two days a year over seven years. So, if you are a parent, a father or a mother with a child below seven, then every year, you are entitled to two days of childcare leave. We will change the law. Which means if your child is sick, you can do it, if your child needs to see the kindergarten teacher, you can take a day off. You want to take a day off with the child, go to the zoo on a Monday. It can also be done. Two days a year, provided the child is below seven, no matter how many children you have below seven.

Then, maids — a lot of parents have asked for maid levy to be made lighter and I think there's something in it because one of the ways we can ease the burden for working mothers, or even non-working mothers in Singapore, is to let them have maids, which they can't do in many other countries. If you are living in America, or in Australia, or in Britain, you won't have a maid help you at home. At most, you have a cleaning lady come in once a week or twice a week, but a maid in the home is something that we're lucky to have in Singapore. But there is a levy and I think it's right if you have a child, we lower the cost. So, we will lower the maid levy for families with children below 12 years old.

Grandparents — grandparents are a tremendous help to families who have children. All the MPs I talked to say so. If they haven't had grandparents, they couldn't have managed, either their own parents or their in-laws. All the grassroots leaders say so. There are even scientific studies of pre-modern societies, Finland and Canada, which showed — they checked all their church records — that if you have a grandmother below 60 living within ten miles, you have two extra surviving grandchildren because the grandmother will help to look after them, will help to guide them, will spot what's wrong and no doubt will nag you to have a few more children. And I can tell you they make a tremendous difference. I have benefited from this. If I did not have my parents or my mother-in-law helping to look after two very young kids in 1984, when Chok Tong asked me to come in, you may feel National Service, you may want to serve, can you do it? But I had the (mother-in-law) at home. I had my parents bringing the children out for walks in the evenings. I come home at night, they are asleep, but I know that they have been fed, attended to, disciplined, if necessary. Everything is in hand. And so, I came in, no maid levy discount, no grandparent incentive, but the grandparents made the difference. And I think for many families, it's like that and so, I think we should have some incentives which are targeted towards families which have old folks at home, on tax and also on the maid levy and this, we will do.

Next, financial support — I won't talk a lot about this. We have various tax breaks, all kinds of them. We will improve them and tidy them up. We also have a Baby Bonus which is now for the second and third child. I think we want to spread it out so that we're not just focusing on this specific child. So, what we will do is we will extend it to the first, second, third and fourth children.

Finally, I think we need a better work life balance. Apart from high expectations being the reason why young people don't get married, another reason is they are simply too busy. They are working. If they are lawyers, they may finish at eleven o'clock at night. If they are civil servants working at MTI, maybe ten o'clock at night. No time to go out, socialise, make friends. Married couples also need good work life balance. I think we are working longer hours. I am not sure why, but hours have become longer, the pace is more intense. Maybe it's the Internet, maybe it's email, maybe it's globalisation, but whatever it is, you wake up at six o'clock in the morning, you check your email. Eleven o'clock at night, before you go to sleep, you check it again and next morning, you come back, somebody replied at 2.00 am. How to have children?

The Government has a solution for everything. So, because of this, we have a Family Life Officer in every ministry. So, one ministry had a Family Life Officer who sent out a notice to the whole ministry, circular, email, cc all, saying you must maintain good balanced family life, stay at home, paid holiday, quality life, so forth and she sent it out at 11.00 pm from her office PC. I don't know whether she's been sacked yet, but I think we have to keep a balance. There has to be on-time and off-time. The US has got a good practice, five-day week. They work like mad, Mondays to Fridays. Breakfast meeting, 7.00 am, dinner, post-dinner meeting, 10.00 pm, 11.00 pm. Friday night, work late; Saturday, Sunday sacrosanct, absolute no-no. Never mind who you are, no business. They will save the time for their family, for their community, they do social work. Totally different personality. They coach a basketball team. They work hard, five-day week. Other countries are different. Five-day week, by Thursday afternoon, your weekend is getting close.

We have always resisted a five-day week. I have made this argument many times. When I went into Monetary Authority of Singapore (MAS), they put up a paper, I said, "No". Last year, they were about to put up a paper. Before they could put it up, I had already answered somebody else "no" in the newspapers. So, they withdrew their proposal. But, in fact, it is one of the most important things for our young people and when we talk to employees coming in or staff coming in and ask them, "What is it which you are looking for?", the first thing they ask us is, "Do you work on Saturdays?" because they want that time. Two days of a weekend is different from one-and-a-half days of a weekend. So, after having said, "No" for a very long time, I think it is time to turn this stone over also. So, the Civil Service will go to a five-day week. I didn't know you were all civil servants! It will apply also to schools and army camps, but we will not reduce the official working hours. So, whatever it is, 44 hours, you have to do, you cover that during the week. And if the public counter is open on Saturdays, has to be open on Saturdays, we will keep it open on Saturdays. So, five-day week doesn't mean everybody is off on Saturday. Some people may be off on Monday or some other day of the week. Now, I wanted to say that I was going to go to work on Saturday, but the civil servants told me, please don't say that, but I can tell you I would be checking my email on Saturday and I'm sure for the ministers and for the people who are in the political leadership, the weekends will be time for them to spend in the community with the grassroots and keeping in touch with the residents.

So, let me recap. Lim Hng Kiang will announce all the details on Wednesday. You can ask him as well as his committee, which includes several ladies — I think Amy Khor is on the committee and Lim Hwee Hua — all the tough questions. My job is just to make the speech. This package by itself isn't going to solve the problem, but if it changes Singaporean mindsets towards marriage, family and children and causes people to think again and reorder their priorities in life, then I think it will contribute to turning the situation around.

Bibliography

Anderson, John E., Cheng, Mark C. E. and Wan Fook Kee. "A Component Analysis of Recent Fertility Decline in Singapore". *Studies in Family Planning*, No. 38, February 1969.

Arumainathan, P. *Singapore: Report on the Census of Population 1970*, Vols. I and II. Singapore: Department of Statistics, 1973.

Berelson, Bernard. "Beyond Family Planning". *Studies in Family Planning*, No. 38, February 1969.

Campbell, William. "Singapore Prepares for A Population of 3.5 Million". *Ekistics* 30, no. 176 (July 1970).

Chang Chen-Tung. *Fertility Transition in Singapore*. Singapore: Singapore University Press, 1974.

———, and Stephen H. K. Yeh. "A Study of Singapore's National Family Planning Programme". *Malayan Economic Review* 17, no. 1 (April 1972).

Chen, Peter S. J. "Family Planning Programme and Policy in Singapore". *Review of Southeast Asian Studies* 2, nos. 1-4 (December 1972).

Chua S. C. *State of Singapore: Report on the Census of Population 1957*. Cmd. 19 of 1964. Singapore: Government Press, 1964.

Chua Sian Chin. "Two-Child Family as A Social Norm". *Mirror* 10, no. 17 (April 1974).

———. "Singapore's Target: Zero Population Growth". *Mirror* 10, no. 35 (2 September 1974).

———. "Speech by Mr Chua Sian Chin, Minister for Health and Home Affairs, at the World Population Conference, Bucharest, Romania, 19-30 August 1974". *Singapore Public Health Bulletin*, No. 15, January 1975.

Chung Ching San. "Evaluation of Progress in Fertility Control in Singapore". In *Proceedings of the World Population Conference, August–September 1965, Belgrade*, Vol. II, pp. 119-23. New York: United Nations, 1967.

Committee on Demographic Aspects of Abortion, International Union for the Scientific Study of Population. *Recommendations for Comparative Abortion Statistics in Countries where Induced Abortion is Legalised*. IUSSP Paper No. 7.

Cox, Peter R. *Demography*, 3rd ed. Cambridge: Cambridge University Press, 1959.

Davis, Kingsley. "Population Policy: Will the Current Programs Succeed?". *Science* 58.

Del Tufo, M. V. *Malaya: A Report on the 1947 Census of Population*. London: Crown Agents for the Colonies, 1949.

Dublin, Louis I. and Alfred J. Lotka. "On the True Rate of Natural Increase". *Journal of the American Statistical Associations* 20, no. 150 (September 1925).

Frejka, Tomas. *The Future of Population Growth: Alternative Paths to Equilibrium*. New York: John Wiley, 1973.

George Washington University. *The World's Laws on Voluntary Sterilization for Family Planning Purposes in Sterilization*. Population Report, Series C-D, No. 2, April 1973. Washington: Department of Medical and Public Affairs, George Washington University Medical Centre, 1973.

Hooi See Choon. "Abortion: A Survey of 1,000 Cases". *Medical Journal of Malaya* 17, no. 4 (June 1963).

Hu, Chow Shun Chia. "An Evaluation of the Intrauterine Contraceptive Device". *Singapore Medical Journal* 11, no. 1 (March 1970).

Inter-Governmental Coordinating Committee. *Sterilization and Abortion Procedures*. Proceedings of the First Meeting of the IGCC Expert Group Working Committee on Sterilization and Abortion, 3–5 January 1973, Penang. Kuala Lumpur: Inter-Governmental Coordinating Committee, Southeast Asia Regional Cooperation in Family and Population Planning, 1973.

Kanagaratnam, K. *The National Programme in Singapore — A Review of Two Years, 1966 and 1967*. Singapore Family Planning and Population Board Paper 1.

_____. "Experiences in Motivation and Promotion of Family Planning in Singapore". *Singapore Public Health Bulletin*, No. 3, January 1968.

_____. "Singapore: The National Family Planning Program". *Studies in Family Planning*, No. 28, April 1968.

_____ and Khoo Chian Kim. "Singapore: The Use of Oral Contraceptives in National Program". *Studies in Family Planning*, no. 48, December 1969.

_____ and Thong Kah Leong. "Role of Post-Partum in the National Program of Singapore". In *Post-Partum Family Planning: A Report on the International Program*. New York: McGraw-Hill, 1970.

Khew Khoon Shin and Mark C. E. Cheng. "Culdoscopic Sterilization — The Singapore Experience". *Annals of the Academy of Medicine, Singapore* (New Series) 3, no. 4 (October 1974).

Kwa, S. B., S. T. Quah and Mark C. E. Cheng. "The Abortion Act, 1969 — A Review of the First Year's Experience". *Singapore Medical Journal* 12, no. 5 (October 1971).

Lee Kuan Yew. "Speech by the Prime Minister, Singapore". In *Proceedings of Seventh Conference of the International Planned Parenthood Federation, Singapore*

1963. Amsterdam: Excerpta Medica, International Congress, Series No. 72, 1964.

Leow Bee Geok. *Census of Population 2000: Advanced Date Release*. Singapore Department of Statistics, 2001.

Lim, Maggie. "Malaysia and Singapore". In *Family Planning and Population Programs*, edited by Bernard Berelson et al. Chicago: University of Chicago Press, 1966.

Lim Teck Beng. "Sterilization in the Female — A Preliminary Report of 636 Cases from Singapore". *Proceedings of the Obstetrical and Gynaecological Society*, Singapore 4, no. 2 (October 1973).

Loh, Margaret. "The Singapore Family Planning and Population Programme with Special Reference to New Directions and Emphasis, 1973/74". *Singapore Public Health Bulletin*, No. 13, January 1974.

_____. "The Two-Child Family — A Social Norm for Singapore". *National Youth Leadership Training Institute (NYLTI) Journal* 7 (March 1974).

Lopez, Alvaro. *Problems in Stable Population Theory*. Princeton: Office of Populations Research, 1961.

Mainichi Newspaper. *Summary of Twelfth National Survey on Family Planning*, Series No. 24. Tokyo: The Population Problems Research Council, Mainichi Newspaper, 1975.

Ng, Y. H. "Shock Following Abortion — A Review of 58 Cases". In *Proceedings of the Sixth Singapore-Malaysia Congress of Medicine, Singapore 1971*, vol. 6. Singapore: Academy of Medicine, 1971.

Pakshong, D. I. "Singapore". In *Proceedings of the Combined Conference on the Evaluation of Malaysia National Family Programme and East Asia Population Programmes, 18–25 March 1970*. Kuala Lumpur: National Family Planning Board, Malaysia, 1970.

Pressant, Roland. *Demographic Analysis*. New York: Aldine-Atherton, 1972.

Ratnam, S. S. "Family Planning and Contraception". *Nursing Journal of Singapore: Berita Jururawat* 7 (1967).

_____, ed. *Adolescent Sexuality*. Singapore: Singapore University Press, 1969.

_____. "Population Control — A Decade of Independence". In *Singapore — A Decade of Independence*, edited by Charles Ng and T. P. B. Menon. Singapore: Alumni International Singapore, 1975.

Saw Swee-Hock. "Sources and Methods of Population Statistics in Malaya and Singapore". *Ekonomi* 5, no. 1 (December 1964).

_____. "Errors in Chinese Age Statistics". *Demography* 4, no. 2 (1967).

_____. "Population Trends in Singapore, 1819–1967". *Journal of Southeast Asian History* 10, no. 1 (March 1969).

_____. *Singapore Population in Transition*. Philadelphia: University of Pennsylvania Press, 1970.

_____. *Estimates of Population and Labour Force by Age Group for West Malaysia and Singapore, 1958–1967*. Occasional Papers and Monographs No. 6, Hong Kong: Centre for Asian Studies, University of Hong Kong, 1971.

————— and Cheng Siok-Hwa. "Migration Policies in Malaya and Singapore". *Review of Southeast Asian Studies* 1, no. 3 (September 1971).

—————. "The Development of Population Statistics in Singapore". *Singapore Statistical Bulletin* 1, no. 2 (December 1972).

—————. "Towards Zero Population Growth". In *The Singapore Environment*, edited by R. S. Bhathal and Peter S. J. Chen. Singapore: University Education Press, 1973.

—————. "The Rising Number of Births in Singapore Since 1970". *Singapore Statistical Bulletin* 2, no. 1 (June 1973).

—————. "Towards Zero Population Growth in Singapore". *Journal of the Singapore Institute of Planners* 3, no. 1 (November 1973).

—————. *Population Projections for Singapore, 1970–2070*. Singapore National Statistical Commission, 1974.

—————. "Population Trends in Singapore". *Journal of the Singapore National Academy of Science* 3, no. 4 (1974).

—————. "Singapore: Resumption of Rapid Fertility Decline in 1973". *Studies in Family Planning* 6, no. 6 (June 1975).

—————. "Development of Population Control in Singapore". *Contemporary Southeast Asia* 1, no. 4 (March 1980).

—————. *Population Control for Zero Growth in Singapore*. New York: Oxford University Press, 1980.

—————. "Too Little Land, Too Many People". In *Singapore Towards the Year 2000*, edited by Saw Swee-Hock and R. S. Bhathal. Singapore: Singapore University Press, 1981.

—————. *Demographic Trends in Singapore*. Singapore: Department of Statistics, 1981.

—————. "Singapore: New Population Policies for More Balanced Procreation". *Contemporary Southeast Asia* 7, no. 2 (September 1985).

—————. "Dynamics of Ageing in Singapore's Population". *Annals of Academy of Medicine* 14, no. 4 (October 1985).

—————. "A Decade of Fertility Below Replacement Level in Singapore". *Journal of Biosocial Science* 18, no. 4 (October 1986).

—————. *New Population and Labour Force Projections and Policy Implications for Singapore*. Singapore: Institute of Southeast Asian Studies, 1987.

—————. "Towards a Stationary Population in Singapore". *Asia-Pacific Journal of Public Health* 1, no. 2 (1987).

—————. "Seventeen Years of Legalized Abortion in Singapore". *Biology and Society* 5, no. 2 (June 1988).

—————. "Muslim Fertility Transition: The Case of the Singapore Malays". *Asia-Pacific Population Journal* 4, no. 3 (September 1989).

_____. "Bring Back the Baby Boom". *Current World Readers* 32, no. 8 (December 1989).

_____. "Ethnic Fertility Differentials in Malaysia and Singapore". *Journal of Biosocial Science* 22, no. 1 (January 1990).

_____. *Changes in the Fertility Policy of Singapore*. Singapore: Institute of Policy Studies, 1990.

_____. *The Population of Singapore*. Singapore: Institute of Southeast Asian Studies, 1999.

Seng, K. M. and S. M. Goon. "Post-Partum Sterilization — A Year's Experience". *Annals of the Academy of Medicine, Singapore* (New Series) 3, no. 4 (October 1974).

Sinha, Hena. "Singapore: Family Planning Association". In *Proceedings of the Seventh Conference of the International Planned Parenthood Federation, Singapore 1963*. Amsterdam: Excerpta Medica, International Congress Series No. 72, 1964.

Singapore. *Abortion Act, 1969*, No. 25 of 1969. Singapore: Government Printer, 1969.

_____. *Abortion Act, 1974*, No. 24 of 1974. Singapore: Singapore National Printers, 1974.

_____. "Abortion Regulations, 1974". *Government Gazette: Subsidiary Legislation Supplement*, No. 58, 27 December 1974.

_____. *Employment Act, 1968*, No. 122 of 1968. Singapore: Government Printer, 1968.

_____. *Employment (Amendment) Act, 1973*. Singapore: Government Printer, 1973.

_____. *Family Planning*. A series of 12 weekly talks broadcast over Radio Singapore and Rediffusion. Singapore: Government Printing Office, 1967, 37 pp.

_____. *Immigration Ordinance, 1952*. Singapore: Government Printer, 1952.

_____. *Income Tax (Amendment) Act, 1973*. Singapore: Government Printer, 1973.

_____. *Parliamentary Debates Republic of Singapore Official Report, First Session of Second Parliament*. Singapore: Government Printing Office, 1970.

_____. *Parliamentary Debates Republic of Singapore Official Report, First Session of Second Parliament, Part III, Vol. 29*. Singapore: Government Printer, 1973.

_____. *Population Estimates of Singapore by Racial Group and Sex and Administrative Area*, No. 1-half-yearly from December 1957.

_____. *Population Estimates by Age Group, Ethnic Group and Sex*, Annual for mid-year.

_____. *Report of Select Committee on the Abortion and Voluntary Sterilization Bills*, Part 6 of 1969. Singapore: Government Printing Office, 1969.

_____. *Singapore — A Country Statement for World Population Conference,*

Bucharest, 19–30 August 1974. Singapore Family Planning and Population Board Paper 22.

_____. *Singapore Family Planning and Population Board Act, 1965*, No. 32 of 1965. Singapore: Government Printer, 1965.

_____. *Voluntary Sterilization Act, 1969*, No. 26 of 1969. Singapore: Government Printer, 1969.

_____. *Voluntary Sterilization Act, 1974*, No. 25 of 1974. Singapore: Singapore National Printers, 1974.

_____. *White Paper on Family Planning*, Command 22 of 1965. Singapore: Government Printer, 1965.

Singapore Department of Statistics. *Monthly Demographic Bulletin*, No. 1, January 1959.

_____, *Monthly Digest of Statistics*.

_____. *Yearbook of Statistics 2004*.

_____. *Trends in Singapore Resident Population, 1990–2000*. 2001.

Singapore, Family Planning Association of Singapore. *Annual Report*, 1949–68 and 1968–76.

Singapore, Housing and Development Board. *Annual Report*, 1965–77.

Singapore, Ministry of Culture. *Singapore*, 1970–76.

_____. *1984 Budget Statement*.

Singapore, Ministry of Communications and Information. *1987 Budget Statement*.

_____. *1989 Budget Statement*.

Singapore, Ministry of Community Development and Sports. *Baby Bonus*.

Singapore, Ministry of Finance. *2004 Budget Statement*.

Singapore, Ministry of Health. *Population and Trends*, 1977.

_____. *Singapore Public Health Bulletin*.

Singapore, Ministry of Labour. *Report on the Labour Force Survey of Singapore*, 1974–76.

Singapore, Ministry of Manpower. *Conditions of Employment 2002*. Occasional Papers, January 2003.

Singapore, Registrar-General of Births and Deaths. *Report on the Registration of Births and Deaths 1940/47 to 1954*. Followed by *Report on the Registration of Births and Deaths, Marriages and Persons*, 1955–65, and *Report on the Registration of Births and Deaths and Marriages*, 1966–77. Singapore: Government Printing Office.

Singapore, Registry of Muslim Marriages and the Shariah Court. *Annual Report*, 1960–77. Singapore: Government Printing Office.

Singapore, Singapore Family Planning and Population Board. *Annual Report*, 1966–77.

Somerville, Neil. *Your Chinese Horoscope for 1985*. Weillingborough: The Aquarian Press, 1987.

Spiegelman, Mortimer. *Introduction to Demography*, revised ed. Cambridge: Harvard University Press, 1969.

Taeuber, Irene B. *The Population of Japan*. Princeton: Princeton University Press, 1958.

Taiwan, Ministry of the Interior. *1973 Taiwan Demographic Factbook*. 1974.

Tan, W. K., M. S. Sidhu and T. H. Lean. "Laparoscopic Sterilization — A Review of 500 Cases". *Annals of the Academy of Medicine, Singapore* (New Series) 3, no. 4 (October 1974).

Teoh, H. K. and C. S. Ong. "A Study of Unmarried Mothers Seeking Legal Abortions". In *Proceedings of the Sixth Singapore-Malaysia Congress of Medicine*, Singapore 1971. Singapore: Academy of Medicine, Vol. 6, 1971.

Thomson, George G. and T. E. Smith. "Singapore: Family Planning in an Urban Environment". In *The Politics of Family Planning in the Third World*, edited by T. E. Smith. London: George Allen & Unwin, 1973.

Thong Kah Leong. "National Family Planning Programme". *Singapore Public Health Bulletin*, No. 2, July 1967.

Tietze, Christopher and Majorie Cooper Murstein. *Induced Abortion: 1975 Factbook*. Reports on Population Family Planning No. 14 (2nd ed), December 1975. New York: Population Council, 1975, 75 pp.

United Nations. *Assessment of Acceptance and Effectiveness of Family Planning Methods*. Asian Population Studies No. 4. Bangkok: Economic and Social Commission for Asia and the Pacific, 1968.

_____. *Manual III: Methods of Population Projections by Sex and Age*. Population Studies No. 25. New York: United Nations Department of Economics and Social Affairs, 1956.

_____. *Recent Trends in Fertility in Industrialized Countries*. ST/SOA/Series A/27. New York: United Nations Department of Economic and Social Affairs, 1968.

_____. *Report of a Comparative Study on the Administration of Family Planning Programmes in the Escap Region: Organization Determinants of Performance in Family Planning Services*. Asian Population Studies No. 29. Bangkok: Economic and Social Commission for Asia and the Pacific, 1977.

_____. *Singapore*. Population Profiles 1. New York: United Nations Fund for Population Activities, n.d.

_____. *The Determinants and Consequences of Population Trends*. Population Studies No. 50, ST/SOA/SER.A/50. New York: United Nations Department of Economics and Social Affairs, 1973.

_____. *World Population Policies 2003*. New York: Department of Economic and Social Affairs, 2004.

_____. *National Population Policies 2001*. New York: Department of Economic and Social Affairs, 2002.

_____. *World Population Ageing 1950–2050*. New York: Department of Economic and Social Affairs, 2002.

Vengadasalam, D., Mukhtiar Singh Sidhu, Choo Hee Tiat and Mark C. E. Cheng. "A Follow-up Study of Applicants for Legalised Abortions Whose Pregnancies were not Terminated". In *Proceedings of the Sixth Singapore-Malaysia Congress of Medicine, Singapore 1971*. Singapore: Academy of Medicine, Vol. 6, 1971.

Wan Fook Kee. *Communications Strategy in the Singapore National Family Planning Programme*. Singapore Family Planning and Population Board Paper 14.

_____ and Margaret Loh. *Second Five-Year Family Planning Programme, 1971–1975*. Singapore Family Planning and Population Board Paper 16.

_____. "Communications Aspects of the Singapore Family Planning Programme". *Singapore Public Health Bulletin*, No. 8, July 1971.

_____ and Quah Siam Tee. "Singapore: A Study of Clinic Continuation Rates". *Studies in Family Planning* 2 (December 1971).

_____ and Quah Siam Tee. "Singapore: A Cost-Effect Analysis of a Family Planning Programme". *Studies in Family Planning* 3 (January 1972).

_____ and Saw Swee-Hock. "The First National Survey on Family Planning in Singapore, 1973". *Singapore Statistical Bulletin* 2, No. 2 (December 1973).

_____ and Saw Swee-Hock. *Report on the First National Survey of Family Planning in Singapore*. Singapore: Singapore Family Planning and Population Board and National Statistical Commission, 1974.

_____. "Sexual Sterilization in Singapore — Some Epidemiological Aspects and Demographic Impact". *Annals of the Academy of Medicine, Singapore* (New Series) 3, no. 4 (October 1974).

_____ and R. Sundrason. "Vasectomy in Singapore". *Annals of the Academy of Medicine, Singapore* (New Series) 3, no. 4 (October 1974).

_____, Chen Ai Ju and Jessie Tan. "Oral Contraceptive Continuation Rates in the Singapore National Program, 1966–1972". *Studies in Family Planning* 6, no. 1 (January 1975).

_____ and Saw Swee-Hock. "Knowledge, Attitudes and Practice of Family Planning in Singapore, 1973". *Studies in Family Planning* 6, no. 4 (April 1975).

_____ and Margaret Loh. "Singapore". In *Family Planning in Developing World: A Review of Programs*, edited by Walter B. Watson. A Population Council Factbook. New York: The Population Council, 1977.

Wu San San. *Singapore Family Planning Programme (1966–1970) and Its Implications on Fertility Decline — With Special Reference to Ethnic Groups*. Singapore Family Planning and Population Board Paper 19, p. 5.

_____. "Family Planning". *Singapore Public Health Bulletin* 11 (January 1973).

Newspapers

Business Times
Eastern Sun
New Nation
New Paper
Singapore Monitor
Singapore Tiger Herald
Streats
Straits Times
Sunday Times
Today

Websites

Inland Revenue Authority of Singapore. <www.iras.gov.sg>, 27 April 2001, 25 August 2004, and 10 October 2004.

Ministry of Community Development and Sports. <www.babybonus.gov.sg>, 17 March 2001.

Ministry of Community Development, Youth and Sport. <www.childcarelink.gov.sg>, 6 October 2004.

Ministry of Health. <www.moh.gov.sg>, 5 October 2004.

Ministry of Manpower. <www.mom.gov.sg>, 5 October 2004.

Index